Understanding Media Theory

Kevin Williams

BLOOMSBURY ACADEMIC

First published by Hodder Education in 2003

This reprint published in 2010 by:

Bloomsbury Academic

An imprint of Bloomsbury Publishing Plc
36 Soho Square, London W1D 3QY, UK
and
175 Fifth Avenue, New York, NY 10010, USA

CIP records for this book are available from the British Library and the Library of Congress

ISBN 978-0-3407-1904-6

This book is produced using paper that is made from wood grown in managed, sustainable forests.
It is natural, renewable and recyclable. The logging and manufacturing processes conform to the environmental regulations of the country of origin.

Printed and bound in Great Britain by the MPG Books Group

www.bloomsburyacademic.com

Contents

PREFACE

Any attempt to document and describe theories of the media faces the complex and sometimes intractable nature of the subject matter. The philosopher Francis Bacon, discussing the advancement of learning (1620), referred to empiric ants mindlessly collecting data and scholastic spiders spinning webs from inside themselves (see Burke, 2000). Bacon was contemptuous of both. He criticised ants for their ignorance of true causes and spiders for conclusions deduced without any reference to the everyday world. Bacon praised the industrious bee who both collects and digests, and beginning from the 'senses and particulars' proceeds by stages to feel its way to general conclusions. For me this book represents the labours of a bee – an increasingly overweight bumblebee – trying to unravel the work of the ants and spiders that inhabit the world of media studies. Collecting and digesting the works of media theorists is fraught with frustration. Painstaking effort is required to unwind the webs of the scholastic spiders, which are sometimes shrouded in impenetrable jargon and obscure language, and unpackage the stockpile of facts and figures heaped together by empiric ants. In doing this, considerable patience and help has been required from others.

First, and most crucially, Lesley Riddle of Hodder Arnold who has waited a considerable amount of time for the delivery of a manuscript. Without her steadfastness and belief in the work this book would never have appeared. Then there was the support of several colleagues in the field of media and communication studies. Chas Critcher played an important part by pointing out the author's limitations in the area of theory. However, his work and lectures on media theory, particularly on stereotyping and audience effects, provided a sound basis from which to learn and develop a structure on which to build. His lectures on the Sociology of Mass Culture module at Sheffield Hallam University in the early 1990s were a major impetus for much of what appears in this book. Geoff Mungham read early drafts and overcame his antithesis to theory to make suggestions about simplifying the text and making it more accessible to readers. His skills at subbing academic prose and his hatred of the word 'that' helped enormously to improve this book. John Eldridge emphasised the importance of theory and the need to critically engage with different theoretical approaches, providing a sounding board at crucial times during the long period of writing the book. I would also like to thank Jenny Kitzinger for her insights, especially in the area of media audiences, and David Miller for his ability to leave no turn unstoned.

Thanks are also due to Terry Threadgold, Ieuan Williams, Mike Bromley and, above all, Clare Hudson whose working knowledge of the media, forensic (and ferocious) intellect, good humour and basic subbing skills have all contributed immensely to this endeavour. Thanks also to Tessa Heath and Lynn Brown for their assistance in the production of this book. Finally several others should be mentioned for their longer-term contributions: Edmund, Margaret, Frances, Alan, Griff, Rowley, Pam and Barry, and Ie, whose reward has been a sedentary job at the BBC. None of these people are responsible for the limitations of this book; these are the author's fault.

INTRODUCTION: □
UNRAVELLING MEDIA THEORY

This purpose of this book is to provide an introductory guide to the key theories that inform debates about the media. The decision to write the guide is motivated by three factors. First, the explosion in the study of the media in British higher education in the last few decades has confronted students, teachers and scholars with a bewildering array of subject matter. Tunstall (1983) notes the study of the media and mass communication can 'cover a dozen disciplines and raise a thousand problems', and with the field being divided 'into many separate media, many separate disciplines, many separate stages in the flow and ... several hundred sub fields' it is not surprising that students are confronted with challenges and problems in trying to make sense of the subject matter. The development of theory, concepts and perspectives is central to the process of making sense of the media, and this book sets out to provide an overview and evaluation of the main theoretical issues involved in the study of the media in a form that is accessible to students and challenging for teachers. The challenges of media theory are more likely to be faced by students and teachers than researchers. The latter have tended to concentrate their efforts on one or another part of the mass communication process or focus their analysis on this or that medium of communication, which has sometimes led them to develop their work unaware of and unconnected to one another. Charges can be made that, as a field of research, 'media studies' is insufficiently reflective about its nature and scope. It is students and teachers that must learn about the full range of theory and to do so they need an overview of the core issues and debates in making sense of the media and the process of mass communication.

The second factor for providing this guide arises from the rapid technological change of recent years, which has brought about considerable turmoil in the media. The burgeoning development of 'new' media such as cable, satellite, the video recorder, compact disc, home computers and the Internet is challenging the pre-eminence of the 'old', traditional media technologies of television, print and film. The growing convergence between the technologies is further changing the 'old certainties' of what we understand by the media and mass communication. These changes pose challenges for those seeking to study the media. They call for new theories, new ways of conceptualising and explaining the role of the media as well as making sense of the changes for the individual and society. The entry of new actors into media studies with their own baggage of theories, concepts and perspectives has contributed to a state of 'ferment' in the field. The attempts by

1

scholarship to respond to the changes is reflected in the way leading academic journals have opened their pages to debate the future of the field (see Levy and Gurevitch, 1994; *Journal of Communication*, 1983; 1993a; 1993b). To follow these debates and make sense of the fundamental changes that are happening, it is essential to have a basic grasp of the theoretical approaches that have shaped the development of the field.

Ferment in the field is not only fuelled by technological change. The last decade has seen the emergence of a divergence of opinion emanating from the struggle between two major kinds of theoretical tradition. A quarrelsome and at times fractious conflict has broken out between what on the one hand are called social/behavioural theories, sometimes labelled the 'communication sciences', and on the other hand cultural theories. While a number of theories will be examined in this book, many have been marginalised in the discussion of media as a result of the contemporary dispute between these two paradigms in the approach to the study of the media. This struggle is part of the fundamental shift or 'intellectual sea-change' occurring within the social sciences and humanities, and even western thought, as a result of the challenges of new approaches to understanding society such as feminism and more particularly the new perspective of post-modernism. Social/behavioural theories are derived from the disciplines of sociology, psychology and social psychology. The focus of these theories is the relationship between mass communication, media organisations and society, or the impact of the media on the attitudes and behaviour of individuals. Cultural theories draw from the disciplines of sociolinguistics, literary studies and anthropology. They focus on the language and meaning of media texts and how they are understood. Within both paradigms there are differences of approach, method and a variety of theoretical positions but there does exist a fundamental difference between them. Social/behavioural theories share the view that theory can be tested through empirical investigation. The emphasis is on quantitative research methods where the validity of a theory can be secured through systematic and rigorous procedures of investigation. Cultural theories place emphasis on qualitative research. The absence of quantitative methods is a feature of cultural studies where data collection has often been reduced to the semiotic or literary deconstruction of specific media texts or more qualitative questionnaires of audience reception of media messages. To follow and engage in this struggle, which promises to dominate our attempts to understand the media for the foreseeable future, it is important to discuss the strengths and weaknesses of both kinds of theory. This is a third factor for providing students and teachers with a basic introduction to media theory.

If these are the factors for providing this guide, there are also other considerations that have shaped the approach taken in this book. The aim is to introduce essential concepts and theoretical perspectives in a way that avoids presenting them as a dictionary-like summary of the field. The theories covered in this text should not be seen as a list of terms to be memorised. Often theorists lay out their work as mantras to be chanted by willing students: learn the language; understand the jargon and you can join the selected priesthood. Such an approach is reinforced by the fear many have of theory. The word 'theory' is anathema to many people, who see it as difficult, complex and detached from their everyday lives. It smacks of abstraction, the obtuse and is shrouded in vagueness. This is often accentuated by the language or jargon that many theorists deploy to outline their grand design to explain the world around them. Matters are further complicated by the present 'post-modern' climate, which dismisses theories or doctrines that present themselves as universal and all-embracing claims to knowledge. There is a problem of the *relevance* of theory. This book seeks to present the relevance of theory to the understanding of media issues in the 'real world'. The applicability of theory in unravelling key issues relating to the role and impact of the media in the everyday lives of people and on the structure of society and the nature of our culture is stressed. To this end different theories are understood in terms of their use in answering key questions about the mass communication process. To do this the book draws on examples from a number of societies and cultures. Anglo-American and European interests, concerns and questions have dominated media theory. This book seeks as much as is possible in the limited space available to engage with the perspectives and debates in media theory at an international level. Many of the illustrations and applications of theoretical arguments will be drawn from a wide range of global experiences. This will enable students to assess the worth of theories and concepts as well as learn about their broader relevance in other societies.

The rest of this introduction is taken up with specific tasks. The first is to clarify in more detail what we mean by media studies. What we are supposed to be studying? Our answer to this question has consequences for our attempts to build theory to explain the media. This is followed by an outline of the main issues and debates in the study of the media. Media theory has had to address certain key issues and enter specific debates about the power and role of the mass media in society. The way in which these issues and debates are approached today is shaped by the contemporary challenges facing the field, which are also discussed. This introductory chapter concludes with an overview of the role and purpose of theory in media studies.

WHAT IS MEDIA STUDIES?

Most academic study begins by discussing what the subject is supposed to be about. This allows the student to know what she is going to study and what issues and topics are likely to be raised. You would expect there to be no difficulty in answering the question 'What is media studies?' We are uninhibited in our use of the word 'media'. The 'media' are all around us and we are familiar with them through their widespread use. The era in which we live is often distinguished by reference to the predominance of the media in our society. A variety of words – for example, 'information', 'communication', 'media' and 'digital' – are used interchangeably to label the age in which we live. Such familiarity breeds contempt as we blame the 'media' for many of our social problems. But the term becomes elusive on definition. According to Meyrowitz (1994: 63) the 'most glaring problem for media studies' is that there is 'no common understanding of what the subject matter of the field is'. He criticises media scholars for their failure to explicitly confront the nature of the media, arguing many have simply adopted 'the belief that everyone knows what the media are and that one can therefore move immediately to other research questions'. This failure has resulted in scholarly confusion over a field of study 'embracing a staggering and often unbounded range of interests and topics' (Golding and Murdock, 1978: 59). Corner (1997: 446) identifies this as the 'knowledge problem'. All fields of study have problems over what they 'seek to find out and the kinds of and quality of data and of explanatory relations which particular ideas and methods might be expected to produce'. Media studies faces an acute problem over what constitutes its 'core knowledge'.

Traditionally the press, film, broadcasting and the record industry have been lumped together as the 'mass media' since their emergence at the end of the nineteenth and the beginning of the twentieth century. They have been the subjects of much media research. However, as the field has grown it has broadened out to take in areas such as popular fiction and literature, comics, advertising, photography, public relations, theatre and dance, and speech. The growing importance of modern media communication in everyday life has led to increasing examination of the media's role in the production and reproduction of popular culture. Interest in the media's involvement in a range of cultural and leisure activities has been a spur to the development of much contemporary research activity. New media are yet another addition to the expansion of the subject matter of the field. The breadth of what is now being studied has led for some to the 'impression of a field that is everywhere and nowhere' (Levy and Gurevitch, 1994: 11). The question is what do these media have in common? Bennett (1982: 30) notes even the media that traditionally constitute the focus of research and theorising have only superficial resemblance to one another. As an example he points to the very different relationships between the state and the press, the broadcasting industries and the cinema. However, the variety of media, which often have little in common, has not prevented the theorists generalising about the 'media'.

The media being only part of the process of mass communication adds further complications. The terms 'mass media' and 'mass communication' are often used interchangeably but there is an important distinction to be made between them. The term 'mass media' refers to the 'organised technologies which make mass communication possible' (McQuail, 1994: 10). But what is mass communication? Communication takes place at a number of different levels from the individual through the group to institutions and organisations and to society at large. The nature of communication – what McQuail (1994: 9) labels the 'reality of communication' – is different at each level. Mass communication is distinct from other forms of communication such as face-to-face, intra-group and organisational communication. What makes mass communication distinct is

4

that it is a process by which media technologies allow information and messages to simultaneously reach a large, heterogeneous mass audience. However, mass communication like all human communication is a process that can be seen in terms of who is producing the messages, the content of the messages themselves, how they are transmitted, to whom they are transmitted and with what effect. One scholar compares this process to a circular building with a number of entrances (Watson, 1998: 3). There are several doors commonly opened by media scholars: often labelled as 'production', 'text' or 'content', 'technology', 'reception' and 'effects'. Where you enter into the study of the mass communication process – that is which door you go through – has implications for what you study and how you study. For some scholars the range and diversity of what is studied is an attractive feature of the field. The interdisciplinary nature of the study of the media can be intellectually stimulating and challenging. But the growth of a field of study that is 'awesomely broad in intellectual sweep' (Golding and Murdock, 1978: 59) means there is confusion and controversy at the very heart of what is being studied. There is no hard-and-fast area of study students can take for granted. Rather than an unchanging field of study we have an area that is constantly changing and developing according to the interests and concerns of media scholars.

These differences over what is studied are reflected in the institutional diversity of media studies courses. The study of the media takes place across the humanities, social sciences and technological fields. However, 'media studies', in Corner's words, only became 'an institutionalised, self conscious grouping' in the British education process from the early 1970s ('communication studies' began a little earlier in the United States, in the late 1950s). Corner (1997: 447) attributes this not only to the growing political and cultural significance of the media but also to an increasing dissatisfaction amongst scholars with what was seen as the failure of traditional social science to address the complexity of how meaning is produced by the media, and the limitations of literary criticism in analysing the output of the media studies. The result was new courses in communication, media, cultural, film, journalism and television studies, as well as media sociology, which brought together a mixture of academics from various backgrounds to work within an interdisciplinary environment. While all these approaches can be seen as generically constituting the study of the media and mass communication, each has its own particular emphasis. There are nevertheless considerable problems in distinguishing between them. As Alan Durant (1991: 418) points out, 'each emphasis is troubled by its own boundaries'. Any attempt to provide a theoretical overview of the field has to acknowledge and embrace the heterogeneity that most students, teachers and researchers experience in their study of the media in the educational process.

This book attempts to address the eclecticism of the field and acknowledge the broad range of approaches that are taken to the study of the media and the mass communication process. However, the primary focus is on media that have shaped the world since 1945

5

and have featured most prominently on media studies courses in higher education – that is, the press and broadcasting. Film is included, but film theory has developed its own distinct niche in higher education. The book also recognises the growing importance of new media. New information technology such as the Internet can be seen as breaking down the distinction between mass communication and other forms of communication. These technologies extend the possibility of enhancing personal communication in the modern world and as a result shifting the focus away from the 'mass', which has been the emphasis in the study of the media in the post-war world (see Corner, 1998). These changes pose major challenges to media theorists. The mass communication process, as has been pointed out, can be entered into through a number of doors. Nevertheless researchers, teachers and students have more regularly entered through some doors than others. Harold Lasswell (1948) provided one of the most quoted descriptions of the mass communication process: *who* says *what* through *which channel* to *whom* and to *what effect*. While many have criticised the emphasis placed on Lasswell's definition of the process of mass communication, his framework conveniently breaks down the areas in which media researchers and teachers have focused their attention. More often than not studies in the field of mass communication and media studies have concentrated on audiences and effects (see Shoemaker and Reese, 1991). What media do to people and what people do with the media have been regular areas of scholastic exploration. In addition to audiences and effects, scholars have also examined the people and institutions that produce media messages, and the factors that initiate and determine the act of communication. The content of the messages themselves and the medium through which they have been communicated is the other division of the communication process on which scholars have focused. However, seeing the process of mass communication in terms of its component parts neglects the broader relationship between the media and society.

The media are an integral and ever-present part of daily life in many parts of the world. They increasingly play a central role in shaping our ways of living, our cultures and our societies. Besides helping us to negotiate the meaning of what is going on in the world, they are important agents of socialisation. They help us to learn about the values, beliefs and norms of our societies as well as assist us to develop our own sense of identity. It is not only a matter of *what* we learn but also *how* we learn. The media mediate our interaction with other social institutions and with each other. They can do this in a number of ways, acting sometimes as a source of conflict and at others as a source of consensus. The media's impact on social life is crucial and it is impossible to discuss social relations without acknowledging their role. As a result understanding the relationship between media and society has become an important component of media studies.

Thus it is possible to identify three kinds of theory that can be discussed in relation to the media and mass communication. First, theories of media and society. Some scholars question whether it is even possible to separate out the study of the mass media from the study of society. For Golding and Murdock (1978) there is no such thing as media and mass communication theory. What exists is nothing more than a subset of social theory. Such theories – for example, mass society theory – attempt to explain entire media systems and their impact on society. Second, there are theories relating to the process of mass communication, the relationship between the various components of mass communication. Third, there are narrower theories focusing on one area of mass communication or one medium of mass communication. They can apply to production, content, reception or effects of media messages as well as particular aspects of these areas. It is not always possible to distinguish clearly between these different kinds of theory. This book includes examples of all and explores the relationship between them. However, the inclusion of different theories reflects the importance attached to them in the study of the media in higher education. The selection relates to the recurring issues and debates within the teaching and researching of media studies in schools and universities. These issues and debates reflect the primary interests and main agendas of those scholars who focus on the study of the media and mass communication process – and serve as the basis for conceptual differences between them.

ISSUES AND DEBATES IN MEDIA STUDIES

The *effects* of mass communication and the media on the knowledge, understanding, opinions and behaviour of audiences has been the primary focus of academic concern and debate. The key question debated is whether the media have the power to shape, change or determine the attitudes and behaviour of individuals. Media scholars have been divided over this question. The notion of an all-powerful media has a long pedigree in the thinking about the media, and has held sway over public and political debate. Many people have over the years attached fabulous powers to the capacity of the media to influence their audiences. They have held the mass media responsible for a range of social ills, including juvenile delinquency, football hooliganism, inner-city riots, terrorism, permissive behaviour, the decline of religiosity, falling educational standards and political apathy. As Connell (1984: 88) says, it is commonplace to blame the media for the 'spread of this or that social problem by being carriers of all manner of distortion or misunderstanding'. Such claims about the impact of the media have been the subject of much academic investigation and speculation. Systematic inquiry into what the media do to people pre-dates the television era. The 1950s saw research into the effects of comic books on children and rock 'n' roll music on youth, while the early part of the twentieth century saw exploration of the influence of film on the behaviour of cinemagoers. Previously political and military leaders as well as poets, philosophers and playwrights have theorised about the effects of different kinds of communication. They were concerned about how audiences were moved to obedience or riotous action, anger or joy, critical thought or deep emotion. Such theorising goes back to the Ancient Greeks who developed theories about the power of the spoken word to influence audiences. Aristotle's *Rhetoric* is an attempt to understand how oratory can excite, ruffle, amuse, gratify and offend (see Cooper, 1932).

However, the history of media studies has also seen a healthy scepticism about the focus on what the media do to people. James Halloran (1969: 18–19) summed up the reservations of many researchers when he stated, 'we must get away from the habit of thinking in terms of what the media do to people and substitute for it the idea of what people do with the media'. What people do with the media has become an increasingly important part of exploring the relationship between the media and their audiences in the post-war period. The view that media audiences are simply passive consumers of what they see, hear and read has been challenged. Emphasis is placed on the audience as active consumers of the output of the media. Individuals are regarded as using the media to satisfy a range of needs, which could include anything from enabling them to escape the daily problems of their lives to helping them construct their sense of who and what they are. By addressing the effects of the media on individuals it is argued that the ability and capacity of those individuals to interpret and make sense of the media is ignored. Thus the key question concerning media effects centres on the relationship between the media and their audiences, and the power of the media to influence their audiences.

Any examination of the impact of the media on their audiences has to be rooted in exploring the ways in which the media report and *represent* the social world. Media studies concentrates on how the media have portrayed the key divisions in modern society. This has meant examining issues such as race, gender, class, sexual orientation and ethnicity. How particular groups in society, as well as how disputes between these groups are depicted by the media and how these depictions have altered has been an important area of study. Many of those portrayed in the media complain of 'bias' in how they are represented. American business accuses the media of being 'anti-business' and 'tending to depict business as greedy, antisocial and insensitive to social needs' (Hoge, 1985). Political parties and pressure groups are particularly vocal in levelling the accusation of bias. The British Labour Party has complained for many years of the 'anti-Labour bias' of the British press, and its leader at the 1992 general election, Neil Kinnock, cited personal attacks on him by the press as being responsible for the party's defeat (see Scammell, 1993). Presidential hopeful Dan Quayle and many of his colleagues on the right of the American Republican Party have spoken of the 'liberal bias' of the press that works against their views and campaigns (see Iyengar and Reeves, 1997). Charges of political and ideological bias are common everywhere in the world. They also operate at a number of levels. Countries of the global South have criticised their representation in the world's media as being dominated by the 'coups, famines and earthquakes syndrome' (see Smith, 1980).

The issue of bias concentrates on the performance of the *news* media. This is the result of the professional and legal requirements for the news media to be objective and impartial. News reporters see themselves as fearless searchers for the truth, and 'telling it as it is' is a central tenet of the philosophy of news journalism. Balance and impartiality are legal requirements of the broadcast media. Such claims and demands encourage evaluation of the content of the media to see whether it meets the test of fairness and accuracy in the representation of issues, events and people. Gunter (1997) has identified several ways in which bias has been analysed. The focus can be on who is quoted or cited (source bias), on the way in which language is used (semantic or discourse bias), on how visual and verbal devices are used to present news (presentational bias), and on the process by which news is selected, reported and given meaning by news organisations (organisational frameworks). The interrogation of objectivity, the cornerstone of the professional ideology of journalism in western societies, has been a feature of media studies, which has concentrated on the performance of the news media.

Another commonly used means to assess media content, particularly in the examination of non-news media forms, is the concept of the stereotype. This term is used to refer to misleading, partial or offensive representations – the 'dumb blonde' or the 'mean Scot'. The concept has dominated popular discussion of the output of the media. However, it has generated debate as to its usefulness as a concept to unravel media messages. The notion of 'genre' has been borrowed from film theory to refine the discussion of media stereotyping. The content of the media can be categorised into different genres or types – such as westerns, thrillers or soap operas – which are organised according to a simple set of rules and a particular format that enables the media to produce a product efficiently and consistently to meet audience expectations. Thus a genre is organised around familiar and predictable storylines or narratives, and represents a set of predictable characters and images. While the concept of genre might help to explain the regularity of media output it is controversial in that it seems to deny individual creativity and authorship at the expense of media formats and rules – it implies 'media determinism' (McQuail, 1994: 267). Bias and stereotyping have increasingly been seen as crude yardsticks with which to assess the output of the news media. They simply tell us that one viewpoint is favoured more than another and that certain parties, interests or institutions are supported by the news media rather that others. As Fowler (1991: 10) argues, the finding that the news is socially constructed and presented from some particular angle is not surprising as this can be claimed about 'anything that is written and said about the world'. However, such concepts excite attention because they relate to the question of ideology.

According to one introductory text, 'in order to understand anything much about the subject of communication and media studies . . . we need to have a working understanding of ideology' (Price, 1993: 57). Ideology has been the subject of millions of books and articles in the social sciences attesting to the vagueness and confusion of the concept (see Van Dijk, 1998). This has not deterred media scholars placing the role of the media in the promotion and construction of ideologies in modern society at the centre of their concerns. Ideology in its classical formulation refers to a system of beliefs, which are partial, misguided and distorted and conceal real social relations. The role of the mass media is crucial in reproducing 'ruling ideas', 'false consciousness', 'hegemony' or 'legitimation', or whatever term theorists have used to conceive of ideology. The media are seen as being biased or reproducing stereotypes, or being organised around formats that construct a particular view of the world. Their role is the 'manufactured production of ideology' (McRobbie, quoted in Watson, 1998: 132). Most media theorists see the content of the media as not being neutral or natural but as manufactured or constructed – as opposed to practitioners who often argue that media content simply reflects what is happening in the world. There is, however, a debate between theorists about how the media reproduce ideology and in whose interest. For some the media are the 'tools' of powerful interests, simply reproducing the messages of their masters and maintaining an ideology that serves to protect their power. Others have argued that the consent of the population has to be won and the media play a role in ensuring this is so by presenting the ideas and views of the powerful as natural and legitimate. Others argue the dominant values and beliefs represented in the media reflect the values and beliefs shared by most people in society. At the heart of the discussion of 'ideology' is a basic problem: the relationship between what is represented in the media and the reality of what is happening out there in the world.

The reproduction of ideology has to be seen within the context of the means of *production* of media organisations. Media production has been neglected by scholars in recent times as the belief that audiences are the main producers of meaning has come to the fore in media studies (Curran, 2000). However, the role of media organisations, personnel and practices in shaping the output of the media has been an important part of the field. Political economy theorists have stressed the role of ownership and control of the media and its ties to the established power structures of society, and the related issues of the role of the market in determining the nature of media production (see, for example, Murdock, 1982a; 1990). The relationship between ownership and control has been a contested part of the discussion of political economy. Others located their discussion of media production in the context of the internal processes of media organisations and the occupational cultures of media workers (see, for example, Tunstall, 1971; Weaver and Wilhoit, 1991). Rooted in organisational theory, such research represents the traditional approach to understanding media production. The degree of individual autonomy that can be exercised by media workers is central to such analysis of media organisations. This debate is often couched in terms of a struggle between creativity and control (Ettema and Whitney, 1982). Recent critiques have argued this approach is too 'media-centric', ignoring the external influences that come to bear on media organisations. Schlesinger (1990) draws attention to the relationship between the media and their sources and suppliers of information, arguing the sociology of journalism should be more sensitive to how this relationship can shape what is news. In the dance between sources and the media there is a debate about who exercises the power to define the nature of what is reported (see Gans, 1979).

The study of the media – and each part of the process of mass communication – cannot be separated from the understanding of the social and cultural context within which they operate. Any description of mass communication or evaluation of the effects, content and production of media messages is inextricably interwoven with a broader discussion of other social institutions and other aspects of social life. As Grossberg and his colleagues say, 'the media make the world even as the world is making the media' (1998: xvi). Hence scholars have been interested in examining the media in relation to broader social and cultural issues. Traditionally debates have taken place around the development of media and the emergence of mass culture. Fear of the 'masses' and mass culture stretches back to the nineteenth century and before (see Carey, 1992; Dyson and Homolka, 1995). The debate about the role of the media in declining cultural standards and the value of 'popular culture' compared with elite art is part of the study of the media in society in higher education. There is also an interest in the role of the media in the democratic process, which has grown in the post-war period, as the media have become a more integral part of the political process. It is in this area that media scholars confront most openly what is a fundamental issue for most of them: the exercise of power in modern society.

Media scholars up until recently have discussed culture and democracy within the national context. However, technological and economic change has led to the growth of global media. The development of satellites for communication and the growth of global information systems allows infinite scope for the distribution of electronic goods around the world (Thussu, 1998). The concentration of media control into the hands of an ever-smaller number of huge western-based transnational companies enhances the flow of western, primarily Anglo-American, media products to other countries. These new electronic empires are having a profound impact on national media systems and cultural sovereignty, and raise the issue of cultural autonomy. Media scholars have become increasingly concerned with the process of 'globalisation' seen to be taking place. They debate over who benefits and who loses from this process, over its impact on global culture – is it building a new global culture in which everyone can participate or are traditional cultures being swept aside by more dominant cultures? – and over the extent to which change is furthering the democratisation of global politics. At the start of the twenty-first century the issue of the media and globalisation is at the forefront of the debates in the field of media studies. Yet as media scholars engage with these issues and debates, and develop their theories to explain the phenomena they observe, the whole endeavour of media studies is being challenged.

CHALLENGES FACING THE FIELD

All theory is a social construction. It is part of an effort by scholars to make sense of what is happening around them. The scholarly 'community' exploring the media and mass communication process has particular characteristics that determine what it wants to achieve with the theories it creates. Of course, it is important to state that the nature of theorising changes over time as new scholars enter the field or as the field of study responds to events in the outside world. But media studies is a relatively new field of academic enquiry. While there are different accounts of the history of the field, it is often stated that the academic study of the media began in earnest in America in the 1930s. As the field has grown it has attracted people from a range of other academic disciplines. Many of these scholars, although coming from different theoretical perspectives and approaches, can be seen as facing certain common challenges. They work in a field often looked down on by their colleagues in the more traditional and established disciplines. Robert McChesney (1994: 342) sums up the disposition of many working in the field in America when he talks of communication being 'regarded by the pooh-bahs in history, political science and sociology as having roughly the same intellectual merit as, say, driver's education'. Such feeling is as much the result of the newness of the field of study as the attitude of traditional academia. However, the insecurity of media scholars is accentuated by the hostility of media practitioners towards the academic study of the media.

Media studies are treated with disdain, ridicule and contempt by many working within the industries. The press bemoans the growing number of students exercising their free choice to take media studies courses. Between 1986 and 1994 there was a fivefold increase in students on media studies courses in British universities which, according to *The Sunday Times* (13 July 1997), is one of the problems facing the British education system. In popular culture 'media studies' is the course followed by the academically or socially challenged characters in soap operas and comedies: it is, in the words of *The Sunday Times*, a 'soft' subject that satisfies the cravings of our media-saturated times 'at the expense of more difficult traditional degrees'. The mutual antagonism between practitioners and scholars has been well documented in media research (see, for example, Schlesinger, 1980; Burns 1977). While journalism has vigorously upheld its right to investigate and scrutinise the working of all institutions in our society, it has been reluctant and often obstructive of attempts to draw aside the veil that covers over the operations of the media. This was noted by one of the pioneers of mass communication research, Paul Lazarsfeld, who wrote:

> If there is any one institutional disease to which the media of mass communications seem particularly subject, it is a nervous reaction to criticism. As a student of mass media I have been continually struck and occasionally puzzled by this reaction, for it is the media themselves which so vigorously defend principles guaranteeing the right to criticise.
>
> (Cited in Burns, 1977: xv)

Nothing much has changed since Lazarsfeld made his comments in the late 1940s.

The disdain media studies receives from popular journalism is encapsulated in the comments of *The Times* 'expert' on media matters. For her, media studies 'reek not only of trendiness ... but of political correctness' (Maddox, 1996). She cringes at 'the myriad of courses on cultural identity and on racial stereotyping, the modish textbooks with titles such as The Gendering of a Leisure Technology (women's use of the domestic video recorder)', which for her 'smack of an in-built message ready to be preached'. Another commentator writing in the *Independent* expresses his angst that if you 'wander into the media studies section of any large bookshop ... you can find vexed and anxious works about the representation of women, blacks, gays and disabled people' (Sutcliffe, 1997). He wonders 'if very little else is being studied in universities but the myriad forms of disadvantage and oppression that the modern world throws up'. Putting aside the stereotypical representation of 'media studies' (see Chapter 5 for a discussion of stereotyping) – and the lack of any hard data to support the assertions about what rests on the shelves of bookshops – the effect of such criticism has been to produce a sense of insecurity amongst media studies scholars. One observer has even talked of a 'crisis of confidence' (Durant, 1991: 428).

The hostility from these 'others' should be expected. Media studies has adopted a critical disposition to the operation and practices of the media industries. Nicholas Garnham noted in the early 1980s 'all schools of thought within British media studies in their different ways attack the media's own cherished self-image as pillars of liberal plural democracy'. For him the process of demystifying the media and raising the consciousness of people about the ways in which the media determine their view of life is 'highly and unavoidably political'. Inside the world of academic inquiry media studies has often presented a brashness and disrespect, which has offended traditional modes of inquiry of the more conservative academic disciplines. It is therefore 'hardly surprising that media studies is not welcomed with open arms by either the media industry or the educational establishment' (Garnham, 1983). The critical approach of media studies has also attracted a number of scholars with their own political and personal agendas, especially around the issues of representation and identity. However, the engagement of media studies with the political should not be exaggerated. One of the objectives of all 'liberal' education as it developed in the post-war period has been to raise consciousness about the way in which the world works (see Hartley *et al.*, 1985, for discussion).

The standing of media studies in the worlds of education and the media industries presents challenges to the scholarly pursuit of the subject. On the one hand, there is the search for academic respectability and the need for some form of disciplinary order. On the other, there is the desire to focus on concerns that are 'oppositional' to the established power structures of society and to defend marginalised groups within society. Gitlin (1991) argues the contradictory pressures on media scholars have resulted in a gap between the rhetoric and reality in the scholarly pursuit of the subject. He points out that media studies 'radiates subversion', 'flatters itself for deep insurgency' and insists that 'interpretation is intrinsically political' while rarely engaging in 'political and intellectual action that extends beyond the protected grazing fields of academe'. This he sees as a betrayal of the traditional link between social sciences and social criticism. As he says, 'considering the thousands of intelligent people absorbed in media studies around the world, their collective output does not do a great deal of criticism at all'. He identifies two developments that have undermined the efforts of media scholars to engage with the public and the political process. The first is what Paul Lazarsfeld labelled 'administrative research' and C. Wright Mills called 'abstracted empiricism'. Mills was critical of social sciences in the 1940s and 1950s for restricting their study to what can be measured – empiricism was abstracted from general ideas about social structures. Thus the larger motives behind social life were neglected. This state of affairs, says Gitlin, has become the 'normal procedure in most of our communications and social sciences departments' in the West, and research that is 'driven by countability too easily becomes hostage to the political project deemed thinkable, fundable and feasible at the moment'. The normalisation of abstracted empiricism has been completed by the technological development of the computer, which enables us to count more quickly. For Gitlin, knowledge produced in this way simply serves the established centres of power in society.

However, Gitlin is also critical of the response to abstracted empiricism. To counter the number-crunching inclination, some scholars began to try to reclaim the world of ideas. The intellectual roots of cultural studies lie in the late 1950s with the freeing-up of intellectual and political discourse, which was to burst out into the spontaneous political actions of the 1960s. According to Gitlin, it began, in part, as an attempt to 'to defend the marginalised and to find a theoretical warrant for their significance'. Those associated with the 'cultural studies' approach, however, began to elevate theory as the central plank in the study of the mass media. Sometimes marching under the banners of post-structuralism or post-modernism, they dismissed number crunching as 'empty headed manual labour' (Lewis, 1997) and proclaimed the supremacy of the theorist who became the 'master of ceremonies' in a world of subjective interpretation that completely marginalised quantitative research (Gitlin, 1991: 330). While criticising the great old men of social science and their grand theories, the grand new men and women of cultural studies searched for their all-embracing meta-narrative. The result, according to Gitlin, has been to produce a club that, in order to join, you have to communicate in dense prose and obscure jargon, and recite the words and thoughts of its leading members. Such prose is seen as incapacitating the scholar from engaging in broader political and intellectual debate. This approach has grown rapidly in the last couple of decades. While not all cultural approaches are riddled with obscurantism, much of what is today labelled as 'critical theory' in the scholarly study of the media has often failed as much as abstracted empiricism to make connections with the public.

Scholarship as silence

> In country after country, academic mass communication researchers have had little to say to those making policy. The field has in fact become largely a culture in exile from everything but itself, a cloistered world of ritual and enclosed performance within the isolation of the annual conference and the refereed journal. The question . . . is what should, and can, be the proper relation of scholar, intellectual and theorist to a changing world.
>
> The issue is not new. In 1944 C. Wright Mills . . . was a 'public intellectual', someone who sought to address a general and educated audience. The field of mass communications, indeed, of the academy in general, is now ironically and overwhelmingly peopled by private intellectuals. The character of the privacy is . . . interior, often self-serving, obsessively careerist, assured, technically proficient. . . . There is the passionless, almost dehumanised technique of the empiricist for whom method and the accretion of data seem more important than the construction of a meaningful question . . . And then there is the ideological technician, conversant in this or that theoretical scripture, disciple of this or that theoretician, for whom too often scholarship is a mask behind which sits an isolated, powerless, broken heart . . . cocooned within the righteous certainty that avoids what Thompson once called 'the collision of evidence and the awkward confrontation of experience' (1980: 15). Both postures put too much distance between academic inquiry and what we will, in a deliberately contentious manner, call the real world that the policy maker inhabits. Both nurture the irrelevant culture of the cloister

Source: Docherty et al., 1993

WHAT IS THEORY?

So far our discussion has addressed the subject matter of media studies and the main issues and debates in the field of mass media and mass communication that have been conducted over the years. These issues and debates reveal the basic problems that media theorists are trying to address. The subject matter is the phenomena they are trying to make sense of. The purpose of theory is to explain, comprehend and interpret phenomena and put forward propositions suggesting why such phenomena occur in the manner they do. In trying to understand how the media work, their role in society and their impact on individuals we cannot survive by observation alone. We have to make choices about what is important, what are the main ideas that enable us to organise our observations and make sense of the variety of information available and provide the best guide as to what to investigate. In everyday life we all implicitly have some sort of working theory to comprehend what is happening around us. We all have some view about the media and the process of mass communication. Theorists simply make explicit this process, enhance our awareness and deepen and develop our understanding of the role of theory in explaining the media.

The first general purpose of theory is to answer the question 'What is going on?' Events and behaviour are often so complex you need a theory to describe what is happening. For example, it is often difficult to differentiate between the process of information and entertainment in the output of the media. However, such theories are often limited and unsatisfactory, which leads people to the second purpose of building theory: explanation. Theory is perhaps most commonly used to try to explain how and why something has happened or why someone has behaved in a certain way. For example, how does television influence children and adolescents? Did the British tabloid press change the way in which many people voted in the 1992 general election? Explanatory theory provides the basis for trying to predict what will happen in the future based on drawing conclusions from a set of premises about behaviour or conditions in the present. Theorists are always trying to predict what will happen next in a given set of circumstances or with certain kinds of actions. Finally prediction helps to guide or inform how people should behave or act in a particular set of circumstances or conditions. It provides the basis for the choice of future action based on the predictions made, thereby helping individuals to manage their environment or negotiate social change. Thus theory can be used in a variety of ways to structure our observations.

Theory operates at a number of levels. It is possible to identify three levels at which theory is discussed – common-sense, practitioner and academic. At the common-sense level we have already described how people have implicit understandings or ideas with which they make sense of the media. Some of these commonly acknowledged and accepted viewpoints serve as the basis for framing the nature of public discussion and debate. Such common-sense theories are not the focus of this book but are important because they figure prominently in public debate about the media, often leading to simplistic portrayals of the role and influence of the media, and are interwoven into a number of theories developed by media scholars. Practitioner theories relate to the ideas developed by those working in the media in the conduct of their work; described by McQuail (1994: 4–5) as 'operational' theory, they cover the accumulated practical wisdom found in most organisational and professional settings. While never formally spelled out, this knowledge is influential in shaping the work of media practitioners and hence the output of the media. The third level of theory – and the primary focus of this book – is academic theory. The media have been studied by a variety of scholars from a range of academic disciplines such as sociology, psychology, social psychology, literary studies, anthropology, sociolinguistics, economics, political science, philosophy, history, law, rhetoric and speech communication, group and systems theory, and even mathematics. The distinctions between the different approaches are not always clear. Each discipline often draws on the work of the others. Some argue that media scholars depend on theory and concepts from other academic disciplines, levelling the charge that there is a 'relative lack of original theory' in the study of the media and mass communication (Berger, quoted in Craig, 1994: 35). Others claim the field is characterised by 'the neglect of theory and the underdevelopment of a conceptual framework to guide research' (cited in Golding and Murdock, 1978: 60), the result of which is a 'theoretical vacuum' into which media scholars pour other disciplines' theories; hence the diverse and often contradictory literature in the area of media theory.

With the number and variety of media scholars, it is not surprising there are conflicts over the assumptions, foci and methods of analysis in the field and that contradictory hypotheses and theories are put forward. It is also the case that while describing similar phenomena and events, scholars present very different ways of understanding and analysing these. They ask different questions of the world and do so because they observe the world very differently. As all social theory is a human construction we should expect to find media theory having different objectives. One important difference within academic theory is that between normative and empirical theories. McQuail (1994: 4) notes that normative theories of the media are 'concerned with examining and prescribing how the media *ought* to work if a certain set of values are to be observed or attained'. Such theories lay down a desired set of conditions or goals for the practice and performance of the media. As a result such theories shape the expectations placed on the media by other social agencies as well as their own audiences. Often, normative theories are encoded in the laws, regulations and policies of any society. They provide a basis for research into the mass media that seeks to assess how they live up to these expectations of social and cultural performance. Empirical – or social scientific – theories make up the more common approach to media theory building. They are concerned with finding explanations based on the 'facts' or observable data. At one level they are concerned with making causal links between the factors (independent variables) explaining the event or phenomenon that is being examined (dependent variables). At another level they can start with a set of premises and deduce conclusions about behaviour or action based on these premises. Empirical theory then seeks to build a model or develop a conceptual framework to explain the phenomena it is trying to understand. A model is a simplified picture of reality that does not attempt to establish a relationship between the variables identified, while a conceptual framework goes further to interpret the relationship. Such a process reduces the richness of reality to a number of propositions and as a result can be criticised. Hence the importance of developing means and methods to assess and judge the competing claims of theories.

Social scientific theory seeks to describe and explain events objectively and to use empirical research methods to evaluate the usefulness and validity of theory (Baran and Davies, 1995: 5). Theories that cannot be verified by empirical observation are rejected. This can sometimes be a matter of controversy as questions are raised about the effectiveness of particular methods of empirical observation. This is accentuated by a growing debate in media studies between those who adhere to a strict interpretation of the scientific research and those adopting a more subjective approach to the study of the media and society. Empiricism, the focus on scientific method and the search for objectivity have increasingly been treated with suspicion and criticised as illusory (see Lewis, 1997). Trying to apply scientific criteria to assess human behaviour is fraught with problems for social researchers; human behaviour is complex, difficult to measure and goal oriented, which confounds efforts to make assessments of cause and effect. Researchers have faced many difficulties in applying scientific method to the study of mass communication, resulting in a dispute between what are the appropriate measures to assess media theory and conduct media research. Testing the validity of theory in a field that includes work 'being done from a range of different disciplinary backgrounds, using different concepts and methods and sometimes applying entirely different criteria about permissible forms of argument, about what constitutes "evidence" and about the conventions for connecting propositions to data' is not easy (Corner, 1997: 452). Whatever the means and methods used to test a theory, it is nevertheless important that judgements are made. The ultimate test of any theory is its usefulness and application to solving problems in the 'real' world.

The *relevance* of theory to the real world of social problems and personal experience is part of making a judgement about its efficacy. Theory is often portrayed as being detached from the day-to-day issues of ordinary men and women. It is seen as separate from the 'real' business of scholars: the process of research. However, theory informs research; without theory research is simply the amassing of lots of facts on a somewhat random basis. Theory guides research by helping scholars to organise how they gather facts and observe the world. But good theory should also help us to understand and make sense of our personal experience and the wider structures and processes of daily life, and how they shape our interaction with other people. The ultimate test, then, of any theory is the extent to which it furthers our understanding of the world in which we live. This applies to media theory as to any other kind of theory. We should test its relevance by how far it furthers our understanding of the role and influence of the media and communication in our everyday lives. Gitlin (1991) calls for communication scholars to be more committed to engaging, animating and provoking a general public. This is what good theory should aspire to. It helps us to develop our knowledge of the mass media, and challenge the misleading ideas that have come to dominate public debate about their influence and involvement.

SUMMARY

Media studies is an area of academic study whose boundaries are not clear and discrete. The range of subject matter is wide, rapid technological change is blurring the distinction between traditional mass media as well as introducing new means of mass communication, and there is conflict within the field between different approaches to the study of the subject. Trying to narrow down the subject material requires making decisions about which media to study and what part of the communication process to concentrate on. This book focuses on the traditional media of press and broadcasting as well as the new media that threaten to change the operation of these media. Film and other popular media are mentioned but are not central to the interests of this book because they have developed a theoretical base separately from the other media. Theory can be applied to the different stages of the mass communication process – production, content, reception and effects – as well as to the relationship between them and the impact of the media and mass communication on society. It can also be applied at different levels, from common-sense understanding of the role of the media through to working theories that inform the way in which media practitioners work, and academic theory, which is the main focus of this book.

The inclusion of theories of the media in this book is determined to a large extent by the major issues and debates that have dominated the development of the teaching of media studies. The main debates centre on the *effects* of the media, their *representation* of the world, the factors shaping the *production* of media messages and the nature of the *audiences* consuming these messages. The broader impact of the media on society is discussed with particular attention paid to the role of the mass media in the processes of *democracy* and *globalisation*. Understanding media theory also requires knowledge of media theorists and the conditions under which they work. The pressures and challenges facing the discipline shape the nature of debate as well as the ways in which the media and mass communication are theorised. Finally there is the role and purpose of theory itself. Theory is not isolated from everyday life. It may take a number of forms and operate at a variety of levels but it is an essential component of understanding the world in which we live. Without theory, research would not be possible and our knowledge about how to act in the world reduced. This book asserts that the effectiveness of any media theory is its usefulness in making sense of the processes and problems of mass communication.

Section 1

Developing the field:
a history of media theory

This section outlines the main ways in which the relationship between the media, society and the individual has been conceptualised since the birth of the media. Present-day theories are drawn from debates with previous theories and often are simply an updated or amended version of older theories. Providing this outline is complicated as only recently have media scholars begun 'coming to terms with the past of the field'. This history is not a 'continuous strand of specialised enquiry' but rather a 'disparate and not fully documented succession of theoretical projects, empirical engagements and often heated debate' (Corner *et al.*, 1998: 2). The past not only includes theoretical paths that have been taken but also those that have been ignored and actively discouraged. Older theories, which have been largely discredited by the academic community, are still accepted by segments of the public and by some practitioners and policy makers. Difficulties also arise, as Corner and his colleagues note, because of the separate kinds of intellectual response to the issues and debates posed by the study of the media in Europe and North America. In recent times this division has been added to by the development of perspectives from the non-western world (see Mowlana, 1996). Thus any attempt to trace the genealogy of media and mass communication theorising can only be a partial account of a rich variety of thinking.

The body of theory that underpins the study of the media today draws on a variety of clues laid down by linguists, mathematicians, sociologists, psychologists, economists and literary theorists, to name but a few. While mass communication has cropped up in a range of diverse academic and scholastic interests, it has nevertheless been neglected in theoretical terms. This is a strange omission given that many see communication as a necessary ingredient for social and human relations. This neglect is particularly true of social theory. Few of the classical social theorists included communication and the media as part of their grand narratives on society. However, this has not prevented media scholars and theorists tracing their intellectual projects back to theoretical perspectives developed in other disciplines such as sociology, politics and psychology. Hardt says this is justified as the 'study of mass communication can only make sense in the context of a theory of society' (quoted in Boyd Barrett and Newbold, 1995: 6) and the most important theoretical roots for media scholars are historically located in the social sciences.

It is possible to suggest several conceptual frameworks or perspectives emerging from the social science tradition that have figured strongly in the development of media theory. These include mass society theory, functionalism, Marxism, the concept of the public sphere and 'freedom of the press'. There is not always a clear distinction between these frameworks in the literature on the media and mass communication, and they are not coherent in their own right – often being sites of struggles of interpretation between different theorists and researchers. On occasions they are used as pejorative labels to attack other writers' work, rather than terms of elucidation. Throughout the historical development of media theory the influence of each of these perspectives has varied. There is also disagreement about the extent of their influence – for example, functionalism is often described as the 'dominant' or 'traditional' approach to thinking about the media and society (Gitlin, 1978), while Marxism offers 'the most often referred to and most seductive theories as far as the media are concerned' (Sorlin, 1994: 8). These approaches have also been re-interpreted and re-formulated according to new circumstances and situations, and in more recent times, have been challenged by new ways of thinking, especially post-modernism and feminism. It is also the case that while each aspires to be an all-embracing theoretical approach, they have often been applied to particular media and particular parts of the mass communication process.

Their application also has to be seen in the context of the social and political concerns of the time in which they were developed. Scholars and theorists are no more immune from the fads, fashions and climate of opinion of their day than ordinary men and women. Theories do not develop in a vacuum, they are a response to the concerns of the period in which they emerge. This section traces several stages in the historical development of media and mass communication theory, and identifies the actors and the particular concerns they were addressing. The divisions are somewhat arbitrary but it is possible to broadly highlight key stages in which certain perspectives are dominant or where a struggle exists between competing theories for supremacy over the field. Such struggles often produced new theories, new perspectives and a re-conceptualisation of the role of the media. By tracing the rise and fall of the different perspectives we can understand how current thinking about the media has evolved.

Chapter One

MASS SOCIETY AND ☐
MODERNITY: EARLY MEDIA
THEORY

Sustained research in the field of mass communication and media studies developed in the United States from the 1930s onwards (Corner *et al.*, 1998: 2). This was some 40 years after the birth of modern media, which happened between 1890 and 1920 with the expansion of mass circulation newspapers, the rapid rise of the cinema and the development of radio (see Williams, 1998; Curran and Seaton, 1997). During these formative years 'the mass media existed without mass communications research as we know it today' (Brown, 1970). While a number of isolated studies of particular aspects of the media were conducted, systematic consideration was limited. However, the prevailing concerns and perspectives of this period have shaped much of our thinking about the media, and any discussion of media theory needs to begin by describing some of the views developed at this time. These views were by and large pessimistic, dominated by a set of notions, often contradictory, later referred to as 'mass society theory' and part of a wider debate about the impact of 'modernity'.

MODERNITY AND THE BEGINNINGS OF MEDIA THEORY

The birth of the mass media coincided with the culmination of widespread, large-scale change in western societies seen by many as representing the arrival of 'modernity'. Modernity is a difficult concept (see Grossberg *et al.*, 1998: 49–57). There is disagreement not only over what it is but also when the 'modern age' began. Some argue it was as early as the late fifteenth century with the onset of the Reformation and Renaissance, while others identify the arrival of the Enlightenment in the eighteenth century. However, it was in the middle of the nineteenth century with the expansion of industrial capitalism, the advancement of science, the rise of mass democracy, urbanisation, colonialism, mass education and public communication that western societies were seen as entering into a period of profound change. By the last decade of the century it was clear these changes and transformations had resulted in the 'search for the new, the turning away from tradition' (Grossberg *et al.*, 1998: 51).

The consequences of modernity were – and still are – a matter of much debate and disagreement. As the nineteenth century progressed social elites, religious and political leaders as well as leading intellectuals, in North America and Europe were expressing their fears about its disruptive impact (see Carey, 1992). They were pessimistic about the break-down of traditional society, and preoccupied with the rise of the 'masses', which they saw as a real or potential threat to the stability of the social order. The potential for social dis-integration was perhaps first articulated by Alexis de Tocqueville who, writing in the 1840s, complained modern society was governed 'by an all pervasive egalitarianism which breeds individualism, materialism and social instability' (quoted in Swingewood, 1977: 3). He believed that mass democracy was bringing about a levelling-down of culture and society and erosion of the influence of the social elite, which traditionally had guaranteed social order. In Britain, Matthew Arnold expressed concern about the debasement of culture in his influential *Culture and Anarchy* published in 1869. Arnold argued that only by maintaining and raising cultural standards could class tensions be alleviated and the threat of revolt from the unthinking, unruly and potentially violent masses be prevented. The German philosopher, Friedrich Nietzsche, was more stark in his warning that 'everywhere the mediocre are combining in order to make themselves master', which would end in the 'tyranny of the least and the dumbest' (quoted in Carey, 1992: 4). Such views typified the position of many intellectuals at the end of the nineteenth century (see Carey, 1992). Modernity was subverting the 'normal order', breaking down established traditional com-munities in which people had a sense of belonging and a sense of their place in the overall scheme of things. Traditional communities were being replaced by a new society in which people were simply a mass of individuals isolated from one another and from the social ties that bound them together – this society is labelled 'mass society'. The severing of tra-ditional social ties and orientations, it was argued, rendered the individual more isolated, with the effect that he or she was more vulnerable and more susceptible to the most base and trivial instincts and emotions being peddled by, amongst others, the new mass politi-cal movements and media.

The coincidence of the rise of the media and the fears of the impact of modernity was important for the initial thinking about the media. The history of mass communication is in one sense a history of the fear of the masses – or those 'dirty people of no name' as the historian Clarendon called them – who became increasingly visible with the growth of the media and communication industries (see Williams, 1998: Chapter 1). Sorlin (1994) points out that when added to other words the word 'mass' provides a pejorative nuance. Thus mass circulation newspapers are full of trivia and gossip, mass art is cheap and lacking refinement, and mass culture is aimed at satisfying the lowest common denomi-nator. The silent movies, the mass circulation newspapers of Northcliffe and Hearst in Britain and America, and cheap novels were the main vehicles for the mass culture so despised by the intellectual and political elites. While proprietors such as Northcliffe pro-moted their enterprises by encouraging their newspapers to 'deal with the interests of the mass of the people' by 'giving the public what it wants' (quoted in Carey, 1992: 6), critics such as Nietzsche were 'contemptuous of every kind of culture that is compatible with reading, not to speak of writing for, newspapers' (quoted in Carey, 1992: 7). Thus the initial thinking about the media was contextualised by fears and concerns about their role in the breakdown of social order and cultural decline.

These fears and concerns were reflected in popular debate at the time about the influence of the media on human behaviour. Children and women were seen as highly susceptible to the 'power' of the silent films blamed for growing juvenile delinquency and rising youth crime. One contemporary observer commented these films were 'a direct incentive to crime, demonstrating, for instance, how a theft could be perpetuated' while *The Times* newspaper opined that 'all those who care for the moral well-being and education of the child will set their face like flint against this form of entertainment' (quoted in Pearson, 1983: 63–4). One of the first attempts to explore such common-sense views was the enquiry set up by the National Council for Public Morals in 1917, which found there was no conclusive evidence either way about the role of the cinema in the growth of youth crime and delinquency (Eldridge *et al.*, 1997: 17). However, such fears and concerns were organised into a loose theory whose assumptions have exercised to a greater or lesser extent a hold over thinking about the media and society ever since. These assumptions centred on the notion of an 'all-powerful' media that have a negative and/or disruptive impact on people and society.

THE RISE AND FALL OF MASS SOCIETY THEORY

'Mass society' as a perspective on mass communication was not systematically developed at the time when the great classical thinkers of the nineteenth century were musing over the consequences of modernity. Rather it was worked up into a theory much later, drawing together the work of a number of classical social theorists and behavioural scientists who came to prominence in the 1930s and 1940s with their view that human behaviour could be conceived as a response to stimuli in the outside world. The initial development of the theory must be seen in conjunction with the birth of modern sociology. Echoes of the mass society resonate in the work of the pioneers of social theory including Comte, Pareto, Mannheim, Durkheim and Tonnies. The contribution of the latter two is crucial. The German sociologist, Ferdinand Tonnies, used the concepts of *Gemeinschaft* and *Gesellschaft* to distinguish between traditional and modern society. Tonnies argued the former society was one in which people were bound together by personal, traditional and communal ties which characterise social relations that are 'reciprocal, binding sentiment . . . which keeps human beings together as members of a totality' (quoted in De Fleur and Ball-Rokeach, 1989: 153). The latter society is one in which personal relations are anonymous, impersonal and isolated. Individuals are seen as rootless, not treated or valued on the basis of their individual qualities but bound together by needs rather than tradition. As Tonnies put it

> everybody is by himself [sic] and isolated, and there exists a condition of
> tension against all others . . . everybody refuses to everyone else contact
> with and admittance to his sphere i.e. intrusions are regarded as hostile acts

> ... nobody wants to grant and produce anything for another individual, nor will he be inclined to give ungrudgingly to another individual.
>
> (Quoted in De Fleur and Ball-Rokeach, 1989: 154)

Emile Durkheim, a French sociologist, developed Tonnies' distinction but with a different interpretation. He was interested in understanding how social stability, or *solidarity*, is maintained, in particular the part that individuals and organisations play in its formation and maintenance. He had a less romantic notion of traditional – or folk – society in which he saw individuals forced to perform certain roles whether they wanted to or not. He referred to this as 'mechanical solidarity'. By contrast, in modern society people have more freedom. Durkheim emphasised the differences between people as well as their capacity to work together. He argued that in spite of the vast array of individual ideas and beliefs there are certain ways of acting, feeling and thinking that are expected and required from people if society is to operate in harmony – what he called 'social facts'. These social facts are the established, expected or conventional ways of behaving laid down in custom, law and precedent. Individuals accept these obligations to ensure that stability is maintained. Durkheim sees a 'collective conscience' underlying the acceptance of these obligations. He used the label 'organic solidarity' to describe modern social relations. In this sense he was more optimistic than Tonnies, seeing new forms of social relations as an improvement on the old ways of doing things. He did, however, warn of dangers in his concept of 'anomie' when individual needs, aspirations and desires get out of hand and are no longer contained by society – in other words, the collapse of the collective conscience. In the works of these two sociologists emerge a number of assumptions about the relationship between the individual and society that have underpinned the application of mass society theory to mass communication. Individuals are regarded as isolated from one another, their interactions are impersonal, and their social obligations and bonds are informal and a matter of choice (De Fleur and Ball-Rokeach, 1989: 159). Such analysis presents people as relatively helpless and open to suggestion.

Support for mass society theory developed between 1930 and 1960 as events conspired to provide some form of support for its main contentions. Crucial was the rise of fascism and totalitarianism in Europe. The rise of Hitler was partly explained by the collapse of the old social values and their exploitation by a skilled demagogue making use of the new, modern means of mass communication to influence ordinary Germans to support his policies. The impotence of the individual and the power of the media were reinforced by the Nazis' use of the mass media, mass rallies and mass bureaucracies to promote their ideology and develop allegiance to the state. Nazi Germany – as well as Stalin's Soviet Union – were identified as mass societies and in the years after the war questions were asked in the United States as to whether mass culture inevitably resulted in totalitarian societies (Grossberg *et al.*, 1998: 35). Such questions were motivated by the rapid development of mass communications in

America. The conclusion identified by many was that America was not vulnerable because of the diversity of its culture. However, the advent of the 'Red Scare' in the 1950s, the role of the media in the rise of Senator Joe McCarthy and the uncritical reporting of his 'witch hunt' raised doubts (see Aronson, 1970). Critics such as C. Wright Mills (1957) did not see American democracy as encompassing a broad range of groups in the political process, but rather as controlled by a small elite representing the 'military industrial complex'. This elite was able to exert its control through the media and other social institutions, including the education system. Mills was concerned with why the average American citizen felt apathetic and powerless, and chose to remain uninformed about democracy.

If Mills was concerned with mass society questions at the political level, others engaged with them at the social and cultural level. In Britain between the two world wars, defenders of high culture were marshalling their arguments against the ways in which the media and other social institutions were pandering to popular or mass taste. The most influential voice was that of the literary critic, F.R. Leavis, who in his text, *Mass Civilisation and Minority Culture*, published in 1930, railed against popular culture, which he saw as simply motivated by the lust for profit and an appeal to the lowest common denominator. Leavis was particularly concerned about the importation of American cultural products, such as Hollywood films, cheap thriller paperback novels and comics, into the United Kingdom. He believed, for example, that cinema involved 'surrender, under conditions of hypnotic receptivity, to the cheapest emotional appeals' (quoted in Pearson, 1983: 93). Leavis's fear of 'Americanisation' – that is, of the cheap, the vulgar and the material – was taken up in the 1950s by other cultural critics such as Hoggart (1958) and has served as the basis for continual concerns at the global level about the increase of American TV programmes throughout the world. Leavis and his *Scrutiny* group found support for their defence of elite culture in the United States. One of the interesting aspects of mass society theory is that it attracted intellectuals of both the Left and Right. Leavis's moralist and conservative argument for the maintenance of cultural standards was echoed by the Frankfurt School, a group of loosely affiliated radical, Left-leaning, Marxist-influenced intellectual émigrés – including Adorno, Horkheimer, Benjamin and Marcuse – who fled from Nazi Germany to America and believed that mass popular culture was sapping creative thinking, reducing individual freedom and promoting false wants through consumerism (see Bennett, 1982). While Leavis and his colleagues were literary theorists or cultural critics, the contribution to mass society theory made in America was less speculative and more empirical. It was conducted by sociologists who sought to test the central tenets of the theory by empirical investigation and examination (Bennett, 1982: 39).

The Frankfurt School

The leading scholars of the Frankfurt School were Max Horkheimer and Theodor Adorno. After fleeing Germany for the United States they were prolific in the 1930s and 1940s but largely ignored. It was not until the 1960s that their work and ideas became more widely disseminated. In their writing they identified with various forms of high culture such as classical symphony music, high art and literature, which they viewed as having innate value. They were critical of mass culture and much of their writings focused on the role of the mass media in the reproduction of high culture. They were sceptical that high culture could be reproduced by the mass media. Adorno argued neither radio nor records could reproduce the authentic sound and experience of hearing a live orchestra. Similarly magazines and the serialisation of novels were inadequate substitutes for literature and diverted people from seeking out the 'real thing'. Horkheimer wrote 'the struggle against mass culture can consist only in pointing out its connection with the persistence of social injustice' (quoted in Inglis, 1990: 39). They emphasised the role of mass culture as shaping the individual in mass society and coined the term 'cultural industries', which became an important term in the vocabulary of cultural studies in the post-war period. Their rediscovery centred on the most detached member of the group, Herbert Marcuse, who became a leading icon of the student protests of the 1960s. His book One Dimensional Man brought together the arguments of the School that capitalism was responsible for the creation of false needs, false consciousness and mass culture, which enslaved working people. The main works of the School relevant for media scholars are Adorno and Horkheimer (1973) and Benjamin (1970), which are reproduced in Curran et al. (1977).

Source: adapted from Baran and Davies, 1995

Mass society theory – as derived from speculation about human nature rather than empirical observation based on research – has encouraged a view of the effects of the media on people's lives and behaviour as straightforward and unambiguous. This perspective has been labelled as the 'hypodermic needle' or 'magic bullet' model, and assumes there is a direct correlation between what people see, hear and read and how they behave. The stimuli-response model was reinforced in the early decades of the twentieth century by the rise in the School of behaviourism in psychology, which saw human action as a conditioned response to events that happened in an individual's environment. Individual personality did not count as behaviourists rejected the view that conscious thought and reflection determines how an individual acts. Behaviourism provided strong support for believing that social action was triggered by external stimuli as opposed to personal choice based on individual beliefs and knowledge. This helped many to account for the effectiveness of the Nazis' use of the media in the 1930s. Mass society theory, with its notions of the helpless, isolated and passive individuals, easily and readily manipulated by messages from an all-powerful media, exercised considerable influence over early media theory. Its popularity, however, decreased from the late 1950s and early 1960s onwards as some of its inherent flaws became apparent and the fear of totalitarianism receded. While debates about mass culture endure, mass society theory in its classic form has virtually disappeared from academic theory. However, as Glover (1984: 4) notes, 'where this sort of thinking does survive is in public discussions about the media which are often haunted by the ghost of theories that have long since passed away'. For example, much of the tabloid press reporting of the child killers of James Bulger (Liverpool, UK, 1993) attributed their act to watching too much violence on television and video.

Mass society theory and the media

1. Mass media are a negative and disruptive force in society and should be controlled.
2. Mass media have the power to directly influence the attitudes and behaviour of ordinary people.
3. People are vulnerable to the power of mass media because they have become isolated and alienated from traditional social institutions that have protected them from propaganda and manipulation.
4. The social changes brought about by the disruptive influence of mass media will result in the advent of more authoritarian and centrally controlled societies.
5. Mass media also bring about the decline in cultural standards and values by promoting trivial and demeaning ideas and activities that threaten civilised behaviour.

Source: adapted from Baran and Davies, 1995: 41–50

PROPAGANDA ANALYSIS AND PUBLIC OPINION

Mass society theory treated the media and mass communication as part of a range of disruptive forces in society. It was not a theory of the media but considered the media as part of an overall process of social change. During the inter-war years a set of theories developed that specifically focused on the contents of the media and their impact. These related to 'propaganda' and the techniques deployed to persuade millions of people, the general public, of particular points of view or opinion. Interest in propaganda was stimulated by the First World War – according to one leading scholar of the period the

'World War led to the discovery of propaganda by both the man in the street and the man in the study' (quoted in Jowett and O'Donnell, 1998: 208). The success of British propaganda during the First World War – on which Goebbels modelled his propaganda efforts – encouraged the belief that the general public was vulnerable to propaganda. This was enhanced by the claims of the advertising and the public relations industry in the 1920s about their ability to sell products and engineer consent (see, for example, Bernays, 1923). The high point for such a belief was reached in the 1930s with the wide-scale use of propaganda by the fascist regimes in Europe and communism in the Soviet Union. This led a number of scholars to examine the impact of wartime propaganda and assess the conditions under which it was effective. The most important of these scholars was Harold Lasswell whose first book, *Propaganda Techniques in the World War*, was published in 1927.

The possibility of manipulating people through propaganda and publicity was raised in the opening decade of the twentieth century. While the word 'propaganda' did not become commonplace until after the First World War, scholars such as the English philosopher Graham Wallas believed that the potential for such manipulation mitigated against democracy being a viable political system (Jowett and O'Donnell, 1998: 104). Wallas argued that men and women were not governed entirely by reason but often acted on 'affection and instinct', which the professional manipulator could arouse and direct to follow a desired course of action. It was left to Lasswell (1927) to develop propaganda analysis, providing meticulous detailing of the techniques and skills required of the propagandist. He drew attention to the role of symbols and myth in the efforts to stimulate large-scale public action, emphasising that the appeal of propaganda was not only in the content of messages and the way in which they were presented but also in the 'state of mind' of the audience. He argued social and political factors, including economic depression and political instability, had affected the psychology of the public in the inter-war years, making them more vulnerable to crude forms of propaganda. Lasswell was implicitly questioning the hypodermic needle model. He argued the media could not be simply used to sway the audience into believing certain things and thereby control them. Rather there had to be certain conditions – political, social and economic – apparent in the public before propaganda could be effective. Lasswell's insights were part of a broader debate in the inter-war years about the nature of public opinion.

One contribution to this debate was from a *New York Times* journalist, Walter Lippmann, whose book *Public Opinion* (1922) has been described as 'the founding book in American media studies' (Carey, 1989: 75). Lippmann and some of his colleagues in the American press were interested in the ability of the public to make decisions in an increasingly complex and manipulated world. His first contribution to the study of the media was a content analysis of the coverage of the Russian Revolution by the *New York Times* (Lippmann and Merz, 1920). From an examination of a sample of stories from over a thousand issues of the paper over a 36-month period the conclusion was that the reporting was 'nothing short of disastrous' for being 'misleading'. Lippmann and Merz argued the newspaper had failed in 'performing the supreme duty in a democracy of supplying information on which the public feeds'. Lippmann believed in the importance of 'sound public opinion' but increasingly came to doubt whether this could be achieved. In his most famous book, the aforementioned *Public Opinion* (1922), he developed his scepticism about the individual's ability to make sense of the world around him or her. He highlighted the discrepancies that exist between the 'world outside and the pictures in our head' – that is, between the factual features of the world and people's beliefs about the world. This gap can be attributed to the interpretation – or misinterpretation – of events provided by the press, of which Lippmann enumerated several examples. But even if the media performed its duty, Lippmann argued that people could not learn enough from the media to help them understand what is happening. There were, in his opinion, psychological and social barriers, including the problems of stereotyping, self-interest, censorship and privacy, which prevent people from developing informed and accurate pictures in their heads, a viewpoint he developed in subsequent work (1925), which portrayed ordinary citizens as living in a world they can not see, do not understand and are unable to direct. Lippmann's work drew attention to the mediated nature of reality. Both he and Lasswell in their different ways argued for consideration of the prejudices, opinions and feelings of the audience in trying to understand how people make sense of the messages they receive. They were, however, essentially pessimistic in their view of the public's ability to cope with processing and understanding information. They both conceptualised the media as external to the community, delivering a vast amount of not always reliable information to individuals not properly equipped to make sense of what they read, heard and saw.

Other theorists such as John Dewey (1927) were more optimistic in their view of the general public. Dewey did not see the public as a mass of isolated and alienated individuals but rather as a group of people with a common purpose, who wanted to communicate with one another about similar problems. He believed people are actors not spectators in what is happening in the world around them and placed greater trust in their ability to call on resources to combat propaganda. He emphasised the power of education through which people could learn how to resist propaganda messages, and argued that the press and radio should act as public educators. It was, in Dewey's opinion, the responsibility of the media to do more than simply provide information about contemporary events; it should also teach people the skills needed to understand these events. Dewey's discussion of the impact of propaganda was underpinned by his faith in the 'power of human relationships and the strength of the community' (Hardt, 1992: 45). Unlike Lasswell and Lippmann he did not believe that communication (and the media) is external to the community, a 'transmission belt' between events and people. He argued that communication is essential to human behaviour and society, 'the foundation and source of all activities and relations that are distinctive of internal union of human beings with one another' that enables people 'to live in a world of things that have meaning' (quoted in Hardt, 1992: 44). Communication, in his opinion, is the process by which individuals and groups of people understand each other and accept one another in spite of their differences. Thus communication and the media of communication are, in Dewey's view, the means through which communities and societies are formed, maintained and sustained. Dewey – together with other so-called American 'Pragmatists' such as Charles Cooley, George Herbert Mead and Charles Peirce – put forward the view that the meaning of events is not inherent in the nature of those events but in the behaviour of people towards them. Pragmatism as a theory proposed that ideas and knowledge are produced in practical situations, when people are trying to make sense of what is happening in order to find a way of acting effectively. There is, then, no reality out there that can be interpreted or misinterpreted but rather the meaning of events is produced through people's interaction with one another and the events.

Such an approach to community, society and communication laid down the basis for the development of what was to be labelled as 'symbolic interactionism', which established a different way of looking at communication and the media. Symbolic interactionism conceptualises human behaviour differently from the stimulus-response model that underpinned much of mass society theory and propaganda analysis. The philosopher Mead and the sociologist Cooley emphasised the importance of communication, defined in terms of language and symbols, as central to the understanding of self and society. Communication for Mead is 'the organising process of community' (Hardt, 1992: 48). Individuals come to know themselves through the process of interaction as well as understand their position in society. Mead stated that the individual could only have attained control over the environment through communication, and 'the very speech he uses, the very mechanisms of thought which is given are social products' (quoted in Hardt, 1992: 47). Cooley was even more clear when he said that communication is 'the mechanism through which human relations exist and develop' and this includes 'all symbols of the mind, together with the means of conveying them through space and preserving them in time' from 'expressions of the face . . . tones of the voice' to 'printing, railways, telegraph and telephones and whatever be the latest achievement in the conquest of time and space' (quoted in Hardt, 1992: 53). Thus society is, according to symbolic interactionism, a system of shared meanings in which people participate through being connected by a language and symbols, and from their interaction came a set of expectations as to how to behave. The media as a central part of modern communication are crucial to the production of shared meaning in contemporary society. Charles Peirce's interest in the role of language and symbols in producing social meaning led him to develop a 'theory of signs', or semiotics, which has come to occupy a central role in the study of the media and mass communications in the post-war period (see Chapter 6).

PARK AND THE CHICAGO SCHOOL

Much of the work of the American Pragmatists – as well as much of the research into society, communication and the media in the years before the 1930s – was qualitative in nature.

The production of facts and data, empirical work, to support the theories and contentions of the approaches we have discussed was limited. Much of the writings cited has been described as 'an undifferentiated mixture of attempts to persuade, to entertain, to interpret meanings, to be literary, to discuss ideas, and to express one's beliefs and prejudices as well as to draw conclusions from reliable data' (quoted in Hardt, 1992: 32). However, a more social scientific approach to understanding communication and society was developed at the University of Chicago. Influenced by the Pragmatists, many of whom were associated with the university, this was the beginning of more systematic media and communication research. The leading figure was the sociologist Robert Park. Park and his colleagues rejected the simple stimulus-response model, favouring instead the more 'cultural' approach outlined by the Pragmatists, and studied the role of social institutions, including the media, in the maintenance of social and community values. They were guided by an optimistic view of the role of communication in the social process. As Park stated, 'it is always possible to come to terms with an enemy . . . with whom one can communicate, and, in the long run, greater intimacy inevitably brings with it more understanding' (quoted in Hardt, 1992: 62). The study of the media and communication by the Chicago School focused on the conditions under which information furthered the improvement of community values and assisted the growth of a democratic public. This also involved issues of social control and the role of the media in distorting community values and behaviour.

Qualitative

> In qualitative research the evaluation of theory tends to be accomplished through debate and discussion between proponents of contrasting or opposing theoretical positions. Theory is advanced through the formation of schools of thought in which there is agreement about the validity of a specific body of theory. Rival schools of theory emerge to challenge and refute opposing theories while defending their own. Proof of a theory's power is its ability to attract adherents and be defended against attacks from opponents. Nearly all research into the social sciences in the late nineteenth and early twentieth century was qualitative in nature, building from the traditional mode of enquiry utilised in philosophy and the humanities.
>
> Source: adapted from Baran and Davies, 1995: 283;
> Jensen and Jankowski, 1991: Chapter 2

Park's most famous study was of the immigrant press in America (1922), in which he examined how immigrant communities in America used the press to gain knowledge and understanding of their environment as well as of themselves and their role in the broader society. He reflected on the function of these newspapers in assimilating immigrant communities into American society. As a former journalist, Park was also interested in the nature of professional

The Chicago School

The University of Chicago was home to the first Department of Sociology in America, founded in 1892. The city was a busy and culturally diverse environment, beset with problems of corruption and crime, which culminated in the empire of the world's most celebrated gangster, Al Capone, who dominated the city in the 1920s and 1930s. In such circumstances it is not surprising that the Chicago School established its reputation for urban studies and symbolic interactionism.

Chicago sociologists were particularly interested in how immigrant cultures coming into the city made sense of their position in the society into which they were entering. They produced a number of studies of groups and subgroups that found it difficult to conform. They were not concerned with the grand picture but with the specific and more concrete problems of how people make sense of the world in which they live. Their focus on the meanings that people give to the environment in which they live led them to the theory of symbolic interactionism. People develop a common identity or group allegiance through interaction, a mutual exchange about what things mean. The theory posited that the meanings people attached to their cultural and social activities were as important as the economic circumstances of their existence and the natural forces that governed them.

Source: adapted from Jensen and Jankowski, 1991: 46–9

journalism and how it could be distinguished from propaganda and advertising. He drew attention – like Lippmann – to the neglect sociology had paid to the newspaper and the news-gathering process. In his article, 'The natural history of the newspaper', published in 1923, he examined the role of the newspaper as a social and cultural force. He outlines the role of print in history, arguing the press is 'not the wilful product of any little group of living men' but 'the outcome of an historic process in which many individuals participated without foreseeing what the ultimate product of their labours would be' (Park, 1923: 273). He tried to make sense of the press by understanding the variety of competing interests and different insights coming from the range of political and social activities of the general public (Hardt, 1992: 62–3). For Park the newspaper was an institution whose output and influence reflected a complex interaction between users and producers, and news was more than just information, it was also an insight into society, a means of promoting social cohesion and identity, and something tied to the daily routines and life of the city, the focus of his research (Tuchman, 1991: 80–1).

Park's approach parallels and draws on the work of the German sociologist Max Weber. Weber, often credited with being the 'founder of modern sociology', in his analysis of the impact of modernity tried to show how new ideas were responsible for bringing about economic change and the rise of capitalism (see Weber, 1976). He argued that the rise of capitalism had resulted in the process of rationalisation whereby individuals adopted a narrow cost-benefit assessment of their actions, pursuing those most likely to achieve the required, specific outcome. His work examined the 'bureaucratisation' of modern life as a result of the dull and repetitive routines that market capitalism demanded. He saw this process as sapping the individual as the increased need for social organisation reduced the control the individual had over his or her destiny. The needs of capitalism were standardising people's lives. Weber mourned the replacement of 'an age of full and beautiful humanity' by this new world filled with 'specialists without spirit, sensualists without heart' and expressed his distaste for the 'mechanised petrification' that accompanied the 'iron cage' of rational-legal organisation (quoted in Webster, 1995: 55). While Weber did not write much about the media he did see newspapers as more than mere suppliers of information and gossip. He saw newspapers as 'political clubs', which by furthering talk about politics in society played an important role in the democratic process. However, he was concerned about the growing influence of press owners and their newspaper chains, which he saw as 'the breeders of political indifference' (Tunstall, 2001). Thus Weber had a more negative interpretation than Park of the role of the newspaper in the organisation of society.

Park and his colleagues in the Chicago School moved the study of the media away from the stimulus-response model to the exploration of the cultural context in which individuals use and produce media messages. In the inter-war years they produced a range of studies (see Hardt, 1992) including a pioneering study into the impact of films on children. Herbert Bulmer and Philip Hauser were part of a group of psychologists, sociologists and educationalists commissioned by the Payne Fund in the late 1920s to examine the impact of movies on youth. Their research sought to 'capture the attitudes or perspectives which mediate the effects of . . . films' (quoted in Jankowski and Wester, 1991: 48). The Chicago School stressed the importance of gathering data through interviews and oral histories. Park advocated – influenced by his experiences as a journalist – first-hand observation. He told students to 'write down what you see and hear; you know, like a newspaper reporter' (quoted in Jankowski and Wester, 1991: 47). Some argue this was the beginning of participant observation in social research. What is less contentious is that the Chicago School developed a more empirical approach to issues of media influence that began to appear alongside the more qualitative and speculative approach to social questions in these early years.

The theories of Dewey and other thinkers associated with Pragmatism – as well as the work of the Chicago School – indicated the role and impact of the media in society was more complex and contradictory than many imagined. One of the assumptions underpinning their work into the media and mass communication was that stability rather than conflict is the most important aspect of social behaviour. This assumption was challenged by another group of early theorists who identified conflict as central to social behaviour and associated themselves with the work of the German philosopher Karl Marx.

MARXISM

Marx, unlike most of the classic theorists of the nineteenth century, had a more positive view of the role of the masses in changing society. For Marx social change was explained by the struggle between competing and antagonistic forces in society that he called – following the work of another German philosopher, George Hegel, on the historical development of ideas – the dialectic process. This struggle was between the 'haves' and the 'have nots' who Marx differentiated in terms of their possession of economic power. The 'haves' were the bourgeoisie, the capitalist owning class, who exercised power through their control of the means of production – that is land, factories and labour. The 'have nots' were the proletariat or working classes, the masses. The power of the bourgeoisie is exercised according to the material exploitation of the working classes through extracting their surplus value and making excess profit. Marxism emphasises the proposition that class struggle is central to the historical development of society.

Karl Marx

Karl Marx worked as a journalist on the German newspaper, Rheinische Zeitung, and acted as the European correspondent for the New York Daily Tribune, before he began his monumental study of capitalism, Das Kapital. His work has strongly influenced the development of thinking in the humanities and social sciences. However, he found writing books difficult and it was only after his death in 1883 that his key works were published, mainly as a result of the efforts of his colleague, Friedrich Engels. Marx's work combines polemical political tracts such as The Communist Manifesto (1848), and philosophical and economic treatises including Economic and Philosophical Manuscripts (1844), The German Ideology (1845/46) and Grundrisse (1858). Marx's ideas are discussed in more detail in McLellan (1971), and his life and ideas are lucidly laid out in Wheen (1999).

In trying to make sense of the vast upheavals of Victorian society Marx left an important legacy to inform the study of the media, a legacy that has been much re-interpreted and re-worked by others since his death. Marx never completed a comprehensive study of the role of the communication and media industries but his work locates the role of mass media in the context of the operation of the capitalist economy, and emphasises the relationship between economy *and* communication and culture. Marx's view of the connection between the economic organisation of society and the process of mass communication is characterised by a famous passage from his works. For Marx and his followers,

> The ideas of the ruling class are, in every age, the ruling ideas: i.e. the class, which is the dominant material force in society, is at the same time its dominant intellectual force. The class which has the means of material production at its disposal, has control at the same time over the means of mental production . . . Insofar as they rule as a class and determine the extent and compass of an epoch, they do this in its whole range, hence among other things they regulate the production and distribution of the ideas of their age; thus their ideas are the ruling ideas of the epoch.
>
> (Marx and Engels, 1974: 64–5)

According to Marx, the capitalist class – the bourgeoisie – control the 'production and distribution of ideas' because of their control of the 'means of material production'. As a result it is their ideas, their views and accounts of the world and how it works, that dominate the outlook of capitalist society. These are emphasised through the means of mental production at the expense of other views and accounts of how the world works. The outcome is that the ideology of the bourgeoisie becomes the dominant ideology of the society, thereby shaping the thinking and action of all other classes in society, including the working class or proletariat. This ideological domination is crucial in the maintenance of the inequality between the social classes. It enables the capitalist class or ruling class to legitimate the established order by hiding the social, political and economic disparities of capitalist society. Marx referred to the creation of a 'false consciousness' in the minds of the other classes about the political and social realities of capitalist society. Marx, therefore, makes a direct connection between the domination of the economic organisation of society and the exercise of ideological control, the control of the ways in which we think. Ideological domination is the outcome of the relentless logic of the capitalist system.

Marx articulates the relationship between economy and ideology in terms of his base-superstructure model. The *base* of any society is its economic foundations, which determine the *superstructure* of the society, that is its political, social and ideological institutions and their interactions. He argued that economic systems do not develop out of people's beliefs and values but rather cultural values are determined by the nature of economic structures. The economic organisation of capitalism determines how capitalist society operates. Education, the political and legal systems, family structure, art and literature, religious beliefs as well as the media in any society are a product of their economic base (see Taylor, 1997: Chapter 3). Marx's work encourages us to see the media as a means to promote a certain set of views and ideas – the ideology of the bourgeoisie – and to exclude or deride alternative or oppositional views or ideas. Miliband (1973: 211) provides a clear outline of the traditional Marxist view of the media when he says that 'given the economic and political context in which they function, they cannot fail to be, predominantly, agencies for the dissemination of ideas and values which affirm rather than challenge existing patterns of power and privilege, and thus to be weapons in the arsenal of class domination'. In other words the images, representations and reports we read in our newspapers, see on our screens or hear on our radios, encourage us to see the established social order as natural, desirable and something that we should support. The media and communication industries, along with other agencies such as the education system and parliamentary political parties, play a part in what Miliband describes as the 'process of legitimation' for the central tenets of capitalism. They serve to defend private property and private enterprise, which are represented as necessary for economic prosperity, freedom and democracy. This is an inevitable outcome of the fact that the media are businesses and are privately owned by the capitalist class.

The history of ideas, of culture, is intimately related to the history of economic production. Hence the media are instruments of social control whose content is manipulated to mislead people and encourage them to accept their subordination. The power of the bourgeoisie over other classes is exercised most crucially through their control of culture and cultural production. Culture – like religion – is, then, in the often-quoted words of Marx, the 'opiate of the people'. It is a drug, injected by social agencies such as the media and education, under the influence of which working people fail to see how they are being exploited. For Marxism *social conflict* is inherent in the nature of production in capitalist societies. The media in this context take sides, so to speak. They are part of the established power structures of society, presenting a picture of the world that reinforces these power structures and offers a false representation of what is happening in the world. Much of the work of early Marxists concentrated on how members of the bourgeoisie exercised control over cultural production, including the emerging media, to serve their own class interests, directly challenging the view of the press as an institution bringing together the community put forward by Park and other members of the Chicago School.

THE LIBERAL THEORY OF PRESS FREEDOM

Rather than seeing the media as mouthpieces for the ruling classes, free press theory highlights the independent role of the media in society. As a concept, 'freedom of the press' has had a long and distinguished history. John Keane (1991) outlines the history of the philosophical treatise in favour of freedom of expression, publishing and reading, many of which have been forgotten in the mists of time. He identifies Britain as the 'birthplace of the modern principle of liberty of the press' and discerns four kinds of argument that underlie free press theory. The theological approach is found most clearly expressed in John Milton's book *Areopagitica*, published in 1644. Milton opposed state restrictions on freedom of expression on the grounds that individual men and women had been blessed by God with the faculty of reason, which allowed them to read and enabled them, according to their conscience, to make choices between good and evil. By censoring what could be read, Milton argued that the individual's freedom to think, to make choices and to decide to follow the Christian way of life were removed. For Milton freedom of the press was necessary because 'the virtue of the individual must be developed and tested continually by engaging contrary opinions and experiences' (Keane, 1991: 12). Thus toleration of a range of opinions was the basis of individual virtue. Milton's religious faith, however, did not mean he was in favour of absolute freedom. He defended the banning of 'popish' books and accepted that abuse or licentiousness of the press should be punished. The political philosopher John Locke, almost 50 years later, articulated another defence of freedom of the press. He argued the rights of the individual should condition the conduct of the press. Press freedom, according to this argument, was not conceived on religious grounds but on the basis that every person had the right to decide for him or herself on all matters, religious, political or whatever. It is the natural right of the individual to publish freely his or her views in face of the restrictions imposed by the state. Such an approach was developed in the two great books of the eighteenth century in defence of individual liberty, Tom Paine's *The Rights of Man* (1791) and Mary Wollstonecraft's *Vindication of the Rights of Women* (1792).

Another argument for the free expression of press and public opinion centred on the theory of utilitarianism. Philosophers such as Jeremy Bentham and James Mill believed the smooth operation of the political system depended on the free expression of public opinion. It was necessary for 'good governance'. Bentham, in the first detailed discussion of public opinion in the English language, argued that the expression of public opinion is 'the chief safeguard against misrule' and 'the abuse of power by the legislators' (Boyce, 1978: 20). Press freedom – as with universal suffrage, secret ballots and regular elections – serves as one of the main mechanisms through which public opinion is expressed. For James Mill people could not choose and criticise their governors without 'the most perfect knowledge relative to the characters of those who present themselves to their choice . . . by information conveyed freely, and without reserve, from one to another' (quoted in Boyce, 1978: 22). Mill argued that liberty of the press ensured that the 'government is always fully apprised, which, by no other means it can ever be, of the sentiments of the people, and feels a decided interest in conforming to them' (quoted in Bromley and O'Malley, 1997: 20). A free press, according to Mill and Bentham, could also scrutinise the workings of power and bureaucracy, and prevent the corruption of legislators and administrators (Keane, 1991: 16). These were radical views in the first half of the nineteenth century when the franchise was limited to a small number of property owners, the press was subject to economic regulation and political control, and ballots were not secret. These arguments became the basis of the theory of liberal democracy with the press seen as playing a central role in the development of the political systems in North America and western Europe in the twentieth century. The ideas of men and women such as Bentham and Mill as well as their actions – both were active campaigners for a free press as newspaper editors or writers – played a significant part in such a development. It is also worth noting that they had a much more positive view of the impact and influence of public opinion than the mass society theorists of the late nineteenth and early twentieth centuries.

The final defence of a free press listed by Keane (1991) rests on the view that the truth can be attained through unfettered public discussion amongst citizens. This view is most associated with John Stuart Mill who outlined his argument for press freedom in his book *On Liberty* (1859), which is 'widely regarded, particularly in the United States, as the founding statement of liberal journalism' (Bromley and O'Malley, 1997: 27). Mill was critical of utilitarianism for placing necessity before truth in the discussion of opinion. He argued that freely circulating opinions are essential for the seeking of truth. He singled out a number of reasons why silencing opinion could have consequences for the search for the truth (see Mill in Bromley and O'Malley, 1997: 22–7; Keane, 1991: 18–20). First, it is not possible to be absolutely certain that any opinion is false. To suppress an opinion is to assume the infallibility of one's own position and deny potential truth. Second, even if an opinion is false it can contain an element of truth. The prevailing opinion on any matter cannot be the whole truth and it is only by confronting contrary opinions, by reconciling opposites, that we can attain the full truth. Third, even if the received opinion is the whole truth 'unless it is … vigorously and earnestly contested, it will, by most of those who receive it, be held in the manner of a prejudice, with little comprehension or feeling of its rational grounds' (Bromley and O'Malley, 1997: 27). Mill believed the diversity of opinions is necessary for truth to prevail. Truth, according to him, 'is so much a question of the reconciling and combining of opposites' and it is only 'by the rough process of a struggle between combatants fighting under hostile banners' that there is a 'chance of fair play to all sides of truth' (Bromley and O'Malley, 1997: 26). Truth would degenerate into dogma and prejudice if not continually challenged and questioned by counter-claims. For Mill the truth required the liberty of the press, which without restriction would supply the facts and opinions, no matter how unpopular or unpalatable, to encourage the questioning of established opinions and thereby ensure truth could prevail.

The writings of these classical thinkers laid down the basis for liberal theory of the press, which is summarised succinctly by Thompson (1995: 238). As he puts it,

> they saw the free expression of opinion through the organs of an
> independent press as a principal means by which diversity of viewpoints
> could be expressed, an enlightened public opinion could be formed, and the
> abuses of state power by corrupt tyrannical governments could be checked.
> A free and independent press would play the role of a critical watchdog; not
> only would it articulate a diversity of opinions and thereby enrich the sphere

of knowledge and debate, but it would also expose and criticise the activities
of those who rule and the principles on which their decisions are based.

Thus we have the view of the press as the 'fourth estate of the realm', an institution that
acts as the voice of the people and is uniquely accountable to it (Curran and Seaton, 1991:
277). Classical liberal theory came not only to provide those working in the press with an
ideology to legitimate what they are doing but also the rationale for the struggle against
state control (see Boyce, 1978). The central tenet is that press freedom and individual
liberty are the natural counterparts of '*laissez-faire*' economic activity in the form of the free
market. As Curran and Seaton (1991: 278) state, 'the hidden hand of the free market' is
seen as ensuring that the newspaper owner's 'pursuit of private interests corresponds to
the public good'. In other words only an 'unrestricted market produces a press that is
diverse, accountable and representative'. This view provided the theoretical underpinning
of the campaign against government press control in the nineteenth century (see Curran
and Seaton, 1991: Chapters 2 and 3). While having exerted considerable hold over the
thinking about the development of the media and their role in society, the conceptual basis
on which the theory was grounded has been challenged by developments since the mid-
nineteenth century. Thompson (1990: 251 *passim*), for example, identifies the growing
commercialisation of the media, the development of new media technologies and society's
growing acceptance of legitimate constraints of freedom of expression. However, as a
model it makes assumptions about the nature of the market in a capitalist society, which
many other theorists reject.

SUMMARY

The work of the classic social theorists of the nineteenth century laid down frameworks
for the later development of different approaches to understanding media and mass communication. While Marx, J.S. Mill, Weber and Durkheim may only have addressed issues
of the media and mass communication in passing, their considerations of the nature of the
transformations western societies were going through in the latter part of the nineteenth
century have shaped – and continue to shape – what constitutes thinking about the media.
The rise of the media and mass communication in the early part of the twentieth century
was not accompanied by any systematic study of the field. Early theorising focused on the
power of the media to influence individuals and society. Dominated by what came to be
labelled 'mass society theory', the media were seen as part of the overall condition of
modernity that was de-stabilising the traditional bonds holding society together, and
making individuals more susceptible to propaganda. Early media theory has handed
down the view of the media as exercising a powerful and persuasive influence over individuals and society. This influence was usually viewed as harmful and early theory was
pessimistic, identifying the media as one of the many disruptive forces de-stabilising
society. This framework for understanding the media was, as Curran, Gurevitch and
Woollacott (1982: 11–12) note, based on several factors including the power of the media

to bring together a mass audience on an unprecedented scale, the view that modernity had created a society more susceptible to manipulation, the belief that individual men and women were defenceless in the face of the power of the media and anecdotal evidence that people had been brainwashed by the media during the First World War and the rise of fascism. Propaganda analysis during the inter-war years sought to examine the conditions under which messages swayed their audiences.

The pessimism of mass society theory was seen as being confirmed in 1938 with the public panic over Orson Welles' spoof radio broadcast of an invasion of Earth by men from Mars. However, research into the actual effect of this broadcast led to a radical re-evaluation of the power of the media. Sociologist Hedley Cantril and his colleagues (1940) found that while some people did respond to the reports of an invasion by fleeing their homes, most were not fooled by the broadcast. The research concluded that there were 'limited effects' as only a small number of people were directly affected by what they had heard. Particular psychological attributes were seen as making those who were influenced susceptible to the power of radio – such as lack of self-confidence and emotional insecurity. The consequence of this research was to lead to a re-conceptualisation of the media as having a limited impact on people's behaviour and attitudes. If thinking about the media in the years between 1900 and the late 1930s was shaped by the broad concerns and fears of sociologists and psychologists about mass society, then in the period after the Second World War it was heavily influenced by the need to generate data about the conditions under which the media are likely to change people's knowledge, attitudes and behaviour. Much of the impetus for such knowledge came from the media industries and governments. It was in such a context that the systematic study of the media developed.

Orson Welles and the men from Mars

At eight P.M. eastern standard time on the evening of October 31, 1938, Orson Welles, with an innocent group of actors took his place before the microphone in a New York studio of the Columbia Broadcasting System. He carried with him Howard Koch's freely adapted version of H.G. Welles's imaginative novel, War of the Worlds. He also brought to the scene his unusual dramatic talent. With script and talent, the actors hoped to entertain their listeners for an hour with an incredible, old-fashioned story appropriate for Halloween.

Much to their surprise the actors learned that the series of news bulletins they issued describing an invasion from Mars had been believed by thousands of people throughout the country. For a few horrible hours people from Maine to California thought that hideous monsters armed with death rays were destroying all armed resistance against them; that there was simply no escape from disaster; that the end of the world was near. Newspapers the following morning spoke of the 'tidal wave of terror that swept the nation'. It was clear that a panic of national proportions had occurred.

Source: Cantril, et al., 1940, The Invasion from Mars

Chapter Two

◻ *SCHOOLS OF THOUGHT:*
DEVELOPING APPROACHES TO
MEDIA THEORY

The liberation of the audience from the role of passive recipients to that of active inter-preters of media messages has been a theme of the development of media theory in the post-war period. The 'limited effects' theory rapidly established itself as the 'new ortho-doxy' in the field. This was accompanied by the development of so-called 'middle range theories'. Unlike the theoretical approach of the pre-war period, which revolved around versions of grand theory such as mass society, these theories developed generalisations based on the collection of empirical data. The stress on empirical research contributed to the intellectual divisions in the field as it encouraged work that was distinguished 'by largely different methods of inquiry, by levels of analysis, by theories that place commu-nication in very different points in the research process ... and even by differences in what phenomena deserved to be called communication ...' (quoted in Baran and Davies, 1995: 350). The practical requirements of empirical research to focus on parts of the com-munication process or on particular media forms inevitably produced fragmentation in media theory. It was nevertheless at the level of grand theory that perhaps the most sig-nificant changes in theorising the media took place in the post-war period. The critiques of Marxism, in particular the advent of structuralism, the challenges of feminism and post-modernism all added to the diversity of theoretical positions on the media. These changes resulted in the emergence of different approaches or 'schools of thought' that have shaped contemporary study of the media.

LIMITED EFFECTS PARADIGM

Several authors have described the 'paradigmatic change' in media theory that occurred in the years between 1940 and the mid-1960s (see Baran and Davies, 1995: Chapter 6). The new paradigm on thinking about mass communication was based on empirical research generated about the media and the mass communication process, which came to dominate the research in North American universities and institutes in the 1950s. Quantitative studies supplanted the older, more speculative approaches to media theory. Baran and Davies (1995: 112) note that the people who led the shift in thinking were not theorists but 'methodologists'. Rather than embrace a grand theory about the role and operation of the media and mass communication in society, they argued theory should be drawn from empirical research. They employed new research methods such as laboratory

experiments and surveys to observe the workings of the media, and argued such observations would provide a more concrete basis on which to develop theory. Researchers
such as Paul Lazarsfeld and Karl Hovland believed that enquiry into the media and mass
communication should be more scientific. They emphasised the systematic gathering of
facts by objective means and methods to gather data that provided empirically testable
generalisations on which to build theory.

Paradigm

According to Thomas Kuhn (1970) a paradigm is defined as the
dominant and widely accepted theories and concepts in a particular
field of study. Kuhn took issue with the view that science evolved
gradually over time with scientists moving closer and closer to the
solution to problems by building on the work and achievements of
their predecessors. He disagreed with this evolutionary view, arguing
that significant advances in science have only occurred historically
when someone has challenged the prevailing paradigm of the time.
Paradigms do not explain everything but offer the best way or most
broadly accepted way of looking at the world at a given time. A new
paradigm 'changes some of the field's most elementary theoretical
generalisations' and causes scientists to 'adopt new instruments and
look in new places'. Kuhn never explained why people come to give up
an old paradigm and adopt a new one.

Source: adapted from Ferrante, 1992

Besides emphasising the importance of 'empirical facts' to media theory, they also drew
attention to the practical application of their research. Hovland's work focused on mass
persuasion and had clear relevance to the world of advertising and marketing, rapidly
developing in the midst of the consumer boom in post-war America. Lazarsfeld labelled
this kind of research as 'administrative research', arguing that empirical research should
provide a guide for administrative decision making. Not surprisingly, much of this
research was funded by the media industries and government – Hovland's work, for
example, began under the auspices of the US Army's Information and Education Division
as part of official efforts to improve the fighting capacity of ordinary infantryman. The
development of more sophisticated empirical techniques could be seen as inhibiting the
development of media theory. It is argued that 'more and more sophisticated empirical
techniques and statistical constructs' led to mass communication research having 'lost
sight of the broader implications of their research and its theoretical significance' (Golding
and Murdock, 1978: 60). Brown (1970: 50) notes that many of the empirical studies of the
media in this period were 'less than fully relevant to the development of grand theory' and

Empiricism

Empiricism places emphasis on the importance of observable, measurable and quantifiable evidence. Such research in the social sciences centres on fieldwork – that is, the collection of evidence about observable human behaviour. Such evidence may be used to test theoretical hypotheses against observable behaviour or to gain insight into certain behaviours. Empiricism assumes that there is an objective reality that we are able to draw up methods of studying, by which we are capable of proving or disproving certain hypotheses or theories explaining this reality.

Source: adapted from Watson and Hill, 1993; O'Sullivan et al., 1994

by the end of the 1950s one leading scholar in the field declared that mass communication research had run out of steam (Berelson, 1959). The trend was to 'middle range theory', and following Lasswell's dissection of the mass communication process into different components – who says what to whom and why – researchers tended to concentrate their efforts in the specific areas of production, content and reception.

Much of the empirical work in the two decades after the Second World War concentrated on the nature of the audience and the conditions under which the media would produce changes in knowledge, attitudes and behaviour. As Brown (1970: 47) points out, the difference in this work from that of the propaganda analysts of the inter-war years, was in the conceptualisation of the nature of the media audience. The picture of the audience as

a mere set of isolated individuals was replaced by one which stresses the structured nature of that audience, the channels of communication within it and the modifying influence which membership in face-to-face groups exerted over external efforts to modify shared beliefs.

This shift accompanied the development of the view of the limited effectiveness of the media in everyday life and over people's attitudes and behaviour. Power was returned to the people who were now seen as being able to choose what they wanted to read or watch and the process of selection shaped by the values of the groups to which an individual belonged.

While much of this quantitative research did not have an overt concern for the relationship of the media to society, it was not necessarily lacking the theoretical underpinning many believed. For Golding and Murdock (1978: 63) the lack of theory was 'more apparent than real'. Many believed American mass communications research was guided by two interconnected theories of society: functionalism and pluralism. These theories laid stress on an uncritical approach to society and polity. Rooted in a view of post-war American society as a 'good society' with a stable democracy, which had mostly done away with major inequalities, functionalism – and its political manifestation, pluralism – conceptualised the role of media as being part of the process of imparting the values that maintained the 'good society'. While the lack of critical engagement was highlighted by a number of observers (see Mills, 1957), by the early 1960s it could be asserted that functionalism had attained a pre-eminent position in mass communication research (Klapper, 1960).

FUNCTIONALISM

Functionalism was established as a theoretical approach to the study of society in the decades immediately after the Second World War. Robert Merton (1949) proposed what he called a 'paradigm for functional analysis' but the roots of functionalism can be traced back to the work of Emile Durkheim. While there is criticism that Durkheim's contribution to the field of media and communication studies has been neglected or misrepresented (see Rothenbuhler, 1994) his work became associated with the notion of 'functionalism' which views the media – as well as other social organisations and artefacts – as being central to the natural, orderly operation of society. As outlined initially by Durkheim, functionalism compares societies to biological organisms. In order to function, a society – just like the human body – requires certain needs to be met, and functional analysis involves identifying the means by which those needs are met. The basic tenet of functionalism is that society is a highly complex system of interrelated activities which, working together in equilibrium, ensures the maintenance of order.

Social order and harmony break down when individuals become dislocated from one another. The collapse of the 'collective conscience' increases the danger of social disorder and in such circumstances individuals need to have their sense of belonging to something wider reinforced and, according to Durkheim, the social process responds to imbalances in society and restores order through change and adaptation. Durkheim was impressed by the ability of society to maintain cohesion in the face of the changes, conflicts and contradictions, particularly as they were manifest in the nineteenth century. He stressed the importance of communication in the process of maintaining and transforming society, and the part it played in the formation and reformation of the consensus on issues and behaviour to maintain equilibrium in society. Durkheim was a 'positivist'; he believed society could be studied by scientific method and emphasised detachment in the method of observation. Social facts – what he saw as the basis of the laws that govern society – could be observed and measured, and their effects gauged. Durkheim rejected social theory that characterises the different parts of society as either 'bad' or 'good'. Rather he believed through empirical investigation it was possible to identify practices that were 'functional' or 'dysfunctional'.

Functional analysis of mass communication centres on the role of the media in the maintenance of social order and social structure, and examines how they perform or do not perform certain tasks necessary for the maintenance of equilibrium in society. Functionalism assumes the media can be examined by empirical investigation to make a judgement as to whether their operation is functional or dysfunctional. Such analysis is not straightforward as it is possible to identify, for example, forms of media content as being both functional and dysfunctional. It is also possible to see functions that contribute to the maintenance of social order being dysfunctional for individuals and particular groups. Merton (1949: Chapter 1) also makes a distinction between intended and unintended consequences of certain practices and actions. While some media functions are *manifest* in that they are observable, others are more difficult to identify, being *latent* and hidden from observation. Thus a news broadcast about the civil war in Sierra Leone has a manifest function in that it might provide information about what is going on in that country but such news coverage can have a latent function in shaping our perceptions and attitudes not only about that part of the world but also the people who live there. Functionalist analysis operates at a number of levels – ranging from examination of the functions (and dysfunctions) of the media for the social system to the individual and particular media, particular media organisations and particular media practices.

Functionalism and the media

1. Functionalism regards society as a system of interrelated parts; an organisation of interconnected, repetitive and patterned activities.
2. Such a society tends towards a state of dynamic equilibrium; if disharmony occurs, forces will act to restore stability.
3. All of the repetitive and patterned activities in society make a contribution of one kind or another to the maintenance of the state of equilibrium.
4. Some of the patterned and repetitive activities in society are indispensable to its continued existence.
5. The mass media and the process of mass communication are one type of patterned and repetitive activity, which make some contribution to stability in a society.
6. Mass communication could be seen as one of the indispensable components of social structure without which society cannot continue.
7. However, mass communication can be dysfunctional when it creates disharmony – for example, in causing forms of deviant behaviour.

Source: adapted from De Fleur and Ball-Rokeach, 1989: 30–1

Scholars in the immediate decade after the Second World War began to identify and assess the functions of the media. Lasswell (1948) argued that the media had three major social functions: surveillance, correlation and transmission. Through the function of surveillance the media enable individuals and society to monitor changes that are happening around them and identify threats and opportunities. The correlation function brings individuals and different parts of society together to respond to opportunities and threats through the process of explanation and interpretation of events. Transmission allows the passing of cultural and social heritage from one generation to another; thus the media can act as agencies of socialisation. Wright (1960) added the function of entertainment, which provides individuals with relaxation, relief and enjoyment, thereby making it easier for them to cope with life and thus assisting the maintenance of social order. Other social functions have also been put forward. Lazarsfeld and Merton (1948) discussed the functions of the news media in the conferral of status and the enforcement of social norms, while McQuail (2000) draws attention to the function of the mass media in mobilising people to participate in social development and change. Distinction is drawn between sociological and psychological versions of functionalism (see Perry, 1996: 49–50), the former concentrating on the media and the social system, the latter on how the media function in the daily lives of individuals. The motivations behind why people use the media and what they receive from such use have been explored since Herzog's study of women's consumption of radio soaps in the 1940s, which was shown to serve a number of functions in women's lives, such as providing emotional release and serving as a source of information and advice to make sense of the world (Herzog, 1944, cited in Grossberg *et al.*, 1998: 246).

The study of the social and individual functions of the media is handicapped by the problem of defining a 'function', which is often described in a variety of ways in the literature. It has been noted 'in the choice of determining what is functional for what lies a good deal of potential for the selective partitioning of the world' (Boyd Barrett, 1995: 73). It is not obvious which media activity is functional (or dysfunctional) to the stable operation of society. Nor it is clear for whom it is helpful and how. For Baran and Davies (1995: 168) such analysis 'rarely permits any definitive conclusions to be drawn about the overall functions and dysfunctions of the media'. As a result functionalists have tended to assume that existing forms of media output and the practices and processes that produced them are functional. Often, the functions identified by mass communication scholars were equated or regarded as synonymous with the aims and objectives of the media industries (Baran and Davies, 1995: 215). This was hardly surprising in the immediate post-war years. It was a period in which society was rebuilt in the wake of the ravages of war followed by sustained economic growth and prosperity in America and western Europe, which provided the basis for social stability. It is argued such an assumption resulted in uncritical acceptance of the contemporary workings of the media and led to findings that legitimated the status quo. If the society around them was in harmony then the operation of the media must be in balance – if there were dysfunctions then they would have had to be balanced by functions. Functionalist analysis of mass communication is based on the belief that all the components of society including the media are organised and structured and operate to maintain social stability. Functionalism is closely associated with 'pluralism', which is concerned with the exercise of power in society.

PLURALISM

Pluralism holds that power in western societies is dispersed amongst a variety – a plurality – of competing groups and interests, none of which is able to dominate society. Everyone has some power and no one can have too much. Competition between groups and interests on more or less equal terms ensures that power is diffused. As one exponent of this theory states: 'all the active and legitimate groups in the population can make themselves heard at some crucial stage in the process of decision making' (Dahl, quoted in Miliband, 1973: 4). The state acts as the referee of the clash between competing social groups such as trades unions, businesses, political parties, civic organisations and pressure groups. The law and an occupational culture of government that places emphasis on the values of impartiality ensure the even-handedness of the state. The media in such circumstances are 'part of the machinery by which ... rival pressures and policy proposals are expressed, made known, brought to arbitration, in a multiple contest that makes for shifting equilibria of influence' (Westergaard, 1977: 98). The plurality or diversity of views in society is reflected in the wide range of media products on offer and the range of opinions expressed in the output of the media. The media operate with a high degree of autonomy, independent of all the competing social groups and interests, and act as a 'watchdog' on the state to ensure its impartiality.

Pluralism conceives of the media as reflecting the diversity of their audiences. Viewers, readers and listeners are regarded not as passive dupes of the media but as agents who can exercise influence over them. They are capable of manipulating media by making choices over what they watch, read and listen to. This choice is exercised through the 'free market', which determines what is served up to audiences by the media. It allows people and groups to have their views represented and advertised. Individuals as a result of 'the plural values of society' react in a number of ways to the media, either conforming to or confronting what they see, read and hear (Curran *et al.*, 1982: 1). In other words, they can use the media to gratify a range of different needs and dispositions. Pluralism thus stresses the notion that everybody has a voice and everybody has a choice, and this underpins the social and political role of the media. The emphasis on political choice, the free market and a free media representing a diversity of views without fear and favour places pluralism at the heart of liberal democratic theory – hence it is sometimes called liberal pluralist theory. Pluralism and functionalism share a belief that the media are an essential component in the workings of liberal democracy. The former sees the media as representing the diversity of competing interests in society, enabling everyone to have the chance to participate and be informed, whilst the latter stresses the integrative role of the media in maintaining a consensus through the reinforcement of a set of shared values about democracy and the democratic process.

Consensus

The term 'consensus' is used to describe a shared set of taken-for-granted assumptions and values amongst all people or a majority of people in a society. Competition and political disagreement in liberal democracies are seen as taking place within a normative framework of agreed rules and shared values: a consensual framework.
According to Wirth (1948, quoted in Manning, 2001: 28), 'consensus ... is not so much agreement on all issues, or even on the most substantial issues, among all members of society as it is the established habit of intercommunication, of discussion, debate negotiation and compromise and the toleration of heresies, or even of indifference, up to the point of "clear and present danger" which threatens the life of society itself'.

Curran (1996: 128–9) draws attention to what he sees as two erroneous premises made in such analysis. First, the assumption there is an underlying unity in society enabling the media to serve everyone's interests in the same way. According to Curran, 'the media's projection of an idealised social cohesion may serve to conceal fundamental differences of interest' that 'repress latent conflict and weaken progressive forces for social change'. Rather societies should be seen as being made up of different interests in conflict over how society should be organised and existing social arrangements encompass 'winners and losers [who] do not have the same investment in the social order'. The second false assumption is that the 'media are independent and socially neutral agencies in society'. Curran says this ignores the close ties that exists between the media and other social institutions, particularly big business and the state, and that the media can be 'co-opted to serve the interests of dominant institutions and social groups'. Such criticisms are informed by the assumption that conflict rather than stability is the most important aspect of social behaviour and process.

REDISCOVERY OF IDEOLOGY

Functionalism and pluralism began to look more problematic with the growing political turmoil of the 1960s. After a period of economic success, and political and social stability in the 1950s and early 1960s, western liberal democracies appeared plunged into industrial unrest and political conflict. As students protested, rioters threw stones and workers picketed their factory gates, the focus on how the media maintained stability and promoted harmony appeared somewhat out of tune with the times. The return of social conflict coincided with the re-emergence of a Marxist perspective in media theory, which took issue with the orthodoxy of the immediate post-war years. Analysis of the media throughout the 1970s pitted pluralism against Marxism. While pluralists criticised the 'theoreticism' of Marxism, the latter mostly dismissed empirical research as 'uniformly uninteresting', and eschewed studies that denied the influence of the media as 'scarcely worth confronting or even reading' (Curran *et al.*, 1982). The reaction against empiricism was accompanied by an emphasis on the importance of ideology in examining the social and political role of the mass media (see Chapter 6). While it is possible to identify several traditions within neo-Marxism, they all emphasised the role of the media as ideological agencies or apparatuses in maintaining and legitimating the power of the bourgeoisie or the dominant group. The matter of dispute was how the mass media did this.

Marxist thinking underwent significant changes in the post-war period, which had profound implications for the way in which the media are conceptualised. The most important shift was from the classical model of Marx, linking ideology and culture to the economic basis of society, to neo-Marxist or structuralist approaches stressing the autonomy of ideological practices. This re-formulation is important for the way in which we understand the media – rather than conceptualise the media as acting as tools of the class that owns and controls them, and serving the interests of this class by concealing and misrepresenting the true nature of society, the media are seen as sites of struggle between competing ideas and interests albeit that some ideas and interests are more powerful than others. Structuralism also saw a change in the focus of media analysis, with examination of the text becoming central to the study of the media. Some argue this shift meant the disagreement between Marxist and pluralist was transformed into a debate within Marxism (see Curran *et al.*, 1982).

Structuralism

Structuralism contends that there are organising principles or structures behind cultural behaviour and inherent in all cultural artefacts. It has been defined as 'an analytical or theoretical enterprise, dedicated to the systematic elaboration of the rules and constraints that work, like the rules of language, to make the generations of meaning possible in the first place' (O'Sullivan et al., 1994: 302). The history of the structuralist enterprise has witnessed the proliferation of positions within the approach, which, some argue, has led to it now becoming so diverse as not to be considered as a unitary approach. Structuralist accounts of the media, therefore, draw on a range of different contributions: the linguistic analysis of Saussure, the anthropology of Claude Lévi-Strauss, the semiotics of Roland Barthes, Jacques Lacan's reworking of psychoanalysis as well as Louis Althusser and Antonio Gramsci's reworking of Marx's theory of ideology. The main concern of structuralism has been the systems and processes of signification and representation that are apparent in media 'texts' such as films, photographs, television, literary texts, adverts and so on. Hence it is often tied to semiology and the study of signs. Although, as Strinati (1995: Chapter 3) points out, there is a difference between structuralism and semiology – the latter is the 'scientific' study of the signs by which people communication with each other through a range of signals such as gestures, language, objects and so on, while the former is a theoretical framework to understand the universal rules and character of mental and cultural structures that underlie social behaviour and activity. Structuralism became very much associated with film studies from the 1970s onwards and in particular the journal Screen.

One of the earliest attempts to move away from examining the economic determinants of the media and focus on the how the media reproduce a particular way of seeing the world was found in the work of Louis Althusser. Althusser's re-working of the theory of ideology represented an important development in Marxist thinking. His article 'Ideology and ideological state appartuses' (1970) drew attention to a distinction between the repressive instruments of state, such as the army, courts and police, which exercise direct coercion to ensure the compliance of people to the established order, and 'ideological state apparatuses' such as the Church, education, religion, political system and the media, which reproduce an ideology that represents capitalism as natural and inevitable. The role of these institutions had previously been untheorised in Marxist thinking. Althusser departed from traditional Marxist interpretations of ideology by emphasising the relative autonomy of the media – and other social and cultural institutions – from direct control by the ruling or dominant class. He argued that if the media were not seen as being independent then they would not be able to perform their ideological task. In other words people would see them as representing a partial view of the world and reject their messages.

Althusser

Louis Althusser was born in Algiers in 1918. He was educated at one of France's most prestigious educational bodies, the Ecole Normale

Superieure, and became in the post-war years one of France's leading intellectual figures. He joined the French Communist Party in 1948. His main publications were For Marx (1977), Reading Capital (1970) and Lenin and Philosophy and Other Essays (1971). In 1980 he was sent to a psychiatric hospital after admitting he had murdered his wife. He died there in 1990.

Source: adapted from Ferguson, 1998

The theoretical basis for Althusser's re-evaluation of ideology, and its implications for understanding the role of the media, is found in the works of the Italian Marxist, Antonio Gramsci. Gramsci's work was completed in first half of the twentieth century and not taken up until the 1970s. According to Gramsci the ruling class maintained its dominance of society primarily by establishing 'hegemony'. He distinguishes

between coercive control which is manifest through direct force or the threat of force, and consensual control which arises when individuals 'willingly' or 'voluntarily' assimilate the world-view or hegemony of the dominant group; an assimilation which allows that group to be hegemonic.

(Quoted in Strinati, 1995: 166)

Gramsci argues the ruling or dominant class rules more through consent than coercion. For Gramsci people did not passively and unquestioningly accept the ideas and beliefs imposed on them by the ruling class and, conversely, the ruling class could not expect automatically to impose its ideas, values and beliefs on the rest of society through its control of the means of production. Hence the ruling class had to win control of their hearts and minds through a process of negotiation, mediation and compromise.

Gramsci

Antonio Gramsci was born in 1891 in Sardinia, attended the University of Turin and left to become a journalist. He was politically active in the factory councils set up by Turin workers in 1917, and in 1924 was a founding member of the Italian Communist Party. He was arrested for his political activities in 1926 and died in prison in 1937. It was during his incarceration that he wrote his major work, Prison Notebooks. His ideas were strongly influenced by his political activism rather than theoretical meditation. However, as most of his theoretical work was written during his imprisonment he had to disguise what he was saying. This sometimes makes it difficult to interpret his meaning.

Source: adapted from Fulcher and Scott, 1999

Roland Barthes made another important contribution to the understanding of the role of the media in the reproduction of ideology. Barthes drew on the work of Saussure and his theory of semiotics, which had entered into the world of media and social research in the 1960s. He argued that the importance of the media in the dissemination of ideology or views of the world rested on their ability to structure signs and images in particular ways. He examined the way in which signs (that is, images, words, music and objects) convey deeper meanings within society and culture than might outwardly appear so. In particular he saw the media, through the process of signification, making certain meanings and views in society appear natural and common-sense. Central to his thinking was the concept of 'myth', which made the ideological nature of media messages appear natural (see Chapter 6).

Barthes

Roland Barthes was born in 1915 in Cherbourg in Normandy, France. His father was killed during the First World War, and his mother and grandparents brought him up. He moved to Paris with his mother in 1924 where he completed his degree in French, Latin and Greek. He suffered from TB during most of his life, spending long periods of time convalescing. His main works include Mythologies (first published in 1957), S/Z (1970) and The Pleasure of the Text (1973). He died in 1980 after being knocked down by a laundry van while crossing the street outside the College de France where he had been appointed a professor in 1976.

Source: adapted from Booker, 1998

The new theories of ideology were 'bitterly attacked' by those who remained committed to a more classical Marxist approach (Curran *et al.*, 1982: 24). Structuralist accounts were seen as over-concentrating on ideological elements at the expense of the 'concrete analysis of economic relations, and the ways in which they structure both the processes and results of cultural production' (Murdock and Golding, 1977: 17) (see Chapter 6). The focus on the reading of media texts and the attempt to extrapolate from these texts conclusions about social relations was regarded as a major lacuna in structuralism (see Murdock and Golding, 1980). This difference between structuralists and their critics from the tradition of political economy has been an important part of the field of media studies since the mid-1980s (see Grossberg, 1995; Garnham, 1995, for a flavour of this debate).

Political economy

Political economy suggests the production of media products – whether news, journalism, film, advertising, drama, popular music or whatever – is structurally constrained by economic and political factors, especially the private ownership of media industries (Franklin, 1997: 34). Political economy sees the content, style and form of media products such as newspaper stories or computer games as shaped by structural features such ownership, advertising and audience spending. The approach emphasises the media as industries and businesses. How they are organised, the ways in which they operate and what they produce are shaped and determined by economic considerations and their attendant political aspects. As two leading political economy theorists, Graham Murdock and Peter Golding (1973: 227) write, 'the mass media are first and foremost industrial and commercial organisations which produce and distribute commodities'. The most important aspect of the operation of media as businesses is that production is geared to the making of profit. What sells most and realises the largest profit is the major determinant of what is produced. Thus the starting point for political economy is the economic and industrial organisation of the media. They believe that the economic base of media is a necessary and sufficient explanation of the cultural and ideological effects of the media. (See Chapters 3 and 6 for more discussion.)

The problem of reconciling cultural texts and social analysis was recognised in the work of Raymond Williams who is regarded, along with Stuart Hall and Richard Hoggart, as one of the founders of British cultural studies, which has made a distinctive and influential contribution to the development of the discipline of cultural studies throughout the world. This approach to the study of mass communication has been labelled 'culturalist'; it argues that the media – and other communication practices – must be placed within the context of society, and the historical conditions and relationships that have shaped social practices. Culturalism rejects the notion that ideals are autonomous from socio-economic conditions but also opposes the economic determinism of traditional Marxism. Leading figures of this approach have throughout the years of their work shifted the weight they have placed on the relative merits of textual and social analysis. The work of Hall and his colleagues at the Birmingham Centre for Contemporary Cultural Studies (BCCCS) at the

University of Birmingham in the 1970s and early 1980s represented the combining of culturalist and structuralist approaches to understanding the media.

The development of structuralism and culturalism represented the erosion of the pluralist/Marxist dichotomy that had shaped debates in media theory in the 1970s. The 1980s saw a growing disenchantment with class interpretations of society. This disenchantment was encouraged by a number of developments. The neo-liberal revival promoted by Margaret Thatcher and Ronald Reagan, and the collapse of 'socialism' in the Soviet Union brought more credence to models and theories of society that were more complex and multi-faceted in their understanding of the exercise of power. Alternative approaches posed theoretical challenges to making sense of the role of media in the reproduction of ideology and maintenance of power. Feminist researchers found Marxism unnecessarily restrictive by its conceptualisation of human behaviour and activity only in terms of class. The differences of gender and sexuality were seen as an alternative to class conflict and exploitation. Other divisions, such as age, ethnicity, nationality and race, were to follow. The writings of Michel Foucault also presented a contrasting view of power, distinct from the 'binary and all-encompassing opposition of class interests'. In face of these challenges Marxism became increasingly defensive (see Murdock, 2000a). Ironically as many celebrate the 'retreat from class', the gap between rich and poor is widening to a situation resembling the conditions of the nineteenth century.

FEMINIST CRITIQUES

Feminist work in the field of mass communication had its origins in the women's movement of the 1960s. A key text in the development of the movement was Betty Friedan's *The Feminine Mystique* (1963), which had at its heart a critique of the media. The media were regarded as central to the pattern of discrimination operating against women in society. Women and women's issues were ignored, downplayed, trivialised or condemned in the media. The women's movement complained about the absence of women in the media, the limited representations of women when they are mentioned, the focus on representing women as 'sexual commodities' and the emphasis on the victim rather than the aggressor in the coverage of violence. This amounted to the 'symbolic annihilation' of women in the media (Tuchman, 1978b). Initially women working in the media industries came together to share experiences, build networks and lobby for change. Groups such as Women in the Media were established (King and Stott, 1977) and it was this political impetus that drove early feminist media research.

Friedan and The Feminine Mystique

Betty Friedan was a former women's magazine editor who accused the media, as well as a range of other expert sources of information in society such as doctors, psychiatrists and sociologists, of fuelling insecurity, fear and frustration amongst women by insisting they live up to the ideals of the 'happy housewife heroine'. She challenged the traditional image of femininity, which emphasised the role of women as housewives, mothers and sexual objects – the feminine mystique – and which worked against women developing their potential outside of the home and household. Her book was in part based on an examination of the content of women's magazines, which showed that the image of women was defined in relation to men, the home and family. Such images reflected the fact that few women worked in media organisations, and the assumption was that they had a detrimental impact on individual consciousness and social life. Such analysis was the basis for the initial challenge of women's groups against the media. For example, the National Organisation of Women (NOW) in the United States declared the media one of the major sites of struggle for the movement and in 1970 over 100 women occupied the premises of one of America's leading women's magazines, demanding the appointment of a female editor, child care for employees and the publication of a 'liberated issue'.

For some it is the 'blurred line between the feminist as academic and the feminist as activist, that distinguishes feminist perspectives on the media from other possible perspectives' (van Zoonen, 1991: 34). Not surprisingly there was little academic research on women and the media. As with other academic disciplines, media research was mainly written by men, about men and for men. The feminist critique is based on two main planks, 'an analysis of structures of power and oppression, in which women are systematically subordinated, and a focus on the politics of representation and the production of knowledge in which women were objects rather than active subjects' (Gallagher, 1992: 2). Most of the early studies in the 1970s and early 1980s, as Gallagher notes, were about the problems and issues associated with the absence of women in the profession and the defects of images of women in the mass media (see, for example, King and Stott, 1977; Tuchman *et al.*, 1978; Janus, 1977; Busby, 1975). Empirical work in the latter area focused on the stereotypical representation of women and its effect on the audience. Underpinning much of this work is the view that societies are characterised by male domination of women. The ideology of patriarchy ensures men benefit at the expense of women, particularly in the domestic sphere where women's responsibility for housework and child care restricts their chances of entering and succeeding in the workplace. One of the key questions for such research is why do women accept this state of affairs. And many feminists have, like Marxists in their examination of the compliance of the working class with the established order, turned to the concept of ideology.

Patriarchy

Patriarchy is a shorthand term for male domination. The structures of patriarchy or male domination are seen as existing in all societies. Men and women comprise 'sex classes' and men as the dominant sex class oppress women and ensure that the distribution of valued goods and services is biased in their own favour. It is the power of men over women, not the dynamics of capitalism, that explains the inequalities between the sexes. The root of male power is in the area of human reproduction and is most clearly expressed in the intimate personal relationship of love, sex and marriage. The constant threat and use of male violence in these relationships – as seen in rape and pornography – is the basis for wider social and political oppression. Patriarchy works through the representation of gender role as being natural, normal and inevitable. Hence men are portrayed as the economic providers and women the emotional providers. The world of work is represented as the male sphere while the home is the female sphere.

Source: adapted from Fulcher and Scott, 1999

As feminist media research developed it produced 'a more complex analysis of the structure and process of representation, the apparatus and economic structures, which support these, the social relations that reproduce patriarchal ideology or discourse and women's place in culture and language' (Gallagher, 1992: 2). Recent feminist work differs considerably from many of the studies of a decade or so ago. The straightforward examination of the 'sexism of media representation', and the neglect of women and women's issues resting on the theoretical basis of patriarchy has been replaced by a plethora of work, drawing on a range of theoretical approaches and concerns. This growth is a reflection of a number of factors. First, the political fragmentation of feminism. Since the 1980s 'the founding principles of contemporary western feminism have been dramatically challenged, with previously shared assumptions and unquestioned orthodoxies relegated almost to history' (quoted in van Zoonen, 1994: 3). Early feminist theory rested on the assumption of a shared notion of women's oppression, which excluded differences between women. The white middle-class assumption of such theory was challenged by class analysis of Marxist feminists and more crucially by 'Third World' women who questioned the usefulness of such feminism to their own circumstances. Later black feminists, psychoanalytical and post-structuralist feminists all challenged the assumption that women's oppression rested at the level of social structures whether capitalism or patriarchy. For example, Juliet Mitchell (1975) was one of the first feminist writers to use psychoanalysis and Sigmund Freud's concept of the unconscious to explain why women accepted ideas, institutions and arrangements that oppress them. She argued that ideas about femininity are so ingrained in the unconscious they are taken for granted and accepted as correct. So deep-rooted are they in one's personality they are difficult to dislodge. Psychoanalytical theory also raises questions about 'identity' as a unified and coherent concept, and leads others to question the usefulness of 'woman' and 'gender' as categories as they intersect with racial, class, ethnic, sexual and so on to constitute personal identity (Gallagher, 1992: 2).

The second factor to account for the development of complexity and fissures in feminist approaches to media theory and research is the resistance of the field of media studies to feminist critiques. By the 1980s it was impossible for communication scholars to ignore the feminist challenge to their field. For some this meant that the feminist media critique had 'moved from the outside to inside the academic disciplines of communication, media and cultural studies' (van Zoonen, 1994: 13). However, this does not mean that gender issues have been acknowledged throughout media and communication studies. There are still many areas of the field untouched by feminist thinking and research (van Zoonen, 1994: 15). This has led to the expansion of feminist scholarship into new areas, accompanied by the increasing desire to develop distinct 'female perspectives' to the field. The traditional theoretical and methodological legacy of (male) scholarship is deemed inappropriate to describe feminist endeavour. Hence new categories and frameworks are sought to develop feminist approaches. The result is that it is impossible to think of 'feminist' theory as a 'consistent and homogeneous field', and attempts to define and delineate feminist approaches are fraught with difficulty (van Zoonen, 1994: 2–3). However, feminist analysis has forced media studies to focus on gender as a mechanism for organising, understanding and experiencing the world.

FOUCAULT

The work of the French philosopher Michel Foucault has had an influential if ambivalent impact on the study of the media and mass communication. Foucault is described as a post-structuralist as he rejects the notion that a person's consciousness or view of the world is determined by either biology or social structures such as class. He breaks with the fundamental view of Marx and many of his neo-Marxist critics, as well as functionalists, that social structures are essential to any understanding of a person's position in the world and his or her view of the world. Foucault thus dismisses a link between social structures and the way in which we see ourselves. Instead he argues that ideology and consciousness, how we see ourselves and the world around us, is shaped by discourses, or ways of seeing, describing and thinking about things. He starts from the same place as Marx in seeing knowledge and ideology as reflecting power relations in society but dismisses the Marxist view that power is essentially tied to economic wealth and control of the means of production and that there is some fundamental truth hidden from people, from the masses. He compares social power to a net that is thrown over society, which surrounds all of us, and he is interested in how knowledge is constructed in particular ways at particular times in history to control groups and activities in society. He sees knowledge as being developed through discourses that represent ideas about or ways of interpreting the world. Foucault's contribution to media theory lies in his evaluation of power and his articulation of the concept of discourse. For him power is not exercised by one group or class but envelops us all and only becomes visible in institutions such as mental hospitals, clinics or prisons where people are most likely to fight against it. Applying his work to media studies – and again it is important to note that Foucault never wrote directly about the media – has led scholars to attempt to identify and interpret the discourses in media texts.

Foucault

Michel Foucault was born in 1926 in Poitiers, France. His father was a doctor and he, like Althusser, attended the Ecole Normale Superieure in Paris where he studied philosophy. He also was a member of the French Communist Party – if only briefly. He developed an interest in psychopathology and wrote his thesis on madness. His main works are The Order of Things (Les Mots et les Choses) (1970), Birth of the Clinic (1973), Discipline and Punishment (1977) and his three volumes The History of Sexuality (1976–84). He became active in campaigns for prison reform and gay rights, and died in 1984 of an AIDS-related illness.

Source: adapted from Booker, 1998

Foucault's work on power and discourse represented a break from the traditional social scientific way of trying to understand and make sense of the world. He made little use of conventional sociological method to support his theoretical position, preferring to use examples drawn from historical sources to illustrate his ideas. His subjective approach stands in contrast to the claims of social science to develop objective methods to test and assess hypotheses. His subjectivity and non-essential approach, which rejected the view that human beings can be reduced to any single essence, characterised what was to be described as post-modernism.

Essentialist theories

Essentialist theories argue that human behaviour and social life can be explained by some essential feature. Thus Marxism sees the nature of human societies as accountable by the way in which economic production is organised and the class relations that emerge out of the

> material inequality produced. Feminism sees patriarchy as the essence
> of society, arising out of the essential biological and psychological
> differences between men and women
>
> Source: adapted from Taylor, 1997

POST-MODERN REVISIONISM

The late twentieth century saw a complete re-evaluation of the way in which society is developing. We are living though a series of substantial social transformations. The nature of capitalism is undergoing a fundament shift – not only is the world of work changing but also the organisation of business. The system of large-scale mass production, which has characterised most of the twentieth century, is becoming obsolete. It is being replaced by a more flexible system in which small firms are subcontracted by larger ones to make products using a workforce that is multi-skilled, able to switch from one job to another at short notice and usually employed on a part-time basis. This has been accompanied by a decline in the power of collective bargaining and trades unions. Politically changes are occurring with the decline of class politics, the rise of new social movements such as environmentalism, feminism and gay rights, the erosion of the nation-state with the globalisation of the world economy and the crisis of the welfare state as governments find it more difficult to fund and operate social services such as education and health care. Another aspect of change is the increased mobility of people and populations around the world with the migration of whole societies and peoples, producing the problem of refugees and migrant communities and the destabilising of cultural identity around the world. In such a world 'people's identities are becoming fractured, pluralised and hybridised, and populations that were marginal in the past have suddenly moved to the centre of the historical and cultural stage' (Grossberg *et al.*, 1998: 53–4). New technologies are seen as fuelling these changes, as they reduce the nature of time and space in contemporary society. For many these changes represent the end of modernity and the advent of a new historical era: post-modernity.

The concept of the post-modern is difficult to define. It has been evident in academic and media theory since the mid-1980s but despite its widespread currency the meaning of the term is variable and sometimes obscure. Webster (1995: 163) describes post-modern scholars and thinkers as those who reject the approach of trying to explain the present using the traditional conventions of established social science. A diverse group of thinkers, often coming from non-sociological backgrounds such as philosophy, literary criticism and cultural theory, they can be associated with a wide range of positions (see Taylor, 1997: Chapter 9). Nevertheless they all appear to reject the notion of the individual as a sovereign agent whose identity or sense of self is clear and coherent and determines his or her attitudes and behaviour. Post-modernists argue that individual identity is a social construction made up of differing and often contradictory components. Hence individuals are the product of class, gender, race, ethnicity, nationality, age and so on, and hence their identity is neither unitary nor unchanging. Rather it is multiple and changing. They do not accept that human behaviour can be reduced to any one explanation or essence and as a result are sceptical of any grand theory. Totalising theories that purport to explain everything that happens in the social world, such as Marx's class struggle or Freud's psychoanalytical theory, which sees all human behaviour as the outcome of the struggle between the unconscious and conscious psyche, or patriarchy are dismissed. They also argue that a social reality does not exist. There is no such thing as a true account of reality. Truth is a problematic concept – or, as Foucault puts it, 'each society has its regime of truth, its "general politics" of truth; that is, the types of discourse which it accepts and makes function as truth' (quoted in Webster, 1995: 167). Post-modern theorists see reality as constructed from different kinds of 'text' – or in Foucault's theory 'discourses' – that operate to convince people of a particular version of reality. As different groups can present reality in different ways through the construction of their own texts, the post-modern thinkers believe all voices should be studied, including those previously neglected.

Post-modernism

In trying to define the 'post-modern' a distinction can be made between 'post-modernity', 'post-modernism' and 'post-modern social theory'. Post-modernity refers to a historical stage in the development of human society, which represents a break with modernity. Post-modernism refers to a cultural movement in which post-modern cultural products such as works of art, films, television and advertisements are seen as distinct and different from the cultural products of modernity. Post-modern culture, for example, blurs the divisions between high and popular culture, abandons notions of a consistent narrative and emphasises style over content. Post-modern social theory refers to a new way of thinking, which challenges the central notion of modernity that rationality underlies human action and change.

Source: adapted from Taylor, 1997

Post-modern thinking has had an impact on all academic disciplines, but none more so than media studies (see Morley, 1995; Stevenson, 1995). One leading post-modern thinker, Jean Baudrillard, argues the media play a crucial role in blurring the distinction between image and reality. He concurs with the view that today we live in a 'society of signs', but unlike semiologists and structuralists does not see signs as having any underlying meaning. While Barthes might argue that the beer a person drinks or the newspaper he or she reads or the clothes they wear might indicate something about their social status, Baudrillard argues that signs have become detached from what they originally signified. He sees representation as having gone through four historical stages: first the image reflected the reality, then it masked reality, then it marked the absence of reality and finally, in post-modern times, it bears no relationship to reality. He rejects the notion of either an objective or subjective reality and labels the situation where images are no longer rooted in reality as 'hyperreality'. With the output of the mass media open to all and any kinds of interpretation, distinctions between what is true or false, real or simulated become blurred. The blurring of boundaries within media content is observable with the collapsing of the distinction between news and entertainment (infotainment) and advertising and editorials (advertorials) (see Harms and Dickens, 1996). In addition people are bombarded with an excessive number of images coming at them faster than ever before, and the sheer volume and variety of information and hype attached to it by the burgeoning public relations and media image agencies is overwhelming rational discussion and judgement (Morley, 1995: 63). In our media-saturated world we have more and more information but less and less meaning. Baudrillard describes the situation as the 'implosion' of meaning. The post-modern media 'communicate an hodgepodge of random images that are not organised so as to say anything or take a position' (Harms and Dickens, 1996: 216). For post-modernists there is no reality outside what we see, hear and read in the media; 'real meaning' is disappearing as our experiences are shaped or 'simulated' by the images and signs of the mass media. Today we live in a 'simulacrum', a simulated world, full of images and all we can do is to use them to amuse ourselves and experience 'pleasure'. Thus, according to Baudrillard (1983: 102) in the post-modern age 'there are no longer media in the literal sense of the term ... that is to say, a power mediating between one reality and another, between one state of the real and another – neither in content nor form'. Surface and style have become the most important defining features of the mass media (Strinati, 2000: 234), as their output – particularly of the most powerful medium, television – is emphasising the playful, the surreal, the superficial and the self-referential at the expense of content, substance and meaning.

In this world of information inflation and diminishing meaning, post-modern thinkers differ over their understanding of the response of media audiences (Harms and Dickens, 1996). Baudrillard has a cynical view of ordinary people, referring to them as a 'black hole' and 'spongy referent'. They are portrayed as passive before the tide of meaningless messages from the media. Paradoxically this provides audiences with power to resist. For Baudrillard people resist by absorbing media messages without responding to them in what he calls a 'refusal of meaning' (Morley, 1996: 63). It is the 'power of silence'. Other post-modernist thinkers have a less contemptuous view of the audience. For John Fiske (1987a) audiences can actively construct meanings from media images. They can make their own messages and resist the intentions of the producers or authors of media messages and as a result can resist the media. The power of audiences to passively or actively resist supports post-modernist claims that audiences cannot be manipulated or duped by the mass media (Harms and Dickens, 1996). This is a move away from traditional views of audiences in media theory.

Thinking and theorising about the mass media has been presented with a challenge by post-modernism. While thinkers such as Baudrillard address the dominance of the media in contemporary life and culture – and capture the increasing tendency of media to merge life and representation into one – their rejection of the ability and capacity of social science to explain and make sense of what is happening and thereby create a better world raises important questions (see Lyotard, 1984; Ang, 1998). However, post-modern media theory has its roots in the work of previous scholars. The post-modern world is above all driven by technological change. The 'blizzard' of images that sweeps over people around the world is the product of new media technologies. Post-modern thinkers, and in particular Baudrillard, draw heavily on the work of Marshal McLuhan who theorised the relationship between the media, technology and society.

McLUHAN

McLuhan was one of the first scholars to examine how people's means of communication contribute to the shaping, character and scope of their society, to economic, political and cultural life (Lorimer, 1994: 1). He emphasises the role of media and communication technologies in influencing the historical development of societies. According to McLuhan the content of the media is largely irrelevant to understanding their influence. Exploring the ideological or semiotic construction of media messages or the nature of media discourses misses the point that it is the technical forms of media communication that shape human perception. For McLuhan, 'trying to understand television by examining the programmes it offers is as futile as attempting to comprehend the impact of the printing press in the fifteenth century by interpreting the contents of Gutenberg's bible' (Adler, 1975). For McLuhan the medium is the message. McLuhan describes how the shift from oral to print communication changed the senses and perceptions of society at that time. For McLuhan media technology changed the balance between the senses of sight, sound, smell, touch and taste. Print stresses sight or 'vision' and this influenced our thinking, making it 'linear, sequential, regular, repeated and logical', which 'allowed human beings to separate thought from feeling' and 'led to a sense of alienation and individualism' (Severin and Tankard, 1988: 315). He also argues written culture shortened human memory since information could be stored in the form of the book. It also provided the opportunity for the emergence of nationalism and the nation-state as the spread of books in languages other than Latin encouraged the development of forms of national legitimacy outside the authority of the Catholic Church, which had dominated medieval Europe.

McLuhan

Marshal McLuhan (1911–80) was a Canadian academic who founded the Centre for Media Studies in Toronto. Trained as a literary scholar he had a fascination with the technology of the mass media. Unlike most media theorists whose work is often never read outside higher education, McLuhan's ideas gained widespread popular attention. He became a pop culture guru of the 1960s, coining terms such as 'the medium is the message' and the 'global village', which have entered our daily language. According to rock star Brian Eno, he 'changed the world in one sentence'. His main books are The Gutenberg Galaxy: The Making of Typographic Man (1962), Understanding Media: The Extensions of Man (1964) and, with Quentin Fiore, The Medium is the Message (1967) and War and Peace in the Global Village (1968). He became a consultant to the media industries, particularly the advertising world of Madison Avenue, and his fame gained him a cameo role in Woody Allen's film Annie Hall. His ideas rapidly fell into disfavour in the 1970s, only to be revived in the 1990s with the growing debate over globalisation.

Source: adapted from Baran and Davies, 1995

The electronic media, according to McLuhan, laid stress on other senses – visual, aural and tactile – and opened up the possibility of people being everywhere at the same time. The electronic media, particularly television, bring people closer together, severing ties to individual nations, and making them members of a 'global village'. Following the work of his Canadian colleague Harold Innis (1950; 1951), who drew attention to the importance of written technology in the establishment and maintenance of empires in the ancient world, McLuhan highlights the 'bias' of time and space built into different media of com-munication. Some media stress time, others space, with different consequences for social life. Thus messages carved into stone, a common feature of the ancient world, are time biased. They are permanent monuments, which preserve messages through many gener-ations but are difficult to transport. Paper, on the other hand, is lightweight and carries messages rapidly across space (see Stevenson, 1995: Chapter 4). The result is that 'the temporal and spatial characteristics of the available means of communication in any society impose boundaries upon the scope and scale of its activities' (Lorimer, 1994: 1). Unlike Innis, who saw the development of new media technologies as enabling elites to exercise more centralised control, McLuhan focused on the potential benefits of such developments. He did not ask questions about who controlled the global village and how they interacted with the villagers (see Chapter 9).

McLuhan's focus on technology leads him to make a distinction, in language redolent of the 1960s, between 'hot' and 'cool' media. Print is a 'hot' medium as it provides those who consume it with all the information necessary to make sense of the world. Television, by contrast, is a 'cool' medium as to make sense of what appears on the screen the viewer must fill in what is missing. According to McLuhan (1994: 23) 'hot media are, therefore, low in participation and cool media are high in participation or completion by the audience'. It is the cool media, especially television, which will reconnect our senses, bringing us together in the global village. For McLuhan the global village was a reconstruction of the communal world of the ancient village torn asunder by the print media. He believed in the power of communication technologies to shape human history, with each medium shaping our senses to produce particular social outcomes. People make sense of the world in different ways depending on whether they read newspapers or watch television. His beliefs have been criticised for their technological determinism and many of his critics accuse him of placing faith in technology to bring about social change while neglecting the need for the reform of social structures.

Technological determinism

> Technological determinism is the notion that technology shapes society, and technological change causes and is responsible for social change. Often technological development is regarded as driving social change and progress. Technology is seen as an independent factor, somehow outside society, and a given technology can lead to particular outcomes. For example, it is argued that computer technology causes unemployment. The assumption that the effects of technology are built in to the technology and do not vary according to the social context in which they are introduced is, however, problematic.
>
> Source: adapted from MacKay, 2001: 29–30

PUBLIC SPHERES

If the approach and arguments of McLuhan and post-modernists led to a rejection of modernity, others defend the 'unfinished project' of modernity (Taylor, 1997: 242). The German philosopher Jürgen Habermas is sympathetic to the attempts of modernity to promote a more rational understanding of the world. In his theory of communicative action, he distinguishes between 'instrumental' and 'communicative' rationality. He argues rationality had been conceptualised in 'instrumental' terms by modernist thinkers who stressed the application of technical means to obtain particular goals. Thus individual decisions to co-operate or participate in actions are determined by a range of instrumental

means such as sanctions, force, gratification and financial reward. Communicative rationality refers to the way people reach agreement and mutual understanding about what to
do through reasoning (Taylor, 1997: 242). People use three kinds of claims or evidence to
convince others of their argument. Habermas identifies claims based on objective and
factual information about the best way to proceed, subjective experience and their guiding
normative views of a situation. In this context Habermas developed the concept of the
'public sphere', which has become a key concept of media studies. For Garnham (1990:
109) 'the principles it embodies represent an Ideal Type against which we can judge existing social arrangements' including the practice and performance of the media.

Habermas

Born in 1929, Jürgen Habermas studied under Theodor Adorno in
Frankfurt where he has spent most of his academic career. His main
works are the two volumes Theory of Communicative Action (1984;
1987), and The Structural Transformation of the Public Sphere
(1989), which was first published in German in 1962.

The 'public sphere' is a forum or arena that mediates between state and society; a forum
in which private individuals can debate public affairs, criticise the authority of the state
and call on those in power to justify their positions before an informed and reasoning
public. The public sphere is independent of government and partisan economic forces and
dedicated to rational debate accessible to all citizens who form public opinion (Webster,
1995: 101–2). Central to the operation of the public sphere is the free flow of information
and communication, and media institutions are essential to its effective working. Not only
does Habermas outline the nature of the public sphere, he also provides a historical
account of its development. He traces its emergence in the seventeenth and eighteenth centuries with the onset of capitalism and the rise of liberal thought. He argues the economic
independence of the bourgeoisie enabled them to struggle for and obtain their freedom
from Church and state, which represented the old feudal order. This freedom was manifest in the growth of critical reflection in plays, novels and letters, and the flowering of
public discussion in outlets such as salons, universities, coffee houses and the emerging
newly independent private newspapers (Curran, 1991: 83). These developments had by
the nineteenth century resulted in the formation of the public sphere with 'its characteristics of open debate, critical scrutiny, full reportage, increased accessibility and independence of actors from crude economic interests as well as from state control' (Webster,
1995: 103). Habermas describes how early capitalism had to struggle against the state.
However, from the nineteenth century onwards the public sphere has been corrupted by
the growth of the power of the state, the emergence of corporate capitalism and transformation of the media into commercial operations, making profit for their owners rather

than acting as information providers for their readers. These developments represent the 'refeudalisation' of the public sphere. Market-driven capitalism had ridden rough-shod over the principle of public communication based on reason and rational discussion. Public opinion is now manipulated and manufactured by publicity, advertising, public relations and social engineering. For Habermas the refeudalised public sphere is a 'faked version', polluted by the lobbying culture of the twentieth century and simply a forum for 'displays of power' rather than the exchange of ideas and sharing of outlooks.

The attraction of Habermas's 'public sphere' for media theory is its focus on the political dimension of the media and their relationship with democracy and the political process. However, critics have drawn attention to a number of weaknesses in his argument. Historians argue that he has a 'very unreal view of the past' and there is little evidence to support his interpretation of the historical development of the press (see Curran, 1991; 2000). Curran (1991: 42–4) argues, 'his characterisation of modern media is positively misleading'. For example, his pessimistic view of modern media is challenged by historical accounts of public service broadcasting. Bodies such as the BBC have been shown at times to broaden political representation and assist the democratisation of the relationship between the government and governed. Feminist scholars have noted the exclusion of women from Habermas's public sphere (Fraser, 1992). The public sphere is also not conceived as inclusive of working people and 'ethnic minorities'. Such criticism led Habermas to re-assess his work, producing a more optimistic interpretation of the modern media and a re-interpretation of whom and what constitutes the public sphere (Curran, 2000: 135–7). His work stands as an antidote to the refusal of post-modernism to make assessments about the media and society.

SUMMARY

This chapter examined media theory in the post-war period. Pluralist and functionalist views initially dominated the theorising of the media. These approaches were rooted in the social cohesion and order that characterised the needs of post-war reconstruction. The growing political and social conflict of the 1960s saw the re-emergence of Marxism to challenge the functionalist-pluralist paradigm. The Marxist-pluralist dispute provided the basic framework within which media theory was developed up to the early 1980s. Limitations of traditional Marxist analysis saw a theoretical shift, which led to new variants of Marxist theory, including the work of Althusser and Gramsci. The splintering of Marxist media analysis centred on the media's role in the reproduction of ideology. Structuralism and semiology became an ever-present part of the neo-Marxist agenda with deeper and more intense readings of media texts becoming more prominent in the field. The focus was on how meanings are produced and pleasures are provided for the consumer of the media. Audiences came to be seen as active rather than passive in their media consumption. The notion of the viewer, reader or listener using the media to gratify their wants and needs was translated into the 'critical reader' deconstructing messages how they liked.

Since the early 1980s the class analysis of Marxism has been further eroded by challenges from feminism, discourse analysis and post-modernism. Curran (1990) sees these challenges as playing a part in the 'decentering of cultural and media research'. It is no longer seen as necessary to relate the media and media-related activities to their political and economic contexts. The role of the media is reduced to a succession of reader/text encounters, which makes no reference to power relationships or situates them in the context of a society in which power is disaggregated. By concentrating on the exploration of the contradictions and ambivalences in media texts and on the power of the audience to actively produce meaning from texts, a more cautious assessment of the influence of the media is encouraged. The focus of media theory has shifted from the political to the popular, on why and how the media are popular and how they create pleasure rather than how they contribute to the political process. Post-modernism takes this one step further by not only problematising the notion of representation but also by attacking the very way in which we approach theory.

Section 2
The production process

This section outlines some of the main theoretical approaches to explaining how media content is selected and produced. The important question media theory asks in this area is who has the power to shape media content and how do they do it. In trying to answer this question, media theory examines the nature of media organisations, their institutional structures and arrangements, their relationship with other social institutions and the work practices and ideologies of media occupations (Curran *et al.*, 1982: 17). Theorising about media organisations and occupations has a long tradition. Max Weber contrasted society's view of journalists as members of a 'pariah caste', with journalistic practice, which he believed required 'as much "genius" as any scholarly accomplishment' (quoted in Tunstall, 2001: 25). Weber, in his essay in 1918, also drew attention to journalists having less and less political influence as press owners gained more and more. The question of ownership and control has been one of the key areas of exploration in trying to make sense of media production and what appears in the media.

Thinking about ownership and control of the mass media has been very much shaped by the theories of Karl Marx and the political economy approach. Marx believed that powerful interests in society exercised control over the circulation of ideas. There was no question for him that these interests controlled the main means of mass communication. They did this by having their hands firmly on the economic levers that operated the mass media. As a result, through ownership of media organisations, and by exercising their will through the chains of command within media organisations, their views of society came to dominate the content of the media. Owners could directly intervene to ensure their views prevailed and media practitioners, regardless of direct intervention, are constrained in what they can report or represent by the economic parameters laid down by capitalist production. Based on Marx's critical perspective, the 'political economy' approach is 'associated with macro-questions of media ownership and control, interlocking directorships and other factors that bring together media industries with other media and other industries, and with political and social elites' and the consequence for media practice and content of the 'working of the profit motive in the hunt for audiences and/or advertising'

(Boyd Barrett and Newbold, 1995: 186). Political economy therefore examines the media and the nature of media activity to identify the extent of corporate reach, the 'commodification' of media products and the changing nature of state and government intervention.

However, there is disagreement within Marxist political economy over the relationship between ownership and control. Classical Marxists argue there is a direct relationship between the ownership of the mass media and control over what we see, hear and read in the media. Neo-Marxists argue owners do not have direct control over the content of the media. It is almost physically impossible for any media owners to exercise day-to-day control over the vast amount of material that is generated by their organisation. Rather control is exercised through the structures and pressures within which media organisations have to operate. These structures are determined by the capitalist system and capitalist ideology. Thus control is seen in terms of structures rather than individuals. Pluralists, on the other hand, do not accept that ownership and control is a matter of concern. They see the consumer of the media being sovereign and ultimately, whatever media owners and controllers want, they have to defer to the wants and needs of readers, listeners or viewers. Through the mechanism of the market the voice of the consumer can be heard and if owners want to acquire an audience and make a profit they cannot afford to ignore this voice. Post-modernists are also critical of Marxists for ignoring the desires and wants of audiences.

Political economy lays stress on economics as a necessary and sufficient determinant of what the media produce, what is in the media. While economic factors are not unimportant, there are also other ways of understanding media production. Rooted in organisational sociology, another approach explores the processes that occur within media organisations and examines the occupational culture of the media in terms of the recruitment, career paths and norms and values of media workers. The autonomy of the individual worker within the organisation he or she works for is central to this examination. The focus on media as organisations has been criticised for being too media-centred. Media organisations, it is argued, should also be understood in the context of forces and agencies external to them. Some stress the relationship between the media organisations and other social institutions and sources of power while yet others see media organisations as reflections of the society and culture within which they operate.

Chapter Three

THE CENSORSHIP OF MONEY: THEORIES OF MEDIA OWNERSHIP AND CONTROL

Walk into a W.H. Smith shop in any city in the United Kingdom and the shelves are full of magazines and newspapers; the street vendor in Dar es Salaam in Africa often has a table piled with publications of different kinds; and the kiosks in Spanish cities appear to be stuffed full of a variety of material. With so many specialised publications such as *What Car?*, *New Yorker* and *Homes and Gardens* through to women's magazines such as *Bella*, *Vanity Fair* and *Hello!*, and news magazines such as *Time*, *Newsweek*, *Far Eastern Economic Review* and *The Economist*, the public across the world seems well catered for. Similarly in music stores such as Virgin Megastore or Tower Records the choice of CDs, cassettes, videos and DVDs appears to be wide. And switch on television or radio and there are programmes and channels that seem to cater for everyone's interests. The impression is that we, the consumers, have an enormity of choice. However, behind this Aladdin's cave of products the choice of what is on offer rests in the hands of a small number of large corporations who produce much of what we listen to, read and see during our leisure time. Choice is apparently determined by the few. Not only do these corporations have the opportunity to influence choice, they also have a crucial role to play in shaping social consciousness. The commodities produced by the media and communications industries are not the same as those produced by other industries. Media goods provide accounts and images of the world in which we live that can determine our ways of understanding that world. Thus the ownership and control of the media is identified not only as an important factor in determining the structure, working and output of the mass media but also in the production of meaning in society. The focus on ownership and control in trying to understand the process of mass communication is usually associated with the 'political economy' approach. Before exploring in more detail how the theory of political economy helps us to understand media ownership and control, let's go back in time and examine its historical origins.

THE HISTORY OF POLITICAL ECONOMY

The term 'political economy' has its roots deep in history. It was first used by a French writer, Monchretien de Watteville, in 1615 when he employed the term to describe the 'science of wealth acquisition common to the State as well as the Family' (Hoogvelt, 1997: 3). However, the political economy approach to understanding society and polity was only formally established at the end of the eighteenth century. Classical political economy is associated with, amongst others, the works of Adam Smith and David Ricardo. These writers were trying to make sense of the vast social changes that were happening in the wake of the Industrial Revolution, an upheaval that transformed agricultural societies into commercial, manufacturing and industrial societies. Trying to understand and explain the transformation, these philosophers and commentators laid stress on the importance of the economic organisation of society, and the ways in which it shaped and determined social, cultural and political relations (see Mosco, 1996). While they differed over the ways in which such organisation shaped and determined society they were agreed on the primacy of economy. Change was explained in terms of the development of capitalism. Smith and classical political economists saw capitalism as the best way to generate wealth, regulate the economy and bring about peace and prosperity. They argued that the mechanism of the market enabled each individual to pursue his or her own efforts to maximise their wealth while at the same time maximising the value of the output to the public. In other words, 'to promote personal greed is to promote the common good' (Pettman, 1996: 11). Smith described the market as the 'hidden hand', which brought together all the myriad of individual actions involved in the production of goods and services to satisfy the needs of society as a whole.

Classical political economy saw private ownership as central to the functioning of capitalism. This applied to all industry, including the press. Up until the early nineteenth century little contradiction was seen between private ownership of the newspaper industry and its public performance. Freedom of the press was primarily defined as the absence of government control. Thus putting newspapers in the hands of private men – and sometimes women – of wealth was not seen as incompatible with the role of the press in providing a channel for political information. Of course, political information in the period was of the partisan persuasion and newspapers were often the organs of political opinion, comment and parties. However, at the start of the nineteenth century, some commentators and critics began to see contradictions between private ownership and public communication. This change in perception was largely the result of the change that occurred in the nature of society and industry and the structure of press ownership. Early newspapers were owned by one individual or rested in the hands of one family. Often the editor and the owner were the same person. It was relatively cheap for an individual to start a paper and thus easy not to see private ownership as a threat to the role of the press. The industrialisation of the press, which began around about the 1850s, led to a gradual rise in the costs of newspaper production, which prevented most people from entering the newspaper market. Small business was driven out, leaving press ownership increasingly concentrated in the hands of large press empires or chains. From the beginning of the twentieth century commentators began to ask whether it was possible to have both a socially responsible press and a privately owned press. An American critic complained, 'it is rationally absurd that an intelligent, self governing community should be the helpless victim of the caprice of newspapers managed solely for individual profit' (quoted in Murdock, 1990). The American novelist Upton Sinclair was more graphic when he said in 1919 that newspapers 'take the fair body of truth and sell it to the marketplace, who betray the virgin hopes of mankind into the loathsome brothel of big business'.

The prostitution of the press to the market-place was a matter of major political concern between the two world wars. The performance of the press was dominated by discussion of the power of press barons around the world – whether it was William Randolph Hearst in America, Alfred Hugenberg in Germany, Jean Prouvost in France or the Lords Beaverbrook, Northcliffe, Rothermere and Cowdray in Britain. Leading figures across the political spectrum expressed their concern. Prime Minister Stanley Baldwin spoke in the 1920s of his worries about the threat posed to British democracy by the press barons of Fleet Street whom he accused of exercising 'power without responsibility'. The left-wing commentator, Norman Angell, spoke for many when he said that

> what England [sic] thinks is largely controlled by a very few men, not by virtue of the direct expression of any opinion of their own but by controlling the distribution of emphasis in the telling of facts: so stressing one group of them and keeping another group in the background as to make a given conclusion inevitable.
>
> (Angell, 1922)

At a theoretical level such criticism of the press is most associated with the works of one commentator, Karl Marx. His analysis, besides dominating the thinking of his contemporaries, supporters and detractors alike, has come to occupy an important position in academic debate today. For some 'argument about the relations between ownership and control has largely been a debate with Marx's ghost' (Open University, 1977a).

MARXIST POLITICAL ECONOMY

Marx's view of the economic organisation of society along capitalist lines was less sanguine than that of classical political economists. While he accepted capitalism created wealth, he also emphasised it generated vast disparities in the distribution of resources and life opportunities within society. For Marx the key characteristic of the growth of capitalism was the ownership and control of the means of production by a small number of people; in other words the levers of economic power rest in the hands of the few. These few constitute a 'capitalist class' or 'ruling class', which uses its power to further its interests and protect its position and influence in society. The main interest of this class is to amass more and more profit. This, however, can only be done at the expense of other classes in society.

In trying to understand the role of the media in modern capitalist society, Marx's work encourages us to see the media as a means to promote a certain set of views and ideas – the ideology of the bourgeoisie – and to exclude or deride alternative or oppositional views or ideas. According to Marx the exercise of political power and the accumulation of wealth are historically intertwined (see Chapter 1). The bourgeoisie as the dominant class controls the economic activities of society. It also exercises a hold over the cultural and media industries, which enables it to regulate the ideas and images that are presented to the subordinate classes in society. In manipulating the output of the cultural and media industries the bourgeoisie seeks to have its view of the world endorsed as well as its position in it. The result is its ideas prevail in social discourse and dominate "the mental horizons of subordinate groups" who consequently view the "prevailing distribution of wealth and power and their lowly position within it as natural and inevitable" (Open University, 1977: 16). The maximisation of profit as well as individual ownership of property is made to appear as the logical outcome of economic activity, rather than particular product of a capitalist system that serves the interests of one group in society. Marx identified ownership of the media and other forms of communication and culture as one of the primary mechanisms by which the bourgeoisie maintains its position of power and privilege. Ownership of the media and cultural industries "rested fairly and squarely in the hands of society's dominant property owners" (Open University, 1977:16) and there are no obstacles to their ability to exercise control over what is communicated. As Marx saw it, ownership, control and class privilege were all linked to one another.

Marx wrote only one article applying his model to the media: 'Opinion of the press and the opinion of the people' was written for the Viennese paper *Die Presse* in 1861 (see Murdock, 1982a: 126–7). In it he explored the relationship between newspaper editors and owners to account for the British press's demand for British intervention in the American Civil War on the side of the South while popular opinion appeared to support the North. For Marx the reason was clear: the close connection between newspaper editors and owners and those in government circles, including the Prime Minister of the day, Lord Palmerston.

Marx on the British press

> Consider the London Press. At its head stands The Times, whose chief editor . . . is a subordinate member of the cabinet and a mere creature of Palmerston. A principal editor of Punch was accommodated by Palmerston with a seat on the Board of Health and an annual salary of a thousand pounds sterling. The Morning Post is in part Palmerston's private property. . . . The Morning Advertiser is the joint property of licenced victuallers . . . the editor . . . has had the honour to get invited to Palmerston's private soirees. . . . It must be added that the pious patrons of this liquor journal stand under the ruling rod of the Earl of Shaftesbury and that Shaftesbury is Palmerston's son-in-law.
>
> Source: cited in Murdock, 1982a

Palmerston exercised his control over the British press by the direct means of owning newspapers and through indirect channels provided by family relations, personal friendship and political patronage. It was through such intervention that the English ruling class exercised its control over the press. Marx underlined the need to 'see the ownership and control of communication as part of the overall structure of property and power relations' (Murdock, 1982a: 127).

To avoid the charge of 'historical or economic determinism' Marx did introduce some important caveats and qualifications to the relationship between economy and society. An economic system created by the pursuit of profit develops a momentum of its own. The analogy is made to a sorcerer who summons up powers that he or she is unable to control. Thus there are limits to the powers of the ruling class. They have to operate within a system that has its own momentum and is subject to periodic economic crises, and the social and political conflicts that flow from them; hence the view of the economic development of capitalism as subject to booms and slumps. Share prices drop and stock markets collapse, and these are followed by depression and bankruptcy. No individual capitalist wants this situation but these events are inherent in the nature of the system.

Marx also argues that the ruling class is not a monolithic entity. The struggle to dominate the market leads to ferocious competition between capitalists and hence gives rise to a conflict of interests. The instability of the capitalist system is accompanied by its inherent ruthlessness. In order to survive and maximise profits in the market-place, capitalists have to keep costs down and exploit their workers. This is the logical outcome of the system and as a result inevitably creates opposition and resistance from those who are exploited. This resistance can often be contained by direct coercion, the use of the armed forces and police service to maintain order, as well as invoking the law. However, as Marx noted, the 'engineering of consent' and building popular support and legitimacy for the established order best guarantee the long term survival of such a system. Thus the means of communication have a vital role to play in capitalism. Those who control these agencies, who control the means of 'mental and cultural production', use them to advance and protect the collective interests of the 'capitalist class'. Those who worked in what he described as the ideological professions, which included journalists as well as doctors, lawyers, university professors, clergymen and clergywomen, teachers, judges and civil servants, were described as worthless parasites who simply uncritically reproduced and disseminated the ideas and values of their masters (Franklin, 1997: 39). Marx's contempt for such hewers of ideological products was a reflection of the importance he attached to ideology in the operation of capitalism. It was the cement that helped hold the system together. Marx laboured most of his life to provide empirical evidence to support his theory. His three volumes of *Capital* attest to the assiduousness of his study. One key development he drew attention to was the tendency in capitalism to monopoly ownership. He predicted that capitalist enterprises would grow in size so that in the future a smaller and smaller number of companies would control the market. This has certainly been a feature of the growth of the media industries since 1945.

CONTEMPORARY PATTERNS OF OWNERSHIP

Political economists have been documenting an inexorable trend in the media industries throughout the world toward monopoly and increased concentration of ownership. Contemporary statistics show that fewer and fewer large companies increasingly own what we see, hear and read. A spectre is haunting the media around the world today and that spectre is Rupert Murdoch. Rupert Murdoch is the archetypal media owner whose interests have attracted a considerable degree of comment and political concern. But, wherever we look, an increasingly narrow range of political and financial interests dominates modern media. In the early 1970s Golding and Murdock, two of Britain's leading political economists, documented the concentration and consolidation of ownership in the publishing, print, broadcasting, film and recording industries in the United Kingdom. They found that the top five companies in each industry held considerable power. They accounted for 86 per cent of the circulation of morning newspapers in Britain, 88 per cent of the Sunday papers, 73 per cent of ITV network production, 86 per cent of all paperbacks sold, 69 per cent of the LP market and 78 per cent of cinema admissions (Murdock and Golding, 1973: 214). This work was one of the earliest systematic analyses of the commercial power of the media (Mosco, 1996: 102) and it not only highlighted the increasing control of the large companies over a particular media sector, or even several sectors, but also the increasing influence over popular leisure time (Murdock and Golding, 1973: 225). The authors sought to establish 'the general and systematic constraints on information and leisure provision which result from the necessities of survival and profitability in the industries providing them' (1973: 223). Since 1974 the authors have continued to document the consolidation of corporate power in the media industries.

In the United States such documentation is associated with the work of Ben Bagdikian. He first published *The Media Monopoly* in 1983, estimating that about 50 media companies dominated the American media. The latest edition of his book, published in 1997, argues this figure had fallen to ten with around another dozen in a position of secondary standing. Bagdikian argues the men and women who run these corporations constitute 'a Private Ministry of Information and Culture' who can determine what America thinks about (1992: xxviii). Herman and Chomsky (1988) develop this point, identifying concentration and nature of media ownership as one of the essential ingredients in their 'propaganda model'. They argue a range of political, economic and organisational filters constrain the reporting of international news in the United States. Their first filter is the 'size, ownership and profit orientation of the mass media' (1988: 3). Specific studies of different parts of the media industries in the United States have contributed to the documentation and analysis of the concentration of ownership (see Mosco, 1996). Similarly in Europe the growing power of 'media moguls' has been subject to examination. Tunstall and Palmer (1991) outline and discuss the ability of media owners in Britain, France, Germany and Italy to 'deliver partisan support at national elections' and 'actively influence the evolving national political agenda' through their ownership of newspapers and TV channels (Tunstall and Palmer, 1991: 107). The influence of owners has also increased in the so-called 'Third World' – although this is less well documented in academic literature. Zee TV's owner Subhash Goel has been described as a 'TV tycoon' whose 'entertainment empire' has 'changed the face of television in India' (quoted in Thussu, 1998: 278).

The degree of involvement of multi-national corporations in the media of the 'Third World' indicates one of the changes in the nature of ownership in the post-war era. Hamelink (1983) has highlighted three economic processes that have increased the reach of media corporations: internationalisation, integration and diversification. Corporations are ceasing to be simply national in their operations and are becoming global players in the expansion of their media interests in different countries. The trend to internationalisation of media ownership is noted by Murdock and Golding (1973: 223) who consider it another aspect of how concentration contributes to 'consolidating the necessary commercial constraints on cultural production'. In Britain media firms are extending their influence into overseas markets while foreign companies, mainly American, are consolidating their interests in the British media. Today, British media interests increasingly are part of larger global empires. The growth of global media giants is part of the process of 'globalisation', which has produced a voluminous literature in the last couples of decades (see Chapter 9 for discussion of theories of globalisation). In every part of the global media industries the dominance of a few corporations is documented. Let's take, as an example, the pop music industry. By 1994 more than 90 per cent of the gross sales of recorded music worldwide came from albums, singles and music videos owned or distributed by six multi-national companies (Burnett, 1996: 2). The power to decide what is played on the 'global jukebox' rests in the hands of these organisations. Sreberny-Mohammadi (1991) notes that at the end of the 1980s the combined revenue of the five largest global media firms was estimated at 18 per cent of the worldwide information industry.

The growing global concentration of ownership is the result of two other developments – diversification and integration. Integration takes two forms – vertical and horizontal. Vertical integration refers to 'the process by which one owner acquires all aspects of production and distribution of a single type of media product' (Croteau and Hoynes, 1997: 38). Sreberny-Mohammadi (1991: 125) discusses how global media giants such as Sony, Bertelsmann, the News Corporation and Time Warner have, through vertical integration, extended 'their power to control the creation, production and distribution of world-wide information and communication'. The Japanese electronics multi-national, Sony, in 1989 bought Columbia Pictures and Guber-Peters Entertainment, two leading US production companies who made films and TV series for worldwide distribution, to combine their capacity to make video/audio equipment with the ability to manufacture cultural products (Wasko, 1994: 61–3). The previous year the company had purchased CBS records for the same reason. Such a purchase enabled Sony to increase control over the market by reducing its dependency on American programme-making companies.

Horizontal integration is 'the process by which one company buys different kinds of media, concentrating ownership across different kinds of media' (Croteau and Hoynes, 1997: 38). Cross-media ownership has developed at a rapid pace in recent years. Take the rise of one media corporation in Britain in the 1990s: United News and Media. It started by owning newspapers, including the Express Group, and then bought into television, acquiring the ITV franchises of HTV, Anglia and Meridian. The group was part of the successful Channel 5 bid and it also had a portfolio of magazines in Britain and abroad, including Australia and the USA – *Exchange and Mart* is one of its main publications in Britain. United also owns the market research company NOP and a range of business information, exhibition and research publications and companies, as well as a money-brokering business in the City. United's ownership of the money-brokering business is an example of the way in which media companies are diversifying into key sectors of industrial and finance capital. The restructuring of ITV eventually led to United selling off its television and press interests. Pearson plc, the owners of the *Financial Times* and *The Economist*, also own Lazard's Bank, Madame Tussauds and Alton Towers, and Reed Tool in the United States (Curran and Seaton, 1997: 80–1). As the media industries have become more profitable, non-media firms have started to buy up media properties. This has further emphasised the role of media as businesses. Further integration into the market brings increased pressures from shareholders, directors and bankers to maximise profit. Herman and Chomsky (1988: 7) point out that it 'has encouraged the entry of speculators and increased the pressure and temptation to focus more intensively on profitability'.

The trend to the concentration of ownership dates back to the end of the nineteenth century. However, cross-media ownership, control by non-media companies, the integration of media companies and the internationalisation of ownership have widened and deepened media concentration to an unprecedented degree. Murdock (1994) notes that 'in many countries and in many central communication sectors, concentration ratios regularly run at levels between 50% and 75% of the market'. One commentator puts it more graphically when he states 'the great media empires spanning the world have subjugated more territory in a decade than Alexander the Great or Genghis Khan did in a lifetime' (Coleridge, quoted in Watson, 1998: 214). The expansion of these empires has been furthered by attendant political factors. The development of corporate control in the past two decades has been assisted by the policies of de-regulation introduced by former Prime Minister Margaret Thatcher in Britain and former President Ronald Reagan in America. They ushered in a new era of *laissez-faire* capitalism that has seen governments of all political persuasions adopt such policies. Freeing media companies from regulations on what they can own and control has been done in the name of competition, choice and quality. A report from a group of European publishers, which included representatives of Murdoch's News Corporation, Axel Springer's group in Germany and Hachette in France, stated, 'large scale de-regulation of national cross media ownership restrictions is a pre-requisite for economic growth in order that media companies can compete in the world market' (quoted in Williams, 1994). As a result of opening up markets to more competition, consumers, it is argued, will be provided with a greater range of products at more affordable prices. It also means the production of better-quality products as companies compete with each other. The emergence of more channels and outlets, increased access to information and knowledge, and more control over when and what people watch and listen to appears to confirm the argument that the free market brings more choice for the individual. Thus any concerns about the increased concentration of ownership are offset by more choice. Supporters of the 'free market' see the explosion of choice as making redundant old-fashioned anxieties about media monopoly as deregulation encourages competition, investment and a growing diversity of product (Curran and Seaton, 1997: 333).

Critics such as Graham Murdock (1992) acknowledge that the 'more choice' argument is 'highly plausible and seductive', but he argues a distinction must be made between plurality and diversity. As he says: 'There may be more communication goods and services in circulation but many of them are versions of the same product in a variety of packages.' While there may be more television channels, they are increasingly broadcasting the same programmes. Murdock argues there are four ways in which media owners limit diversity and thereby pose a threat to democracy. First, they use their resources to support certain political or ideological causes. Second, they can insist their outlets support their general business interests by giving publicity to success and suppressing coverage that is potentially embarrassing. Third, they use their power to shape the terms and nature of the competition of the markets in which they are major players. Thus Rupert Murdoch can drop the price of *The Times* in order to drive his competitors out of the quality newspaper market in Britain. He can support the losses incurred in such an operation through profits from other parts of his media empires. The result of a competitor newspaper closing down would be a decline in diversity in the quality press. Fourth, by attempting to maximise the complementarities, or 'synergies', between various components of their media and business operations, media owners can limit people's perspectives. Murdock cites the case of Time Warner and Batman. By owning the rights to the comic character the multi-media giant can orchestrate the development of the product to maximise its profits. Batman was developed into a film publicised by Time Warner through its magazines and promoted via its cable and television networks, the soundtrack of which was released on its record labels and whose merchandising included children's toys produced through its manufacturing interests. For political economists such as Murdock and Golding who have documented the expansion of the global media giants there is a direct relationship between ownership and control. They accept the basic viewpoint developed by Marx that there is a correlation between the economic structure of the media industries and their ideological content.

CRITICISM OF MARXIST POLITICAL ECONOMY

Marx's theory about the relationship between ownership, control and the exercise of power in industrial, capitalist society was challenged after his death in 1883. Critics argued that property as a basis for the exercise of social power was becoming less significant for two main reasons: the growth of a new managerial class and the development of a new kind of capitalist enterprise. The rapid growth in the nature and size of industrial production gave rise to the emergence of new professional groups who, as a result of their expertise, organisation and knowledge, would have the ability and competence to manage modern capitalism (Murdock, 1982a: 128–9). Control was seen as passing to those managers whose objectives were no longer simply the pursuit of profit. They would have other concerns including the interests of consumers and employees. The power of these managers, it was argued, was increased by changes in the nature of finance capital. Owners, in order to remain competitive and maintain profits in a rapidly changing climate, had to raise more and more money. To do this they began to sell shares in their companies and businesses to outsiders. This was the birth of the joint stock company. Ownership, as a result, was diluted and its nature changed. Owners were now more likely to be shareholders who left the responsibility of managing their companies to professionals. Adolf Berle and Gardiner Means in 1932 examined America's top corporations to find that nearly two-thirds of them were under management control, which they claimed was a 'bloodless' revolution that had swept the professional manager to power. They argued the power of managers rested on the fact that shareholders were a disparate, disorganised and uninformed group who were in no position to challenge the managerial elite who ran the corporations. Critics of Marx's theory of ownership emphasised this shift in power in capitalist enterprises – the era of the individual owner, they argued, had been replaced by the era of the professional manager. This 'managerial revolution' challenged Marx's ruling class theory and raised questions about where power resides in modern society.

Marx recognised joint stock companies had an 'increasing tendency to separate this work of management from the ownership of capital' and was aware of the argument that the manager, by taking on all the functions of the capitalist, will make 'the capitalist appear as superfluous from the production process' (quoted in Murdock, 1982a: 130). He did not believe, however, the rise of the new managerial elite was a challenge to the power of the ruling class. The manager was simply a 'functionary working for the capitalist' and real power still rested with the capitalist for whom the manager worked. Marx did not see the spread of share ownership as undermining the structure of capitalism. The ability of the manager to exercise control 'ultimately depended on their willingness to comply with the interests of the owners' (Murdock, 1982a: 131). While managers may have autonomy and control at the day-to-day level, 'allocative control' still rests with the owners. Recent developments in capitalism have made the relationship between management and ownership even more complicated. The modern corporation has witnessed a huge increase in the scale of production. These organisations are characterised by their vast size and complexity. The considerable expansion of the popular base of shareholdings in our society – the rise of so-called 'popular capitalism' – is seen as having democratised the nature of ownership. These factors, it is claimed, have diluted proprietorial control. Stephen Koss (1984) argues the modern proprietor is 'a businessman first and foremost', more concerned with commercial considerations than political or ideological interests. John Whale argues proprietors do not have the time or interest to do anything but deal with the 'global problems of trade and investment which occupy their mind' (quoted in Wagg, 1987). These views raise a major theoretical debate as to whether ownership automatically means owners have control over the products and content of the media.

DOES OWNERSHIP MEAN CONTROL?

The argument that media ownership is more concentrated than ever before is largely uncontested. The dispute is whether and to what extent the 'potential for control is actually realised in practice' (Golding and Murdock, 1978: 28). Murdock (1980) identifies two approaches in Marxist thought to analysing the relationship between ownership and control – what he labels as 'instrumental' and 'structural'. In its most crude or vulgar form instrumentalism focuses on 'conspiracy and direct intervention'. The relationship between ownership and control is seen as straightforward and illustrated most commonly by reference to the relationship between individual proprietors and their newspapers. Owners and managers are seen to conspire to 'determine which person, which facts, which version of the facts and which ideas shall reach the public' (quoted in Parenti, 1986: 32). Examples such as the dictum by Victor Matthews, owner of Express Newspapers in the 1970s, that 'editors will have complete freedom as long as they agree with the policy I have laid down' are cited (Baistow, 1985: 5). The policy of owners is seen as working as a whole to produce a press that, according to the *Morning Star* newspaper in its evidence to the Royal Commission on the Press in 1977, 'strongly defends private enterprise ... and are overwhelmingly biased in favour of the Right Wing in politics' (quoted in Murdock, 1980: 43). Ralph Miliband (1973) develops this version of control at a theoretical level. He accepts the impact of the views and prejudices of those who own and control the capitalist media is 'immediate and direct ... by the constant and ever daily interventions' (Miliband, 1973: 204). He believes the right of ownership 'confers a right of making propaganda and where that right is exercised, it is most likely to be exercised in the service of strongly conservative prejudices' (Miliband, 1973: 204). Miliband does not simply examine how owners influence particular papers but focuses on the ways in which the press as a whole represent the interests of the ruling class. There are a number of pressures apart from capitalist ownership – for example, advertising censorship, the consensual values of people working in the media, the 'official climate' – which 'all work in the same conservative and conformist direction'. For him the mass media are 'weapons in the arsenal of class domination' and as a result 'predominantly agencies for the dissemination of ideas and values which affirm ... existing patterns of power and privilege' (Miliband, 1973: 211). Instrumental approaches thus focus on the control exercised by individual capitalists to extend their own interests, and ways in which the media as a whole work to reinforce the general interests of a capitalist class (Murdock, 1982a: 124).

Critics see such analysis as too simplistic. It presents the mass media as 'servants' – or more graphically as the 'cudgel of oppression' – of a ruling class with little or no autonomy (Seaton and Pimlott, 1987: ix). The media simply act as a conveyor belt for the ideas of the ruling capitalist class. This ignores the ability of journalists and media workers to resist the intervention of owners. Examples of a proprietor stopping a story can be countered by others of editors running a story that is critical. While owners often try to exercise control over editorial content they do not always succeed. Negrine (1989: 75) points to the anecdotal nature of the evidence to support the contention that ownership translates into control. He believes these instances are 'anything but the basis for generalisable statements across fields and decades'. He also questions whether it is possible to see owners as a unified group with common interests. He asks what are these common interests? Are they anything more than a desire for success and survival? Owners are also seen as unlikely to exercise their power without taking into consideration commercial and marketing factors, which can produce differing media accounts of the world. Negrine also doubts the ability of a single individual to oversee the empires of the contemporary global media firms.

The other strand of Marxist thought is the 'structural' approach, which locates discussion of ownership and control in the context of the 'mode of production or political economy and the limits it places on the choices and actions of press proprietors and personnel, whatever their origins, social connections or personal commitments' (Murdock, 1980: 54). Analysis is not centred on the activities and interests of individual owners but on the constraints and limitations placed on owners, managers and workers by nature of the capitalist economy. In other words structuralists examine the 'ways in which the policies and operations of corporations are limited by the general dynamics of media industries and capitalist economies' (Murdock, 1982a: 124). Economic structures shape the activities of media owners, controllers and workers and the pressures under which they work. These pressures emanate from the emphasis on the need to maximise profit and the demands of competition. Thus Murdock (1980: 57) argues there is no need for owners to intervene directly because 'the logic of the prevailing market structures ensures that by and large the output endorses rather than opposes their general interests'.

Garnham (1990) argues to understand media content it is essential to analyse the context in which it is produced and distributed. The process of production, the deployment of media workers, the division of labour, the means of distribution need to be considered in order to make a decision about 'who can say what to whom'. It is only by understanding the organisation of the industry that we can comprehend why certain media products are made and distributed as well as their content and form. Garnham identifies a number of features of the media industries that are determined by their specific means of production and distribution. For example, he points out the unique nature of the product manufactured by the media industries, which has shaped the methods used to find markets. Media products have ambiguous uses. They are unlike most other products in that they need to have novelty value – a newspaper has to be new every day, while music recordings have to have different sounds; and they are not destroyed in the process of consumption – reading a film or watching a book does not make it unavailable to other people (Garnham, 1990: 160). Media products are, then, costly to produce with a high degree of initial investment, but cheap to reproduce, which encourages the industries to seek to maximise their audiences as 'the preferred profit maximisation strategy'. Garnham argues this is the reason for the concentration, internationalisation and diversification of ownership. Concentration allows owners relative freedom in their attempts to maximise audiences; internationalisation allows them to search for markets across the globe and diversification allows them to reproduce the same product across a variety of media. The risk to initial investment is thus minimised in these ways.

Curran and his colleagues (1980) illustrate the relationship between economic and market factors and media content through their analysis of the growth of the 'human interest' story in the press. They trace how such stories have increasingly replaced public affairs and political coverage in the press but in particular in tabloid newspapers. They document this decline over four decades in a range of newspapers – although Negrine (1989: 83–8) raises some questions about the methods and interpretations of their research. Human interest stories are not 'news' in that they do not attempt to explain events in terms of social, economic or political forces (Curran *et al.*, 1980: 306). Rather events are portrayed in terms of the outcome of the interactions of individuals whose lives are 'strongly governed by luck, fate, and chance within a given, naturalised world, which merely forms an unchanging background'. This change is attributed to the growing 'economic pressures to maximise readers and the pattern of reader demand' (Curran *et al.*, 1980: 301). To remain economically viable tabloid newspapers have to attract the maximum number of readers they can and to do this they concentrate on human stories, which are popular amongst their target audiences. Thus the economic realities of tabloid newspaper production necessitate proprietors and workers adopting a product that presents consumers with a particular way of learning about events. This is not a deliberate act by owners to spread particular views but the outcome of economic necessity.

The structuralist approach addresses some of the criticisms directed at instrumentalists – although in the literature sometimes the distinction between the two approaches is blurred. It enables us to see those who work in the media as having some autonomy. Structuralists accept it is impossible for owners to have direct control of the day-to-day operation of media industries and they do not directly intervene in editorial content. Media workers do have control over the output of the media but they have to operate within an economic environment, which shapes their decisions and actions. The nature of this environment is such that the decisions they make and actions they undertake are conditioned to producing views that are by and large pro-capitalist, pro-business and hostile to alternative or minority opinion. Both approaches, steeped as they are in their Marxist roots, stress a connection between ownership and control, between economic production and ideological reproduction. They have established an important position in media theory but they challenge popular and professional understanding of the role of the media in society and the relationship between ownership and control.

The traditional liberal-pluralist approach represents the media as independent of state and political, economic and social interests. Workers in the industry are seen as possessing a high degree of autonomy to reflect or to represent what is going on in society. As far as ownership and control is concerned, liberal-pluralist theory does not see it as a central issue in trying to account for the output of the media. It agrees that owners and managers are constrained in how they can represent the world. It also sees the market as an important mechanism in determining the content of the media. However, it argues the content and form of the media is determined not by the actions and options of the owners but by the choice of consumers. The ultimate arbiter of what the media serve up is the consumer and the market guarantees consumers get what they want. This view is not only expressed by academic analysis but is also central to the way many in the media industries justify what they do. For the former *Sunday Times* reporter John Whale (1980: 85), 'the broad shape and nature of the press is ultimately determined by no one but its readers'. He argues owners' and editors' decisions 'would be nothing without the ratification of readers'. They have to 'defer to the influence of readers' as readers can go elsewhere if they do not like what they read. For Whale the British press is predominantly conservative in tone and right wing in inclination because its readers are. If people wanted society rebuilt then they would buy more radically inclined newspapers. Alastair Hetherington, former editor of the *Guardian* and controller of BBC Scotland, echoes this view when he says that 'a daily newspaper or news bulletin . . . must strike a responsive chord in the minds of viewers and readers . . . without all this, communication is not achieved' (1985: 39). In the market where the consumer is sovereign the media are thus merely 'giving the public what they want'.

Liberal-pluralists are critical of the focus on the concentration of ownership. They see it as irrelevant; the most significant factor is the ability of the audience to ensure that its needs and wants are reflected in the output of the media. Some even see it as beneficial to the performance of the media in meeting consumer demand. Collins and Murroni (1996: 75) argue 'large, concentrated media organisations are not intrinsically undesirable' as 'large size tends to bring the resources required for comprehensive high quality reporting'.

Whale (1980: 81) believes there is 'positive virtue in a newspaper's belonging to a larger commercial group'. Liberal-pluralists also reject the Marxist approach on two other grounds. They argue Marxists fail to distinguish between different kinds of media, especially between private and publicly owned media. They point out public organisations are not driven by the profit motive. The largest media organisation in Britain, the BBC (British Broadcasting Corporation), is not financed by commercial activities but through the licence fee and is therefore free from the need to make a profit and satisfy shareholders. Both the BBC and independent TV are regulated by statutory bodies, which commit them by law and practice to impartiality in their output. Thus Marxist theory is not seen as applying to all media. Liberal-pluralists also point out that the media regularly report minority interests critical of capitalism. Both the BBC and ITV have regularly broadcast views critical of the major political parties and programmes critical of political orthodoxies (Franklin, 1997: 42). Not only are there radical programmes but also channels such as Channel 4, which is committed to creating space in its schedules for alternative and minority views. Elsewhere in the media it is possible to find capitalist companies willing to publish the works of Karl Marx or cut discs calling for revolution in the streets.

Marxist theorists reject these criticisms. They argue public and private media may be differently constituted but they are both subject to the pressures of the market. Organisations such as the BBC still have to compete in the market. With the introduction of competition the BBC has had to improve the ratings of its programmes in order to justify the licence fee. Thus the Corporation is making the same decisions in the process of production as private media about how to maximise the audience. ITV, while subject to regulation, is driven by the need to satisfy its main source of revenue – advertisers. Winning and keeping large audiences is essential to its viability and profitability. Thus both the BBC and ITV are committed to the same goals, which are steeped in market and commercial considerations. Miliband (1973: 209) points out that public institutions such as the BBC are dominated by those who represent the establishment. He argues that those who control the BBC are drawn from the ranks of the good and the great. Of the 85 governors of the BBC in its first 50 years, 56 came from a university background, and 40 of these had gone through Oxbridge, while 20 had been at the three leading public schools in Britain: Harrow, Eton or Winchester (Franklin, 1997: 41). Miliband argues this elite has run the BBC in the interests of the capitalist class. They are not representative of the British people but the class that runs the country. He also argues what is critical on television tends to 'remain within a safe, fairly narrow spectrum'. Research findings showing that viewpoints favourable to the status quo are given preference in BBC TV news are cited as evidence to support this argument (see Glasgow Media Group, 1976; 1980).

THE POWER OF ADVERTISING

Many of the decisions media owners and managers make about the commercial viability of their operations are influenced by the growing dependency of the media on advertising. For instrumentalists advertisers intervene directly into the operation of the mass media to ensure their interests are preserved or promoted. Herman and Chomsky (1988) in their 'propaganda model' highlight how advertisers discriminate against certain political messages and viewpoints appearing in the media. Golding and Murdock (1991) criticise the propaganda model for concentrating on 'strategic interventions' by advertisers and owners while overlooking 'the contradictions within the system'. Both advertisers and owners operate within 'structures which constrain as well as facilitate, imposing limits as well as offering opportunities'. Golding and Murdock argue that analysing these limits is the 'key task for a critical political economy'. Herman (1998) rejects this criticism, arguing that if such opportunities do exist they are of secondary importance. Constraints and choices are internalised and enforced by the structures of power within which the media operate. Curran (1977; 1978; 1980) has analysed and theorised the structural impact of advertising on the media.

The discrimination of advertising

> Working-class and radical media suffer from the political discrimination of advertisers. Political discrimination is structured into advertising allocations by the stress on people with money to spend. But many firms will always refuse to patronise ideological enemies and those whom they perceive as damaging to their interests, and cases of overt discrimination add to the force of the voting system weighted by income. Public service station WNET lost its corporate funding from Gulf+Western in 1985 after the station showed a documentary 'Hungry for Profit' which contains material critical of multinational corporate activities in the Third World. Even before the programme was shown . . . station officials 'did all we could to get the programme sanitised'. The chief executive of Gulf+Western complained . . . that the programme was 'virulently anti-business if not anti-American' and that the station's carrying the programme was not the behaviour 'of a friend' of the corporation. The London Economist says, 'Most people believe that WNET would not make the same mistake again.'
>
> Source: Herman and Chomsky, 1988: 17

Curran (1977) argues working-class newspapers in Britain, such as the *Daily Herald*, collapsed because of the low purchasing power of their readers. This is the result of the importance of advertising in determining the profitability of the press. Newspapers – as well as other media – depend on two sources for their revenue: sales and advertising. Advertising is an increasingly important constituent in the finances of the media. According to Miliband (1973: 207) the direct political influence of large advertisers upon the commercial media need not be exaggerated ... their custom nevertheless is of crucial importance to the financial viability, which means the existence of newspapers and, in some but not all instances, of magazines, commercial radio and television.

Media with small sales can only survive if their audiences are seen as possessing sufficient purchasing power to attract advertisers. Curran (1978: 246) points out advertisers are not interested in reaching all the people as 'some people have more disposable income or greater power over corporate spending and are consequently more sought after by advertisers'. Thus the broadsheet newspapers continue to survive in spite of relatively small circulations because their readers are mainly drawn from the wealthier sectors of society. The best-selling quality newspaper today has about the same number of readers the *Daily Herald* had when it folded in 1964. Advertising also accounts for the bias of media products to certain kinds of audiences. For example, women's magazines focus their attention on the lives and loves of women between the ages of 16 and 34 because their spending power makes them the most attractive to advertisers. Thus it is argued there is a bias in the mass media towards more affluent audience groups.

The importance of advertising in media markets 'turns the ideal of "consumer sovereignty" on its head' (Murdock, 1977: 145). It makes the relationship between supply and demand for media products more problematic as it is the demand from advertisers for particular kinds of audiences that is the major determinant of supply. The preference of consumers is thus secondary to the need for media to satisfy their major source of revenue, the advertisers. Curran (1978: 234) presents ways in which advertising finance has shaped the nature and content of the press. Not only have newspapers adjusted their content to attract the kind of readers that advertisers want but have also introduced 'specialised features ... in order to segregate readers into the groups that advertisers want to reach and to direct their attention to particular parts of a paper where they can be efficiently picked out by advertisers'. Thus, British students and educators are targeted by the *Guardian*'s education supplement on Tuesdays. Advertising has helped to determine the very structure of the modern newspaper. Curran (1977; 1979; 1980), in his analysis of the newspaper industry, has gone further; he sees advertising as acting as a system of 'licensing' or 'patronage'. The dependence on advertising has contributed to a de-politicisation and de-radicalisation of the British press. Newspapers with radical or left-wing inclinations are often those whose readership has low purchasing power. Commercial decisions by advertisers, which discriminate against such newspapers, have political consequences. The effect on advertising has been to contribute 'to producing and maintaining a press weighted to the centre and right' (Curran, 1980: 109). For Curran the emergence of a free press in the middle of the nineteenth century 'introduced a new system of press censorship more effective than anything that had gone before' (Curran, 1977: 198). In the United

States the licensing power of advertising extends beyond the print media. A former head of NBC TV has observed that television is 'an advertising supported medium, and to the extent that support falls, programming will change' (quoted in Herman and Chomsky, 1988: 16). The more de-regulated – or more 'free' – the market, the greater the opportunity for advertisers to influence the output of the mass media.

For theorists such as Curran market forces are a much better mechanism of exerting social control than political and legal repression. Negrine (1989) is sceptical. While acknowledging the importance of advertising, he rejects the determining role ascribed to it by Curran, and Herman and Chomsky. He comes back to the point made by liberal-pluralists that such analysis ignores the audience. As he puts it:

> Without readers, no newspaper can survive; with sufficient readers and willing advertisers, the chances of survival are greater but the medium still has to prove itself. Unless it does so, it is likely to lose both readers and advertisers. It is this complex environment that decides the fortunes of the media.
>
> (Negrine, 1989: 88)

The focus on the process of production at the expense of any understanding of the nature of the audience has been singled out as a weakness in the political economy approach.

CONSUMPTION NOT PRODUCTION?

Some critics have argued the political economy approach to the media is unnecessarily rigid and deterministic. This, as we have discussed, is a charge made by liberal-pluralists, and acknowledged and addressed by structuralists. However, in recent years, theorists working from the perspective of post-modernism and cultural studies have levelled this charge against political economy. Strinati (1995: 143) argues that ultimately theorists such as Murdock and Golding opt for economic determinism by minimising any sense of interplay between communicative activity and economic dynamics. He criticises political economy for having no sense of a struggle for meaning. People are simply portrayed as passive actors in the ideological process. In other words political economy is charged with reducing everything to the importance of the economy and neglecting any sense of struggle in the production of media messages. Writers such as Fiske (1989a) are critical of the obsession political economy has with the process of production at the expense of any understanding of how people consume the media. He believes media diversity is not an issue because the content of the media, whether information or entertainment, is polysemic, by which he means it is subject to mulitple readings or interpretations. People have the power to choose what sense they make of what they see, hear and read, regardless of the intentions of those who produce the messages. Media concentration is thus not a problem for Fiske, as it does not restrict diversity, which he sees as determined by those who consume the output of the media not by those who produce and distribute it (see Mosco, 1996: 259). For Fiske, political economy is handicapped by what he calls its 'productivism'.

Cultural theorists celebrate the power of the audience to resist the 'preferred reading' of the producers (see Chapter 7). They are optimistic about the capacity of people to resist corporate power. Fiske in giving power to the people coins the term 'semiotic resistance' – that is, the 'power of people in their various social formations of subordination and disempowerment to resist the colonisation of their consciousness by the forces of social power' (quoted in Watson, 1998: 226). Political economists counter that such criticism fails to understand the nature of their analysis. They argue it is possible to accept that people have the opportunity to understand the media in different ways. However, they believe the 'romantic celebration of the individual's power to evaluate media content' (quoted in Mosco, 1996: 261) neglects the power of the producer to set limits on the process of audience resistance. As Mosco (1996: 260) says, 'audiences are not passive, but neither are producers dumb'. Limits are set by the media industries on the power of the audience to resist. They also argue the ability of the individual to resist is determined by socio-economic and demographic factors. Thus more knowledge, education and purchasing power make it more possible to resist the power of the media. There is, then, a debate between where the boundaries lie between the power of the audience and the power of the producer.

NEW MEDIA, OLD OWNERS?

The development of new media technology such as the Internet is seen as shaking off the shackles of the problem of ownership. The net is one example of how new technology combines old-fashioned, face-to-face communication with mass communication, and as a result allows individuals more control over what they say, what they are told and whom they talk to. Howard Rheingold (1994) is an advocate of the democracy-enhancing nature of the Internet. He argues it is a means by which the domination of information flow by large corporations and the state can be repelled, and the management of public opinion can be resisted. The Internet provides the potential of the unlimited and unrestricted flow of information. Everyone can have access to the Internet and its riches of information, and the opportunity to use the technology to criticise freely government policy and the actions of the state and powerful interests in society. The Internet and other technologies are seen as spelling the end of the large, monopolistic media corporations by widening choice and empowering individuals (Toffler, 1980; Negroponte, 1996). Digital television is seen as expanding the number of media outlets from which people can gain information and enjoy entertainment. Expansion is tied to the enhancement of the capabilities of viewers to select programmes they want to watch at the time they want to watch them. Interactive services, as one media manager argues, are 'taking people where they want to be, when they want to go there and with people they want to be with' (quoted in Murdock, 2000b:

46). The TiVo system, for example, enables people to search out all their favourite pro-grammes whenever and wherever they are being screened and establish their own per-sonalised viewing schedules. Such technology thus promises much, not only the revolutionising of the way in which we consume the media but also the empowerment of the individual's control over information and entertainment.

ntl advertisement

The media industries are strongly promoting the liberating potential of the new technologies such as digital television. An advertisement for ntl in Britain in February, 2000, stated that:

We're transforming the face of TV with a host of interactive and enhanced services, from interactive shopping and banking services to tele-voting and the chance to control a camera angle on a football match, or even your favourite drama.

Source: Murdock, 2000b: 51

Political economists are sceptical of such promises and the rosy picture of the digital future. They reject the optimistic beliefs that new media technologies will bring about more choice and the empowerment of media consumers, and disagree with the claims of writers such as Negroponte that 'the monolithic empires of mass media are dissolving into an array of cottage industries' (Herman and McChesney, 1997: 106). Golding and Murdock (2000: 87) draw attention to the differential access to communications and cul-tural goods, which they point out is 'more sharply true for recent innovations in informa-tion and communications technology'. The 'digital divide' in the United States and Britain is not only wide but widening. It is the affluent that have greatest access to the new tech-nology, a position exacerbated by the process of de-regulation and privatisation of the media industries, which represents a 'shift in the provision and distribution of cultural goods from being public services to private commodities'. For political economists such as Golding and Murdock this shift signals a significant change in the opportunity for differ-ent groups to have access to the modern mass media. Having to pay for new television services will make it more difficult for those on low incomes to afford the services and will, increasingly, reduce the diet of material available to them (Golding and Murdock, 2000: 88). Robins (1996) notes that Internet usage shows not only a bias to the wealthy but also to men and America. Only 12 per cent of Internet usage is in the global South where two-thirds of the world's population live (Thussu, 2000: 248).

Political economists warn about the new technologies becoming increasingly absorbed by the existing media corporations and incorporated into their commercial world.

Wise (2000) describes how the multi-media revolution is the result of the technological developments fuelled by both the military needs of the 'Cold War' and the ideas of personal liberation of the 1960s counter-culture. He notes many of the original computer revolutionaries, influenced by the thoughts of Marshal McLuhan, believed in the potential of the new technology to change the world. Seduced by this potential, the early inventor-entrepreneurs and their guru can be accused of neglecting the social and economic conditions under which the technology is developed. Herman and McChesney (1997: Chapter 5) argue the convergence of the media, computer and telecommunications markets and the de-regulation and privatisation of the media industries around the world are encouraging the further concentration of ownership. Mergers and acquisitions are the name of the game as the larger media giants seek to 'control the transmission of three basic communications products – voice, data and video' (Herman and McChesney, 1997: 134). The merger between Time Warner and America Online (AOL) in 2000 indicates that in a market-driven system control of new technology will be dominated by large media conglomerates, only now they will be larger than before. The euphoria of those who celebrated the Internet and the digital revolution is seen as misplaced as large corporations develop new means to exert their control. The future of new media is, according to political economists, 'a subject to be determined by politics, not technology' (Herman and McChesney, 1997: 135).

Napster and the net

> The music-swapping Internet service Napster has lost its court battle to provide free access to music. In an historic ruling with implications for the music industry and the estimated 50 m Napster users a US Federal appeals court in San Francisco decided yesterday that the company must stop distributing material it knows to be copyrighted. ... The five largest record labels – Warner, Sony, EMI, BMG and Universal – brought the action ... claiming that the unauthorised use of the music was theft and was costing the companies billions of dollars in lost profits. The five companies control about 90% of popular music worldwide. In May 1999 Napster released software that made it easy for personal computer users to find and swap songs they had stored as computer files ... The record companies have been exploring their own systems of supplying music via the internet, albeit ones that require a subscription payment. ... [A]nticipating that the case might go against them Napster reached an agreement with Bertelsmann, the parent company of BMG music company that was one of the quintet suing them. The German media company has agreed to inject capital if Napster switches to a 'subscription-based

> service' paying royalties. . . . Napster was deluged by users at the weekend ahead of the court decision. Nearly 2 m song files were traded on Sunday.
>
> Source: Guardian, 13 February 2001

SUMMARY

Choice of what we see, hear and read in the mass media resides in the hands of a small number of companies. Political economy theory stresses the primacy of the economic organisation of the media industries – especially private ownership – as a determinant of the content and structure of the media. Classical political economy sees capitalism with its emphasis on the market as the most efficient way of generating wealth and maximising the public good. Marxist political economy sees capitalism as creating vast disparities in the distribution of resources and life opportunities within society. For Marx the key characteristic of the growth of capitalism is the ownership and control of the means of production by a small number of people who constitute a 'capitalist' or 'ruling' class. The levers of economic power rest in the hands of this class, who as a result control the means of mental production. The output of the media, according to Marx, reflects the interests, concerns and perspectives of this group of people.

The concentration of ownership in the post-war period at the national and international levels is seen as increasing the power of the owners of the means of production. However, Marx's critics point to changes in the nature of capitalism, in particular the rise of a new kind of industrial organisation – the joint stock company – in which ownership has passed from the hands of the individual to those of the shareholders. With the dispersal of ownership, control of companies became the responsibility of the professional manager whose interests could be divergent from that of owners. Marx noted this development in its early stages and responded by saying that while managers had control at the operational level, the power to shape the overall policy of the company still rested with the owners. Modern capitalism and industrial production is much more complex than in Marx's day. This complexity is seen as weakening the link between ownership and control. Contemporary Marxist theorists have responded to change in one of two ways. Instrumentalists re-assert the basic tenet of Marxist political economy that there is a direct link between ownership and control. Structuralists, on the other hand, acknowledge it is impossible for owners to have direct, day-to-day control over the operation and output of media organisations. They stress the importance of 'allocative control' whereby an individual or group has the power to define the overall goals of the media organisation and control its financial policy. This power has to be exercised within the constraints of the general political, economic and cultural environment within which the organisation has to operate.

Both pluralists and post-modernists reject Marxist views of ownership and control. Both of these approaches emphasise the power of the audience or the consumer to determine the output of the media. Pluralists say the consumer is sovereign in a market system – it is he or she who decides what to read, watch or hear, and owners must respond to what their audiences want if they are to make profit. Post-modern critics say audiences have the power to choose what sense they want to make of the output of the mass media regardless of the messages. They criticise political economy for placing too much stress on production at the expense of the consumption process and proffering an erroneous image of the viewer, reader and listener as a passive dupe.

Chapter Four

☐ *INSIDE THE IMAGE FACTORY:* THEORIES OF MEDIA ORGANISATION AND MEDIA WORK

What we see, read and hear in the media is the end product of a complex process. Films, television programmes, pop music, advertising copy and newspaper stories are made within media organisations according to a particular set of activities and practices, and by a number of different kinds of people. While the consumer is encouraged to see the output of the media as simple, straightforward and natural, the makers of media products are engaged in a highly organised and multi-layered system of production. Economic pressures are a key determinant in shaping this production process but other factors are also important. The organisational structure and occupational culture of the media also shape the process of mass communication. The context in which media practitioners work has been identified by some scholars as not only being central to explaining media content but also to understanding their relationship with other social institutions and with their audiences. They argue study of media organisations and media work enables us to build a more complete picture of the role of the media in the re-production of ideology. Rather than see media simply as businesses and analyse them in terms of economy and industry, this approach places emphasis on those who work in the media and how their work is organised. Media content is therefore not simply determined by the relationship between owner and employee but by organisational and occupational factors, from the individual prejudices of media workers to the rules, routines and values of media organisations, and their relations with other social institutions.

LEVELS OF ORGANISATIONAL ANALYSIS

The study of media organisations and media work has its roots in the early observations of journalists undertaken by Weber (2001 [1918]) and Park (1923). The first research on media workers was by Leo Rosten (1937) who studied the Washington Press Corps. Four years later Rosten (1941) examined those working in the movie industry in Hollywood. Rosten's studies focused on the personal attitudes and social background of media practitioners. It was not until the late 1950s that systematic study of media organisations and occupations began. This was due to a number of factors outside media studies (Curran *et al.*, 1977). First, the emergence of a sociology of complex organisations in the 1950s yielded theories about organisational structure and behaviour, and provided analytical tools that could be applied to the study of media organisations and media work (see

Morgan, 1992). Second, the struggle between functionalist-pluralist and neo-Marxist approaches focused attention on the extent to which media organisations and those working in them had autonomy from the dominant power structures of society. Third, the political climate of the 1960s increased attention paid to the role of the media in politics, with scholars examining the interaction between media organisations and political institutions, and the way in which political communication is shaped by this interaction (see Gurevitch and Blumler, 1977). The empirical research generated since this time on media organisations and media work, and their impact on media content has been conducted at three different levels.

1. The first focuses on the individual media worker and his or her preferences, the social background and experience that shape these preferences, the professional ideologies under which he or she works and the practices that are adopted in daily work. Shoemaker and Reese (1991: 54) identify three different kinds of factors influencing the performance of the individual media worker: personal attitudes, values and beliefs; social background and experience; and professional orientations and practices. Studies have examined the psychological and political disposition of individual workers who act as decision makers in the production and editorial process, as well as the social characteristics and political values of those who work in the media. They have attempted to ascertain whether there are particular characteristics that single out those in media occupations. One key question in the study of the beliefs, values and characteristics of media personnel is whether they possess the attributes of a profession, such as law and medicine, in which there exists a set of guidelines for accepted behaviour that regulates their practice and performance (Curran et al., 1977: 19)

2. The second concentrates on organisational structures and routines and their influence on media practitioners and their work. The focus is on the roles assigned to media workers by their organisations and how individuals fulfil the goals of the organisations for which they work. Media organisations are complex entities whose goals, structures and rhythms determine the production process. Media content is less shaped by individual actions, enterprise and creativity than it is more the outcome of the routines and policies adopted by media organisations to inform and entertain (Manning, 2000: 52). Media organisations, like other large organisations, are 'characterised by hierarchy, division of labour, and routinisation of working operations through relatively standardised rules and procedures' (Paletz and Entman, 1981, quoted in Ward, 1995: 102). This is seen as responsible for the remarkably similar products that emerge. As Golding and Elliott (1979: 207) conclude from their study of newsrooms in Ireland, Sweden and Nigeria, 'news changes very little when the individuals who produce it are changed'.

3. The third level is the interaction between media organisations and the wider social, political and cultural environment within which they operate. The focus here is on forces external to the media shaping media organisations and work, and hence what is

produced. Shoemaker and Reese (1991: 147) identify factors such as the media's sources of information, revenue sources, technology, political and legal environment, and perceptions of what audiences want. Examining the power other social institutions can exert over the media is seen as countering the limitations of the 'media centric' focus of the previous levels (Schlesinger, 1990). The broader 'cultural' context is also seen as important extra media influence (see Schudson, 2000). Media workers and organisations are part of a culture that determines how they interact and what they produce.

There are overlaps between these levels but at each of them empirical research has wrestled with one overriding concern: who has the power to influence the processes by which media messages are produced and how is this power exercised? Each level of organisational analysis identifies a broad question addressed to this concern: to what extent do media workers influence media content and the working of media organisations? How far do the structures and processes of media organisations influence what media workers do and what they produce? To what extent do other social organisations and social forces affect the workings and output of the media? In attempting to provide answers to who exercises power and how, scholars focus on the individual, the organisation and the socio-cultural environment.

Attempting to analyse media production, social science research has primarily focused on one kind of media organisation, the newsroom, and one kind of media practitioner, the journalist. Most of the early work into media production concentrated on news. Only much later were other kinds of media subjected to scrutiny, and they still remain an underdeveloped component of organisational research and analysis. The claim of the news media to simply reflect what is happening out there by holding up a mirror to the world, throws out a challenge to media scholars to test the veracity of such a claim. Whether journalists only follow their 'nose for news' and live up to their professed aim of producing an objective account of events is a focus of numerous empirical studies of news organisations. Concentrating on how news organisations work raises the question of whether it is possible to generalise about the variety of media organisations that exist and the different kinds of media work done. The starting point for many of those who study media organisations is that there are differences between media – for example, in the audiences they are trying to reach and the product they are producing – but the production and distribution of media are concerned with many of the same basic issues. Hirsch (1972: 14) acknowledges the 'distinctions between types of symbolic content' of media and accepts 'these are mutually exclusive, as well as internally differentiated according to which of the mass media they are created for'. But, he argues, categories such as 'news', 'entertainment', 'print' and 'broadcast' are used to 'distinguish and segregate media and types of content that are nevertheless strikingly similar in the manner that each is organised'. The organisational perspective assumes there are 'clear analytical similarities among the constraints on and organisational context in which reporters, writers, artists, actors, directors, editors, producers, publishers, executive vice presidents and others learn and carry out activities characteristic of their respective role, crafts and occupations' (Hirsch, 1972: 15). What is crucial in the study of media organisations, whatever form they take, is the extent to which the 'autonomy' of media practitioners to act is influenced by social structures and organisational practices (Manning, 2000: 53).

Theoretically the discussion at each of these levels is couched in terms of the concepts of structure and agency. While structure refers to the limitations and constraints placed on human action, agency suggests human action is independent (Croteau and Hoynes, 1997: 20). The actions of individuals can either be seen as conforming to what is expected of them by society, the organisation they work for or the group or class they identify with, or coming out of the power of individuals to freely define situations and freely decide their behaviour. Functionalism, which dominated research into media organisations and media work in the early years, focused on 'the impersonal processes through which organisations function rather than on the motivations of the participants' (Open University, 1977b: 7). Organisational goals are considered paramount and the emphasis of research is on how individuals are integrated into the organisation to realise these goals. Individual workers are motivated by a number of means, such as inducements and coercion to carry out their organisational roles. Each worker plays a clearly defined role that enables the organisation to efficiently and effectively execute its goals. The failure of the functionalist approach to examine the relationship of the organisation to the broader social structure, to explore the possibility of conflict within organisations, to consider the aims and goals of individuals inside organisations and to account for the ways in which organisational goals are decided and how they can change resulted in a very narrow conceptualisation of media production. This criticism is also levelled at Marxist approaches, which see media organisations as inextricably tied to the dominant social institutions (Gallagher, 1982: 153). As such those working in the media have little or no autonomy in their work, simply serving the interests of the capitalist or owning class and acting as mouthpieces or megaphones for their views, opinions and interpretations -- although neo-Marxist approaches sometimes stress the day-to-day 'relative autonomy' of journalists and news producers (Ferguson, 1990: 117).

Others take issue with the emphasis on structure permeating Marxist- and functionalist-based analysis of media organisations. Pluralists see media practitioners as autonomous individuals whose creative and interpretative skills are encouraged and valued by the organisations for which they work. As a result they are 'left to get on with the job' (Whale, 1977, quoted in Curran: 1990, 117). Another approach, which draws on Weber's work on bureaucracy, presents a dynamic picture of media organisations. Labelled the 'social action' model, this approach portrays media organisations as made up of competing groups and individuals with different interests who conflict with authority both inside and outside the organisation. Media organisations are sites of struggle, and the bargaining process between different groups and individuals shapes what the media produce. The outcome of this process is not pre-determined but 'relative to a particular and evolving balance of interests' (Open University, 1977b: 10). Culturalist or post-modern perspectives see this explanation as problematic. While not necessarily rejecting the argument that media content emerges from interaction between people in organisations, cultural accounts see the work of media organisations and practitioners shaped by the broader cultural assumptions of the society in which they exist. Schudson (1989: 275) argues there is a difference between the social construction of news through the interaction of news workers with one another in an organisational context and the production of news within the broader 'cultural givens' within which everyday interaction must occur. Thus 'the generalised images and stereotypes in the news media ... transcend structures of ownership and patterns of work relations' (Schudson, 2000: 189).

INDIVIDUAL MEDIA WORKERS

Arguing media content is determined by the decisions of the individual media worker accords with the common-sense assumption of media audiences and the self-image of many of those working in the media. Journalists, for example, often see themselves as rugged, independent individualists, an image promoted in popular culture. Hollywood films seldom portray journalists in routine, desk-bound, dead-end jobs (Zynda, 1981: 10). Films are usually discussed in terms of the talent of their stars, the reputation of their directors and the acumen of their producers. Leo Rosten in his 1940s study of Hollywood highlights the importance of the film stars in the success of the cinema. He believed 'no group in Hollywood receives as much attention from the public as the men and women whose personalities are featured in films and around whom entire movie organisations have been geared' (Rosten, 1941, in Tunstall, 2000: 93). An assumption made for all media is that the personality, work and talent of the individual is primarily responsible for shaping what they produce. This is familiar to those working in the industry as it reinforces their notion of the freedom and autonomy of individual communicators as well as their audiences, who are encouraged to see media content as reflecting the diversity of voices in society. One of the first ways of understanding how the work of the individual is transformed into media products was to conceptualise the manufacturing process as a series of 'gates' through which ideas had to pass.

GATEKEEPERS

In his classic study of the process of news selection, published in 1950, David Manning White introduced the concept of the 'gatekeeper' into the theoretical lexicon of mass communication research. He drew on the work of the psychologist Kurt Lewin who in his research into decisions made about household food purchases identified certain points in the communication process he called 'gate areas' when certain pieces of information are filtered out. White believed 'no aspect of communication is so impressive as the enormous number of choices and discards which have to be made between the formation of the symbol in the mind of the communicator and the appearance of a related symbol in the mind of the receiver'. Hence his emphasis on the process of selection that occurs within the newsroom. He examined the choices made in the selection of news stories on a small city newspaper reaching 30000 families in the Midwest of America and argued the news selection process involves a large number of gates through which news stories must pass. Gatekeeping means 'a story is transmitted from one "gatekeeper" after another in the chain of communication' each of whom opens gates to let some stories through and closes them to others. White's first task was to identify people inside newsrooms who act as the 'gatekeepers'. This is not straightforward given the large numbers who participate in the news selection process. He identified the news wire editor as one key decision maker and this person became the focus of his research. White found his news wire editor selected only one in ten of the stories that came across his desk for printing in the newspaper. In rejecting stories he relied on 'value judgements based on the gatekeeper's own set of experiences, attitudes and expectations'. About a third of the stories were rejected on his personal evaluation of their merits while the other two-thirds because of lack of space or being too similar to stories already published. White accepted basic journalistic beliefs about newsworthiness played a part in the selection of news but argued the process was 'highly subjective'. The result of his work was that 'public information was seen to be determined by editorial gatekeepers who chose what news to use, with this selection procedure inevitably being a reflection of the personal background and beliefs of those individuals' (McGregor, 1997: 49).

Mr Gates

White's study, The Gate Keeper: A Case Study in the Selection of 'News', was based on decisions made by one news wire editor – whom he called 'Mr Gates' on what should appear as national and international news on the front and 'jump' pages of a small city newspaper. Mr Gates, a man in his mid-forties and with 25 years of experience as a journalist, selected stories from the incoming copy from the news agencies, Associated News, United Press and International News Service, which appeared on the wires every morning. White persuaded the editor to keep all the material that came in for one week in February 1949 and provide written explanations for the stories not used, which accounted for nearly 90 per cent of the material received. Explanations for the non-usage of stories included 'dull writing', 'too vague', 'not interesting', 'too far away', 'too regional', 'no space', 'too much already on the subject', 'he's too red', 'don't care for suicide stories' and 'out of good taste'. Mr Gates acknowledged his prejudices played a role in the selection

> process, stating, for example, his antipathy to 'a publicity-seeking minority with its headquarters in Rome', which meant 'I don't help them a lot'.

White's model of gatekeeping was widely applied to the process of mass communication, with its emphasis on the role of the individual not the media organisation in the process of narrowing down the large array of messages that can be communicated. Thus the book publisher must choose from a large number of book titles, the television commissioning editor from a large number of proposals from independent TV companies, the record executive from a large number of demo tapes by bands and pop groups, and the network scheduler from the wide range of programmes to make up the output of a TV channel. These are crucial decisions that directly shape what audiences see, hear and read. White's model draws attention to the personal whims, idiosyncrasies and prejudices of the gatekeepers as important in the process of mass communication. A number of studies have updated the model in light of changing circumstances. Snider (1967) found 17 years later that Mr Gates' story selections were still based on what he liked and what he believed his readers wanted, while Bleske (1991) showed how Ms Gates in spite of technological, organisational and social change did not differ appreciably from her male predecessor in allowing her own personal values to act as an important determinant of news selection.

White's model is today seen as naive and simplistic, dismissed as being 'of little utility' (O'Sullivan *et al.*, 1994). The focus on a single gatekeeper watching over a single gate ignores the complexity of modern media organisations as well as 'minimises the complexity of newsmaking' (Schudson, 2000: 177). Subsequent work attempted to develop the model beyond the simple individual level of White's study. Bass (1969) distinguished between different types of gatekeeping functions. He divided news workers into two types: 'news-gatherers', such as reporters who go out and get stories, and 'news-processors' such as the newsdesk, sub-editors and news editors who 'filter' stories to fit the space available. His work presents a more sophisticated view of gatekeeping, focusing on multiple gatekeepers 'acting as representatives of an organisation in fulfilling certain functions necessary to the flow of news within the organisation' (see Shoemaker, 1991: 14–16). This formulation does not satisfy critics who argue the model underestimates the part played by journalists in manufacturing the news. Chibnall (1977: 6) argues 'the reporter does not go out gathering news, picking up stories as if they were fallen apples', but rather 'creates news stories by selecting fragments of information from the mass of raw data he or she receives and organising them in conventional journalistic form'. News does not exist independently of the news organisation. He also adds by the time the story reaches the newsroom many of the important decisions in the selection process have been made. As he notes, reporters rarely witness events and rely on the 'selected and selective accounts of others' (1977: 7). The gatekeeping model is criticised for its oversimplification of the news production process and neglect of the pressures on media workers in doing their jobs. The model was also challenged by the findings of subsequent research. White's emphasis on the personal characteristics of an individual as the explanation for Mr Gates' decisions leads to the expectation of variety in what is selected as news, but Gieber (1956), after analysing the selections made by 16 newspaper wire editors, did not find any significant variation in the news items selected. He concluded editors are 'caught in a strait jacket of mechanical details', which prevents personal whims being a major determinant of what is selected. For Gieber the gatekeeper is essentially passive, selecting news according to particular organisational routines and policies.

While the autonomy of the individual worker to make decisions shaping media content remains part of the mythology of the media professions, media theory began to place more emphasis on the collective nature of the production process. Purely individual decision making is seen as a rare occurrence and rejected in favour of understanding the group dynamics characterising media work. Hood (1972: 417) in his discussion of TV news production shows how news passes through many gatekeepers, official and unofficial, direct and indirect:

> A news bulletin is the result of a number of choices by a variety of gatekeepers. They include the editor who decides on the day's coverage, or the organiser who briefs the camera crews and reporters and allocates assignments, the film editor who selects the film to be included in the bulletin, the copytaster who chooses the stories from the tape to accompany the film, the sub editor who writes the story and the duty editor who supervises the compilation of the bulletin, fixes the running order of the stories and gives it its final shape. Each of these gatekeepers accepts or rejects material according to criteria, which obviously, under no system, can be based on individual whim.

As a result it is not possible to make sense of the different contributions to a TV news bulletin because of the variety of employees involved. The collective nature of media production means, as Van Zoonen (1994: 46) points out, that no one communicator can be held responsible for the final product. The group dynamics of the process are more important in trying to explain what appears in the media. This requires knowledge of the social characteristics of media practitioners, their socio-demographic features, their political and cultural convictions and values, and their professional roles and conceptions. Such an approach still accords the individual discretion in the selection and decision-making process but emphasises the characteristics of media workers as a group. As a group media practitioners can be seen as having *general* characteristics, those pertaining to their view of the world, and occupational or professional characteristics, those relating to how they see their job being done (Grossberg et al., 1998: 68).

SOCIAL ATTITUDES AND VALUES

Studies of the social background of media occupations show, in one way or another, the industry is unrepresentative of broader society. Media professionals, for example, have been characterised in some research as liberal or left wing. Lichter *et al.* (1986) found in their study of 'elite' reporters in American television and the press that journalists are more likely to see themselves as political liberals compared to the public in general. Gans (1979) suggests American journalists share a set of 'enduring values' that shape the nature of news. He argues these values cannot be classified as either conservative or liberal but represent a kind of progressivism. He identifies ethnocentrism, altruistic democracy, responsible capitalism, small town pastoralism, individualism, moderation, social order and national leadership as the values guiding the American news journalist in his or her work.

Gans' work echoes that of scholars in Britain who identify the media with consensus values and the status quo. Support for these values is seen as a product of the class background of those working in the media. Hood (1972: 417) refers to individual whims being determined by class background, upbringing and education. He argues to understand the output of the BBC it is crucial to know the social origins of executives and programme makers in the organisation who are 'predominantly but not exclusively middle class' and 'if of working class origins they will in all probability have been assimilated into the middle class by their education' (Hood, 1997: 18). Their class background encourages them to support the dominant structures and ideology of British society. Hence their support for parliamentary democracy, the law, the family and Christian morality as well as the capitalist system (Connell, 1978). The BBC's role in 'holding the middle ground' when there are threats to these values can in part be seen as a reflection of the background and attitudes of those who work in the Corporation (see Kumar, 1977; Burns, 1977). The BBC is seen as one example of a wider phenomenon. Tunstall (1971) found most of the prestigious positions in British journalism were filled by graduates from Britain's two leading universities – Oxford and Cambridge – while Curran (2000) emphasises the narrow class and education background, occupational values and social networking of literary editors, which in part accounts for the limited book reviewing agenda in the British press. Johnstone *et al.* (1976: 28) found American journalists were urban, young, white, male and from solid middle- or upper middle-class social backgrounds. Hence it is no accident the news in large measure reflects male perspectives, is disproportionately centred on urban places and events, and pays little attention to minority or disadvantaged groups.

Other media are seen as shaped by the social characteristics of those who work in them. The urban and Jewish background of Hollywood producers and screenwriters is seen as shaping the content of American movies and television (see Grossberg *et al.*, 1998: 67). Feminist critics draw attention to the 'gendered structure of media production'. They argue 'male bias' in the media reflects the pattern of male dominance of the media industries. Around the world 'women are very much a minority presence in ... the "man's world" of the media' (UNESCO, 1987, quoted in Van Zoonen, 1994: 50). The under-representation of ethnic minorities in the media workplace is another example of social bias. What all these studies of the social background of those working in the media industries have in common is the assumption that group attitudes and values explain the pattern of coverage in the media. Hence to change the media's representation all that has to be done is to change who works in the media. Bringing in people from different social backgrounds and with different attitudes will lead to new forms of representation. This raises a number of issues at the theoretical level.

Drawing on empirical tests to build a theoretical position demands some degree of consistency in the evidence produced. While there are numerous studies of the social background and political attitudes of media workers, no clear pattern emerges. More significantly, 'empirical tests of the extent to which communicators' personal attitudes, values, and beliefs influence their work provide conflicting results' (Shoemaker and Reese, 1991: 71). Research also indicates different media allow for more scope for individual and personal attitudes and values to shape the production process. Murdock (1980) argues the backgrounds, lifestyles and commitments of those working in TV drama make up an essential component in the process of drama production. The changing position of women in the industry provides some measure of whether people determine content. Since the 1980s the number of women in the media industries has increased considerably (see Weaver and Wilhoit, 1996). New hiring policies have made journalism, for example, more representative of women in society. As a result it could be expected this would not only change group dynamics but the representation of women in the news. However, research shows the growth of women's numbers in newsrooms has not brought about significant changes (European Commission, 1999). Despite some differences in the choice of spokespersons and the compiling of background information women in journalism differ very little from their male counterparts in their selection of what is newsworthy (Van Zoonen, 1994: Chapter 4). It should be pointed out that there is a debate over whether sufficient women have attained positions of power in the industry to influence the production process. The empirical data to show social background and values influence the selection of news or the rest of the media's output are not conclusive.

PROFESSIONAL ROLES AND CONCEPTIONS

Media workers' understanding of what their job entails could also determine choices made in the production process. People's view of their job can be separated from their own personal views and attitudes as well as their social background and experience. Professional work is seen as comprising certain conventions and norms that enable people to do their job. Media professionals are no different. They can be seen as taking on a role and behaving accordingly. By examining the roles of media professionals some scholars argue we can understand media content. The position of journalists has been subject to much speculation. Is there a set of work values, attitudes and behaviours associated with being a journalist and doing the job that shapes what is produced? Is there a set of norms and values people entering journalism must learn and perform accordingly? Attempts to answer these questions have centred on whether it is possible to consider journalism as a profession, with a set of rules that orientates individuals to particular ways of working and results in particular kinds of content.

Roles

The concept of 'role' helps clarify the relationship between society and individuals, between forces of structure and agency . . . Sociologically roles can be thought of as bundles of expectations associated with different social positions. For example, students know the basic requirements of their role: attend lectures, complete essays, sit exams etc. . . . We rarely think about the specific content of roles, because we have largely internalised them. A person who has learned a role tends to 'just do it' and not think about it. In fact roles become part of a sense of self . . . However, sometimes the socially constructed nature of roles becomes apparent – for example, when role expectation is breached seeing what we shouldn't be doing reaffirms what we should be doing . . . The process by which we learn the basic ground rules of a role is called socialisation. Every media occupation – journalist, photographer, writer, film-maker, musician and so on – requires socialisation into that role. We tend to think of this kind of work as creative, done by people who have special talent. However, even these creative media jobs are performed by people who must fulfil the expectations of their roles, . . . but roles are not rigid: they do not dictate specific behaviour, . . . individuals often have a good deal of room for negotiation within the framework of the roles they occupy. Roles are also not static, . . . changing social conditions both create and eliminate the need for particular roles.

Source: adapted from Croteau and Hoynes, 1997: 109–10

While many consider journalism as a profession, including most of those working in the news media, the criteria used to define professionalism do not apply very well to journalism (Shoemaker and Reese, 1991: 73–4). Above all, there is no mechanism to enforce an agreed set of standards governing the behaviour of journalists, nor is there any prescribed body of knowledge and formal training practitioners must acquire before entering the field. Whether journalism meets certain objective requirements to be deemed a profession is not as important as whether individual journalists share a conception of what the role of a professional journalist should be and how far this determines how they select, write and edit news stories. Common-sense presents the professional role of the journalist as being one of neutral observer of the events unfolding in front of him or her. Nick Nolte, as a photojournalist in the film *Under Fire*, sums up this position when he utters the words, 'I don't take sides, I take pictures.' This is how many journalists see their role. They consider themselves as 'neutrals', simply acting as channels for the transmission of information (Johnstone *et al.*, 1976). The emphasis is on speed, accuracy, accessibility and entertainment as the criteria to judge whether they are doing their job in a professional manner. Objectivity is perhaps the central tenet of this conceptualisation of the role of the journalist.

Not all journalists, however, define their professionalism in terms of neutrality. Cohen (1963) distinguishes between two different role conceptions for journalists from his examination of American journalists and the foreign policy process: neutral and participant. Journalists who define their role as participants do not see news as emerging naturally from events but from their efforts to investigate and analyse what is going on. Only by the imposition of their point of view will news come to light (Van Zoonen, 1988: 39). The role of 'participant' is more apparent amongst younger, better-educated journalists who worked for large well-resourced news organisations (cited in Shoemaker and Reese, 1991: 75). The distinction between the neutral and participant roles has developed since the 1960s with the evolution of participant journalism into 'new' journalism with its focus on advocacy. In parts of Africa and Asia it has been incorporated into what is known as 'development' journalism (Aggarwala, 1990) while in many European countries the interpretative function of journalism has always been central to the profession (Chalaby, 1996). Empirical research indicates journalists have more than one understanding of their professional role, of how they should do the job. Some argue a shared sense of professionalism is beginning to emerge in global journalism. Spichal and Sparks (1994) in a study of 22 countries found professional values are similar in spite of differences of national culture, educational qualifications and training, social background and political affiliation. They conclude some kind of universal standard is beginning to emerge. This coincides with the argument that the 'globalisation' or 'westernisation' of the media is producing a shared set of professional values amongst journalists everywhere. Golding (1977: 292) argues media professionalism in the countries of Asia, Africa and Latin America 'is an ideology that has been transferred ... as part of the general stream of cultural dependence' from the industrialised countries to the rest of the world. Such findings are contradicted by other studies. Kocher (1986), from her investigation of British and German journalists, concludes they 'differ in their perception of their roles, their professional motivation and their evaluation of the norms connected with work in journalism', with German journal-

107

ists placing more value on opinion while their British counterparts see their role primarily as transmitters of facts. In recent years surveys of journalists have found both roles being embraced by a majority of journalists. Weaver (1998: 468) found more disagreement than agreement between journalists in different parts of the world as to their roles, including over the importance of reporting objectively. Schudson (2000: 187) notes it is 'best to be cautious' about all this data, as it is based on what journalists say or think. It is not based on actual practices, on what journalists do, and discrepancies can exist between what journalists *say* they should do and what they do.

The perspective that personal values or professional roles explain media content is rejected by scholars such as Epstein (1974: xiv) who believes individuals modify their behaviour 'in accordance with the requisites of the organisation', and Hood (1972) who argues individuals' work is determined by what they believe to be 'possible, tolerated and approved by the organisation'. They see 'the key to explaining the particular "outputs" of organisations . . . [lies] in defining the basic requirements which a given organisation needs to maintain itself'. Professional and personal practice must be interpreted in accordance with the requirements of media organisations.

ORGANISATIONAL CULTURE AND CONTROL

Media organisations, like all organisations, develop techniques to transform the unpredictability of the world into a set of routines. Universities, for example, transform the process of higher education and learning into subjects, courses or modules, timetables, lectures, seminars, essays and examinations. News organisations similarly have a number of routines and conventions to transform their raw material into news. The millions of events happening every day around the world are the basic raw material. The chaotic and varied nature of these events is packaged into a number of routines for the gathering, selection and processing of news. To be newsworthy events must be compatible with these routines. The crucial question is how news organisations – and more generally media organisations – whose workers and employees are committed to the goal of objectivity and the free expression of their creative talent, are able to impose their influence.

Routines

> Routines are patterned and repeated practices people learn in order to carry out certain tasks. We all have routines to cope with most aspects of daily life. Without them we would have to think carefully every time we did something. Individual workers in organisations do their jobs according to certain routines. News workers have routines for news gathering, processing and transmission. News work is focused on the 24-hour news cycle, deadlines, inverted-pyramid story writing (see box on page 110), news beats, and space and time

> constraints. Within all media organisations routines develop as a way of minimising the risks of production, which can include a range of considerations from being involved in a libel suit, protecting individual workers from criticism by their peers and the public, the duplication of efforts or increasing costs.
>
> Source: adapted from Shoemaker, 1991

One of the first attempts to examine how news organisations exercise influence over their employees was by Warren Breed (1955). He examined how news policy is enforced amongst newspaper journalists. He identified the particular problems newspapers have in ensuring employees conform to the policy and singled out three reasons why conformity is not automatic. There are ethical norms about how journalists should do their job; newspaper staff are more 'liberal' than their publishers and there is a professional understanding that publishers should not directly intervene to tell their employees what stories to cover and how to report them. These factors mean overt compulsion is not a method easily deployed. Breed sought to understand how policy is maintained when 'it often contravenes journalistic norms, that staffers often personally disagree with it, and that executives cannot legitimately command that it be followed' (Breed, 1955: 327). He identifies several means by which news workers conform to the policy of their newspaper and in so doing shows how news work cannot be done by the individual in the detached and isolated way portrayed by the gatekeeping model.

Breed places emphasis on the 'socialisation' of reporters and news workers with regard to the norms of the job. New reporters on newspapers are never told what policy is or how they should do the job; they learn it through a process of 'osmosis', on-the-job training by which they internalise what is expected of a reporter to gain reward and avoid punishment. The new journalist 'discovers and internalises the rights and obligations of his [sic] status and its norms and values'. The process of discovery is through observation and experience, listening to superiors and learning which actions produce rewards from editors and respect from co-workers. The internalising of the values and norms is seen in the status and aspirations of the individual, the structures of newsrooms and the operations and tasks they have to perform. Breed highlights six factors that can prevent acts of deviance: institutional authority and sanction; feelings of obligation and esteem to superiors; mobility aspirations; absence of conflicting group allegiance; the pleasant nature of newswork; and the satisfaction of producing a tangible product called news at the end of the day. However, enforcement cannot always be guaranteed and acts of deviance occur. Breed discusses the reasons for this. The two most important are when a story departs from what is typically covered by the newspaper and when the reporter's reputation is of such a high status that he or she can question and challenge the norms of news gathering and processing.

The need to enforce policy is seen in the hierarchical nature of newsrooms, which 'limits and shapes the discretion that reporters have in their newsgathering and news reporting activities' (quoted in Ward, 1995: 103). The clear delineation of chains of command inside newsrooms is seen by some as intrinsic to how reporters work. For example, the hierarchical nature of the newsroom can be seen as entrenched in how news stories are written. News stories take the form of the 'inverted pyramid' that can be 'easily cut . . . without re-writing by simply deleting the last paragraphs' (Ward, 1995). The emphasis on the hierarchical nature of news organisations assumes conflict between news workers and their managers and the organisation is inevitable. Sigelman (1973) argues tensions between reporters and their superiors do not characterise newsrooms as much as co-operation between individuals to produce the news. Several studies see news as the unintended result of the widely accepted practices of news gathering rather than the result of a policy of enforcement from above (see, for example, Epstein, 1973; Fishman, 1981; Gans, 1979; Golding and Elliott, 1979).

Inverted pyramid

> The writing of news stories usually emphasises the structuring of the story in the form of an inverted pyramid, which means the most important elements are placed at the top of the story while the least important, often referred to as 'background', are put briefly at the bottom. It is traditionally the job of the newsdesk to fit reporters' copy on to the page or into the bulletin, and this format enables them to exercise control more easily.

News 'is the result of the methods newsworkers employ', which have been developed in co-operation between reporters and their employers (Fishman, 1981: 14). Tuchman (1978a), in an influential study, outlines how news workers in their work are 'routinizing the unexpected'. The unexpected is the millions of events that happen every day in the world – the basic raw material of the reporter's work – which must be transformed into the product called news. Reporters have to select certain events and produce news stories about them by a certain deadline. For news organisations there is a need to minimise the risks in this process. They require a regular and reliable flow of news to fill the space and time within the daily cycle. Tuchman suggests they do this via the 'news net'. Journalists strategically organise themselves around certain locations more likely to generate news stories they can catch in their net. Hence the establishment of 'news beats'. News organisations organise their news-gathering efforts around other social institutions. Reporters are assigned to cover institutions such as the courts, police, No.10 Downing Street or the White House, and government departments or particular areas such as the arts, science and sports. This system reduces costs, promotes efficiency in the news-gathering process and alleviates psychological wear and tear on the individual reporter. The news beat system means 'the world is bureaucratically organised for journalists' whose reliance on bureaucratic organisations enables them to have at their disposal a method for the 'continuous detection of events' and a 'map of relevant knowers for any topic of newsworthy happenings' (Fishman, 1981: 51). The consequence, however, is the preference given to official accounts of what is happening in the world. Research has found official sources of information dominate the news agenda (see, for example, Sigal, 1973). The casting of the 'news net' has implications for who is considered newsworthy and how they are covered.

The 'news net' is not the only way news organisations make the gathering of news more predictable. Tuchman draws attention to how events are categorised inside newsrooms into particular types, enabling editors to decide immediately how to assign them and allocate the human and technical resources to cover them. Tuchman identifes several 'typifications' of news that have implications for how they are reported, understood and explained. Assigning a pre-determined typification of 'hard' or 'soft' news, 'spot', 'developing' or 'continuing' news, women's or financial page story, shapes the treatment and placement of a news story in the paper or bulletin. These distinctions assist news organisations to control work through prediction. Unscheduled news, that is unexpected or unanticipated events – what we most commonly think of as 'news' – constitutes the smallest part of what is reported as news. Most news is scheduled or predicted in advance – it could be labelled 'olds'. Newsrooms work from a news diary listing a range of upcoming events to cover, such as press conferences, set speeches and the publication of reports. These events figure prominently in the news because they are essential for the maintenance of continuous production. From Tuchman's perspective the day-to-day work of journalists is often being desk bound, telephone dominated and handout dependent with little opportunity to follow what practitioners call their 'nose for news'.

If the news net enables journalists to locate where news happens and the typifications of news determine the strategies for covering events then, according to Tuchman, objectivity assists reporters to report news in ways acceptable to other organisations. Turow (1997: 212) suggests objectivity helps media organisations to avoid placing themselves in political jeopardy and provides individual reporters with the confidence their story will not be rejected by editors and their organisation. Tuchman (1977) describes objectivity as a 'strategic ritual' by which individual reporters and news organisations can defend their product. There is also an economic rationale for objectivity. Perceptions of the product as 'biased' can lose news outlets some of their audience and threaten their economic well-being. Elliott (1978) describes how 'powerful factors in the technology and economics of journalism lay behind the drawing of this distinction between fact and comment'. The growth of news agencies in the late nineteenth century, with their desire to provide a service for subscribers with different political opinions and commitments and different national allegiances is seen as promoting the ideal of objectivity (see Schudson, 1978, for a discussion).

Strategic ritual

Tuchman studied the work of a newsroom of a major US newspaper, following round reporters and observing what they were doing. She concluded journalists evoke objectivity much as 'the way a Mediterranean peasant might wear a clove of garlic to ward off evil spirits'. She identifies several forms of 'strategic ritual' deployed by reporters to combat criticism of their lack of objectivity. First, when a reporter cannot tell what he or she is being told by an informant is correct, he or she can find an alternative point of view to report and then leave it to the reader to make an assessment as to whom is right. This enables the reporter to report the 'facts', satisfy the editorial pressures to meet deadlines and maintain the notion of being objective. But no attempt is made to investigate the 'truth' of the matter. Another strategic ritual is the 'presentation of supporting evidence'. Facts can be added together to appear to shed light on a topic without making any firm conclusions as to the 'truth'. Tuchman provides the example of a reporter's description of someone as a 'master musician'. When asked to justify this statement, the reporter tells his editor the musician once played with a famous composer, which satisfied the editor but did not add up to a completely objective statement. Finally, there is the 'judicious use of quotation marks', which distance the reporter from the reported statement. This may enable the reporter to escape the charge of not being objective but can colour the reporting of the events and thus readers' understanding of what is going on.

Source: adapted from Tuchman, 1977; Glover, 1984

Gitlin (1980) develops the discussion of coping with the pressures of uncertainty in news work with his examination of the 'persistent patterns of cognition, interpretation, and presentation, of selection, emphasis and exclusion', which organise and structure what is reported. He argues 'frames' – also labelled as 'referential structures', 'themes', 'preferred readings' and 'definitions of situations' – exist which shape how the news media understand and explain events. Drawing on the work of sociologist Erving Goffman, who showed how we all frame reality in order to negotiate, manage and comprehend the complexities of everyday life, Gitlin argues media frames 'organise the world for both journalists who report on it and ... for us who rely on their reports'. They make information understandable by assisting journalists to process large quantities of information and numerous details and facts quickly by enabling them to be packaged in a particular way. Numerous studies have examined how news is shaped by frameworks of interpretation –

for example, Halloran *et al.* (1970) show the news reporting of the 1968 anti-Vietnam war protest in Grosvenor Square was determined by prior definitions of the event as violent and directed by outside agitators. Gitlin sees frames as an 'unavoidable' and 'necessary' part of managing the production of news. Events will not be reported if a framework for understanding them does not exist (Ward, 1995: 112). But different frames can be applied to make sense of events, and one of the key questions for Gitlin is how to explain why a certain frame is adopted. Hall *et al.* (1978) do precisely this when they argue the 'routine structure and practices of the media in relation to news making serve to "frame" events within dominant interpretations and paradigms'. Working with a neo-Marxist approach they argue the routines of news gathering give preferential access to official sources of information, what they label as the 'primary definers' of events and situations, and their view and interpretation of what is going on.

Understanding media content in terms of the goals and needs of the organisation has limitations. First, what is a typical media organisation? Tunstall (1970: 8) asks the question 'When is a media organisation an organisation?' Should a chain of newspapers be regarded as one organisation or a federation of several organisations? Should the vast array of media interests that make up Rupert Murdoch's empire be seen as separate organisations or units within one large organisation? Much of the research into media organisations has concentrated on the editorial or creative departments employing people to make a product for their audience. The focus on this part of the enterprise ignores the other parts of media organisations such as the technical labour force who service the technology and machinery to deliver the product of creative and editorial departments. Tunstall (1970: 11–12) points out the 'great majority of a media organisation's employees perform technical, administrative, commercial and clerical functions' and are not involved in programme making or editorial production. Editorial and creative departments are part of larger organisations and the individuals who make decisions about what is produced are independent from those making the product. Hence actors whose interests in news coverage are minimal can shape news selection. Those involved in the technical, financial, advertising and marketing activities have different orientations to the news. For advertising executives the product should be tailored to satisfy the needs of advertisers and hence advertising departments promote conditions to maximise advertising revenue, which inevitably brings them into conflict with editorial or creative departments seeking to satisfy the needs of viewers, listeners or readers. The focus on the creative side of media production ignores a range of other factors as important, if not more so, in shaping media content.

That media organisations are not monolithic entities raises a second problem. Can we talk with any certainty about what are the needs or goals of media organisations? What are the needs of media organisations? How do we assess 'organisational needs'? Is it appropriate to talk about *the* goals of media organisations? Given the diversity of activities in a

113

media organisation it is clear different and often contradictory goals can be pursued, and that a range of different and contradictory needs exists. Compared to other types of organisation, it is possible to argue media organisations have an 'unusually broad mixture of goals'. Tunstall (1971) distinguishes a particular struggle between revenue and non-revenue goals in news organisations. He stresses non-revenue goals – for example, political partisanship, educational, cultural and prestige objectives – play a more important part in media than other organisations. For him the key question is how far the organisation is driven by the commercial imperatives of raising revenue and maximsimising profits, as opposed to more ethically or politically defined objectives. Tunstall stresses the process of bargaining over goals that goes on inside media organisations. The balance between revenue and non-revenue goals has changed in recent years with the commercialisation of the media working against non-revenue goals (see Curran, 2000). Advertising and marketing departments have become more powerful inside media organisations.

Much organisational theory, particularly Marxist and functionalist, presents the goals of media organisations as self-evident and a given. This has sometimes been accompanied by the reification of the organisation, attributing human motivations to inanimate objects. Foucault's notion of the 'carceral organisation', controlling people through discipline and surveillance (1977), or Goffman's 'total institution' in which individuals surrender self for the organisation are examples of how organisations can be conceived as black boxes with clear goals, unproblematically serving the interests of society or a particular group.

Reification

Reification is the process of converting an abstract mental object into a material thing or person. For example, we are regularly told that the government thinks or the government believes. A government cannot think or have beliefs. Similarly politicians and civil servants can be reified as 'the City', 'the state' or 'the country'. Tuchman (1977) argues the news can often be seen as reifying social phenomena. She says news presents economic activity or civil disorders, such as riots, as alien forces, akin to the fluctuations in the weather, as natural phenomena outside of human control or involvement.

The focus on what happens inside media organisations is also seen as obscuring the broader cultural and social context within which media production happens. Often driven by the notions of social construction, organisational studies are accused of appearing to 'abandon any strong claim there is a 'reality' out there' (Schudson, 1989: 274). More consideration, it is argued, should be paid to how other social institutions shape media production, the impact of audience, or perceptions of audience, likes and dislikes on the production process and the cultural air media practitioners breathe.

SOCIAL AND CULTURAL ENVIRONMENT

The relationship between media organisations and the external world has been conceptualised in a number of ways. Central to this is the question of media power. On the one hand media workers and organisations have the power to shape media content, whereas on the other external forces, in particular other powerful social institutions and the audience, determine what is reported and represented in the media. Organisational approach has tended to adhere to the former. By focusing on individuals and their organisational environment, a picture is painted of the media in control of what emerges from the production process. Approaches that see the media from without tend to see the control lying outside the media, giving 'the impression that the media are little more than panes of glass through which it is possible to discern the structure of society, its values and innermost tensions, in ways that are wholly unaffected by institutional mechanism' (Curran, 2001: 10–11). This debate is most clearly laid out in analysis of the relationship between the news reporter and his or her sources of information.

Sources are central to news production as most events are never witnessed by reporters. They depend on others telling them what has happened. Reporters must 'cultivate sources' to obtain their information (Ward, 1995: 114–15). Sources most successful at gaining access to the mainstream news media are those who are well organised, well resourced and able to supply a regular and reliable flow of newsworthy information. These tend to be powerful groups and organisations in society, usually official bodies and, in particular, government. It is only recently that studies have focused on the role of sources in the construction of the news. The relationship has been under-conceptualised as organisational approaches 'largely, although not exclusively, focused on how media organisations, especially those producing news, have made use of sources of information' (Schlesinger, 1990: 62). The growth of 'promotional culture' has made the study of sources and their influence more central to analysis of media production. Central to the study of sources is 'the exercise of political and ideological power, especially, but not exclusively, by central social institutions which seek to define and manage the flow of information in a contested field of discourse' (Schlesinger, 1990). The focus has moved away from the individual media worker's autonomy inside the media organisation toward the autonomy media organisations have from other powerful groups and interests in society.

Pluralists and Marxists have both come to see official sources as dominating the news agenda. Preference is given to the opinions of those in authority as 'news privileges the privileged' (Ward, 1995: 114). If pluralists see this dominance as a breakdown of the normal operations of media organisations, Marxists argue it is a natural outcome of the 'structured relationship' between the media and the powerful, the ruling or dominant class

(Hall, 1978). Both approaches stress the power of official sources comes from their ability to exploit the organisational routines of the news media. This is complemented by the lack of financial and cultural resources at the disposal of non-official sources. The 'resource poor' face almost insurmountable hurdles in gaining access to the news (Goldenberg, 1975). Official sources acquire status not only through spending money on the provision of 'information subsidies' (Gandy, 1982) but also through the accumulation of cultural capital (Bourdieu, 1984). With their resources, power and capital, official sources are the 'primary definers' of the news agenda while the media are 'secondary definers'. Not only are reporters and their organisations reliant on official sources for their information, these sources also provide the frames and themes the media use to interpret the news (Hall *et al.*, 1978; Paletz and Entman, 1981). The emphasis on how official or elite sources dominate has been the focus of a number of studies, particularly in the area of politics, which explore how these sources have developed their ability and capacity to manage the news. The growth of professional groups whose job is to promote official source organisations and improve their media relations is central to this evaluation (see Curran, 2001: 29).

Cultural capital

> Just as there is an unequal distribution of economic capital and thus material power between different people, groups and classes so it is argued there is a corresponding unequal access to cultural capital and symbolic power. The ideas, opinions and voices of some people are deemed more credible and reliable than others because of their accumulation of cultural capital and their symbolic standing within society. Therefore my grandmother from the Rhondda Valley does not possess the same amount of cultural capital as Prime Minister Tony Blair.
>
> Source: adapted from O'Sullivan et al., 1994: 73

Schlesinger (1990) is critical of the concept of primary definition on which much of this research is based. He argues the concept neglects how official sources sometimes attempt to impose different interpretations of problems and their solutions. For example, inside government, ministers often compete to promote different policy options and in such circumstances it is not always possible to identify who is the primary definer (see also Blumler and Gurevitch, 1986). Schlesinger takes issue with the uni-directional way in which official or elite sources are supposed to impose their definition. The primary definition model allows 'no space to account for occasions on which the media may take the initiative in the definitional process by challenging the so-called primary definers and forcing them to respond – as, for instance, in investigative journalism' (Schlesinger, 1990:

Primary definition

> Hall and his colleagues in the book Policing the Crisis (1978) first
> articulated the concept of primary definition. They argue the media is
> 'structurally biased' to official sources. The 'result of this structured
> preference given in the media to the opinions of the powerful is that
> these spokesmen become what we call the primary definers of topics'
> and they 'establish the initial definition or primary interpretation of
> the topic in question'. For Hall et al. this interpretation dominates all
> subsequent treatment of the topic and sets the parameters within
> which further coverage must take place. Arguments contrary to the
> primary definition of the topic must be located within the primary
> definition of 'what is at issue'. They must begin with this framework
> of interpretation as their starting point.

67). There is also no space for oppositional definitions to dislodge the primary definition, which assumes a never-changing situation or as Schlesinger (1990: 66) puts it, 'primary definition ... involves a primacy both temporal and ideological'. These limitations mitigate against any sense of negotiation or competition prior to primary definition, which seems to run counter to the efforts made by official and non-official sources alike to mobilise resources to manipulate the media. Schlesinger sees the model as deterministic and static, but he does accept journalistic routines are generally organised so as to promote the interests of the powerful. He proposes a less rigid theory of domination that does not accept the triumph of official sources as an inevitable, pre-determined outcome but something to be struggled over and which in certain circumstances can fail.

The re-conceptualisation of primary definition generated numerous studies examining the competition between sources for definitional advantage in the news (for example, Anderson, 1993; Deacon and Golding, 1994; Schlesinger and Tumber, 1994). Such research reflects dissatisfaction with the deterministic approach of many organisational studies and a rejection of the pluralist accounts, which see the media as a forum for debate between parties with equal access to the process. Rather it emphasises 'the fissures and tensions within the dominant power bloc and the wider context of ideological competition and resistance from below' (Curran, 1990: 144). It also holds out the possibility of political action producing the opportunity for change neglected in the primary definition model.

If some researchers are critical of the determinism of primary definition, others are dissatisfied with explanations of what is in the news – and the media more generally – which focus on the actions of individual journalists, news organisations and source organisations. They reject the view that media workers and organisations deliberately disseminate official ideology or promote the views of the elite while discrediting those of their opponents. Rather media workers and organisations unconsciously reproduce thinking and talking about the world that draws on the dominant and established 'modes of discourse' in society (Ward, 1995: 119). All organisations, media and otherwise, are part of the broader culture in which we participate and, as such, reporters and officials go about their work within and in relation to this culture (Schudson, 2000). The images, language and discourses in the news transcend the structure of media organisation, the patterns of media work, and the interaction between sources and reporters by reflecting the cultural air we all breathe. It can be argued, for example, that the reporting of race in the British media is drawn from the British cultural tradition, which contains elements derogatory to foreigners, especially people of different race and colour (see Hartmann and Husbands, 1974, quoted in Schudson, 2000: 190). Media organisations and media workers operate within a culture from which they are obliged to use cultural symbols. This is most clearly captured in the relationship journalists and other media practitioners have with their audiences. Most media workers do not have any direct contact with their audience but they 'may resonate to the same cultural moods their audiences share' (Schudson, 2000: 190). The culture we live in, the taken-for-granted values that permeate society, are seen as shaping news judgement, news selection and news values. The knowledge that is the basis for decisions about what is newsworthy is too complex and intrinsic to human beings to be explained in terms of professional ideology or organisational operations. It is much more deeply ingrained in human consciousness. Thus sexist or patriarchal outlooks in the media are not simply a result of a particular form of social organisation but a reflection of values much more widely distributed in human societies (Schudson, 2000: 191).

Cultural accounts of media organisations see what media practitioners do as structured by cultural influences that are inscribed in their work routines, including their relationship with their sources, rather than dictated by hierarchical supervision and control (Curran, 1992). The myths, symbols, rituals and archetypes of modern society as a result are expressed in the media. Such accounts are able to make sense of changes in the nature of media work and media content over time as well as across societies. Culturalists see media workers as having relative freedom inside the media organisation, within the confines of the broader culture, but consider them and the production process as secondary to the contests and engagements within the culture. It is these contests and engagements that are expressed in the content of the media, with media workers and organisations as mere cyphers. Such a view provides little or no scope for political action by media workers to change matters. Power rather resides with the media audience who can interpret what they see, hear and read in a number of ways.

Another external force influencing media production is technology. Rapid change in information and communications technology is fundamentally changing the production process. New technologies are transforming organisational structures, changing management–employee relations as well as patterns of work. The scale of the change means working practices in the media and cultural industries are 'almost unrecognisable' compared to a couple of decades ago (McRobbie, 2000: 258). There is a dispute about the impact of this change. Optimists stress the greater autonomy for individual workers, less rigid job demarcations and more flexibility in the workplace, while pessimists point to less job security, lower wages, longer hours and fewer rights in the workplace as unionisation disappears (see Curran, 2001: Chapter 1). From a political economy perspective Curran (2000: 34) highlights the growing gulf within the media between those extremely well-paid stars at the top and the vast majority of those working in the industries who have seen a decline in their autonomy and conditions of work. Working in a more cultural studies-oriented framework, McRobbie (2000: 258) stresses the creative dimension, the dynamics of self-promotion and the 'glamour' of modern media work, which enhances the role and autonomy of the individual media worker.

New technology is also seen as increasing the ability of governments and other social entities to strengthen their hold over the media. Individual media workers can be seen as subject to increased surveillance in their work from inside their organisations as well as from outside by government agencies. The interactivity of these technologies, such as the Internet, is seen as a direct threat to the continued role of the specialised communicator. The capacity such technologies provide for consumers to find information for themselves and for breaking down the barriers between journalists and the technical functions of news gathering and processing in the form of multi-skilling is considered by some to be 'the end of journalism' (Bromley, 1997). Much of the debate about the impact of technology on media organisations and media work is steeped in technological determinism. But the combination of technological, social, economic and political change that is occurring in the world outside the media is having a profound impact on the nature of media organisations and media work, which media theory and research has been slow to address.

SUMMARY

People in organisations manufacture what appears in the media. Who these people are, how they work and the nature of the organisations they work for are important factors in accounting for the content of the media. Research into media organisations and media work is undertaken at three levels: the individual, the organisation, and the broader socio-economic and cultural environment. At each of these levels it is possible to identify a corresponding theoretical approach. Some scholars adopt a 'communicator-centred' approach, emphasising the background, experience, beliefs and values, and work routines of individual media workers as central to explaining how the media works and what it produces. Other scholars adhere to an 'organisational-centred' approach, which explains media content by the ways in which the media organise work, the roles and routines laid down by media organisations for individual workers to follow. Yet other scholars suggest factors external to the individual media worker and the organisation that shape media production and content. They see other social institutions, technology and sources of information, as well as the broader culture, as crucial. All these approaches contrast with the common-sense assumption the media simply reflect what is happening around them.

Central to all these approaches is the question of who exercises control over what we see, hear and read. In media theory the debate is examined in terms of structure and agency. How much autonomy do individual media workers have? How free are media organisations to follow their own goals? To what extent does the media shape social structures? Different theoretical perspectives provide different answers to how far structural constraints, as opposed to human agency, account for the nature of media organisations and media work. Providing empirical evidence to support any of these answers is limited by the vast amount of research being concentrated on one type of media organisation: the news organisation. Steeped in the study of news journalism, much theorising into media production emphasises the role of the media in manufacturing or constructing reality. As organisational research branched out into other media industries – film, drama, popular music and entertainment – the idea of construction has been maintained. Organisational theories see the knowledge people gain of the world around them through the media not as a product of the reproduction of what is happening out there, in a direct and unproblematic way, but a reflection of how media organisations work and what individual workers do.

Section 3
Media content

This section examines theories that explain the nature of media content. How the media represent the world and what is happening in it is often controversial and usually a matter for dispute. Individuals, groups and peoples regularly complain about the ways in which they are portrayed in the media. Their sensitivity stems from the view 'to be imprisoned inside the misrepresentation and misunderstanding of others can be a withering form of incarceration' and such a fate can 'afflict whole nations and cultures as painfully as individuals' (Smith, 1980: 27). The media are the focus of such attention because they occupy the space between viewers, listeners and readers, and the world outside. We depend on them to tell us what is happening and provide us with a picture of the external world. The crucial question is what kind of picture do the media present. In answering this question a vast amount of literature has been devoted to exploring the content of the media. Central to this analysis is the concept of representation.

Social life is made up of representations. We need them in order to understand our social environment as well as to communicate with one another. Lippmann (1922) stresses the distinction between the world of actual events and our mediated knowledge of those events. What we think and how we act is often based on what we perceive to be true, not on what is actually true. He spoke of people acting according to the 'pictures' in their heads. How the media represent the outside world is a matter of debate. Media representations are not reality, even though some audiences judge them as if they are and some media workers claim they are. As we have seen in the previous section media representations are the end product of 'processes of selection that invariably mean that certain aspects of reality are highlighted and others neglected' (Crouteau and Hoynes, 1997: 134). The 'organisational bias' of the media is only one approach to assessing how the media misrepresent or misreport. Other analyses of 'media bias' focus on the content of the media, using a range of criteria to assess bias from how pictures are placed on a page or how visual devices are used in television news to the use of language to convey the meanings of events and issues. Questions of media bias are usually asked of the factual media. Most fiction and entertainment media do not try, or claim, to accurately and truthfully represent reality. They provide people with pleasure and fantasy, which allows them to escape from the trials and tribulations of their everyday life, their reality. It can neverthe-less be argued fictional and entertainment media forms provide insights and pass obser-vations on the particular social conditions in which they are made. Stereotypical representations in such media contribute to people's knowledge and understanding of the world as much as what appears in media charged with the duty of factual representation.

Much of the research into 'media bias' concentrates on the extent to which the media reflect the realities of the social world. In particular the media's representation of key imbalances in social power, around race, class, gender, sexuality and age, is central to these studies. The ways in which certain social groups are represented, how these representa-tions have developed over time and across cultures, as well as how they relate to inequal-ity in society, are the main lines of investigation taken into media content (Croteau and Hoynes, 1997: 133). Several issues can be identified in such research but the main issue that has exercised media studies most is the question of what is the 'real'. Is there such a thing as reality and if so how do we measure it? Recent theoretical approaches challenge the notion of a 'knowable reality', arguing no representation of reality can be accurate and true (Croteau and Hoynes, 1997: 135). This is opposed by those who point to a variety of social facts against which media content can be assessed (see Philo and Miller, 2001). Media theory in recent years has placed more emphasis on understanding the role of the media in the construction of reality. How meaning is determined by the formulas and formats – media genres – adopted in the production process and by the way in which media tell stories – their narrative structure – has been analysed. For some the question of meaning has made redundant the concept of ideology and in the 1990s the concept of discourse became more important in trying to understand media representation.

Assessment of media representation is located within an evaluation of the meaning of media messages. The meaning attached to media texts by those who manufacture or create them is not necessarily the meaning drawn from them by readers, viewers or lis-teners. The struggle for meaning is central to understanding media content. It is also the basis for a difference of opinion between media scholars. For some scholars meaning is apparent in the content of the media (Berelson, 1952) while others argue that meaning cannot be simply read off from what is manifest in what they label as media 'texts'. Rather, they argue, meaning is 'hidden' or 'embedded' in media texts and the task of the researcher is to reveal the deeper meaning latent within the content of the media. They also argue meaning is not fixed. It changes according to who the reader, viewer or listener is. Different people bring different experiences, knowledge and backgrounds to the process of unravelling meaning. The former position is associated with 'content analysis', the latter with 'semiology or semiotics'.

Chapter Five

TELLING IT AS IT IS? □
QUESTIONS OF MEDIA
REPRESENTATION

We live in a media-saturated world (O'Sullivan *et al.*, 1998: 1–15) and the continuous flow of images and information from the media is the most important source of people's understanding of the world around them and those who live in it. But what views of the world does the media represent? The two concepts most commonly used to discuss representation are 'bias' and the 'stereotype'. Bias is one of the few terms used in common-sense conversation about the media that also drives attempts by scholars to understand media content. Charges of bias are regularly thrown at the media. Politicians are perhaps the most vociferous in accusing the media of being partial in communicating what is happening. But other groups complain about how they are reported or represented. Individuals in conversations across the world criticise the media for its lack of accuracy or fairness in their coverage. Celebrities, in particular, accuse the media of presenting one-dimensional pictures of their lives and work, and even of fabricating news about what they have done. Such accusations of bias are usually levelled at factual forms, such as news, current affairs and documentaries. These media are committed to the goal of objectivity through the professional ideology of journalism (see Chapter 4) and the legal obligations under which they work. However, fictional media are increasingly subjected to similar accusations.

In the 1980s TV dramas such as the BBC's *The Monocled Mutineer* and the series *Casualty* were charged with bias. The former was accused of misrepresenting events that happened during the First World War when sections of the British army mutinied, while *Casualty*'s concern with the daily workings of a hard-pressed, under-staffed hospital was seen by some as having an anti-government bias (*Listener*, 13 November 1986). Charges of historical inaccuracy have been levelled at films such as *Michael Collins* and *In the Name of the Father*, which were accused of 'supporting' the IRA, even though the former was about events that occurred nearly a century ago. Fictional media forms are not bound by any obligations to fairness and impartiality, and there is doubt as to whether the concept of bias should be applied to them as they are built on the imagination and subjectivity of the writer and others involved in the production process. Fictional media forms are more commonly subjected to the charge of stereotyping. The term 'stereotype' is used to indicate representations that are misleading, incomplete or negative of a group of people in society. Through stereotypical representation the media have been criticised for portraying women, young and old people, gays and lesbians, drug users and a range of other 'minority' groups in a simplistic and derogatory manner. The result is the potential to marginalise such groups and give rise to social prejudices. Thus to frequently portray students as heavy drinkers, recreational drug users and partygoers can contribute to the lowering of their standing and acceptance in society. The news media is also seen as contributing to stereotypical representation, and media research has subjected both the fictional and factual media to scrutiny to assess accusations of bias and stereotyping.

Regulation and media impartiality

The legal obligation to be impartial in the reporting of events is placed on broadcasters in America, Britain and most west European countries. In news and programmes of political comment, broadcasters are obliged to pursue a policy of objectivity, fairness and impartiality. In the United States the television code states that broadcasters have 'to give fair representation to opposing sides of issues which materially affect the life and welfare of a substantial segment of the public', while in the United Kingdom an Act of Parliament lays down that 'due impartiality' must be preserved in respect of coverage of political, industrial and social policy matters. Regulatory bodies such as the Federal Communications Commission (FCC) and the Independent Television Commission (ITC) are responsible for ensuring that broadcasters comply.

Source: adapted from Gunter, 1997: 6

Since the late 1960s media research has generated a voluminous literature examining a range of bias and stereotyping critics claim to see in the output of the media. Much of this research concludes that the 'entertainment and news media do not reflect the diversity of the real world' (Croteau and Hoynes, 1997: 161) and the 'media reflect and support the existing patterns of social and economic inequality' (Tunstall, 1983: 141). However, this research has caused controversy. Trying to prove individual journalists or particular news or current affairs programmes or certain media are biased or stereotyping has led to a 'bottomless morass of disputed examples and counter examples' (quoted in Mungham and Williams, 1987: 18). Bitter arguments broke out between researchers and media practitioners as the former engaged in the dispute on the same terms as the aggrieved parties and their opponents (see Schlesinger, 1980). In the process the notions of bias and the stereotype have been increasingly challenged as inadequate formulations for assessing media content (Brunt and Jordin, 1982: 142). They have been replaced by concepts such as genre and narrative, which examine the role the media play in constructing rather than reflecting the world around them

WHAT IS BIAS?

The term 'bias' at a common-sense level refers to the tendency to depart from the straight and narrow. It is sometimes claimed to have its origins in the game of bowls in which a ball can have a in-built tendency to deviate or to be made to deviate by the player either to the right or to the left (McQuail, 1992: 191). Bias in news and information means the systematic inclination to favour 'one side in a dispute, or to favour one interpretation or to sympathise with one cause' (Street, 2001: 17). Arguments about bias tend to be most commonly articulated in political terms when a newspaper, channel, programme or reporter is accused of being too left or too right wing (Brunt and Jordin, 1982: 141). The traditional response from the media, primarily from broadcasters who are most subject to the charge, is to argue that charges of bias from both sides must mean their coverage is unbiased. The assumption is that straight-down-the-middle is where the path of objective truth lies. In politics the middle way or the middle ground is occupied; it is not a neutral position and holding the middle ground can be seen as an act of partiality (Kumar, 1977). All charges of bias are predicated on a belief that an unbiased, objective reality exists from which the media are deviating. The problem is identifying this position. For Brunt and Jordin (1982: 142) the concept of bias 'assumes some non-existent middle ground of political reporting, an illusory neutrality and a naive realism that looks for an impossibly transparent reflection of real life'. Discussion of media bias cannot be separated from notions of objectivity and an objective reality to report on.

Journalism and the news media are committed to the concept of objectivity, which came to be considered by the early twentieth century as the yardstick by which to judge the performance of the press. Smith (1978: 153–71) describes the long road along which the British press travelled to establish objectivity as a quality expected of journalism. The advent of television saw objectivity cemented as a 'routine norm of good practice' (McQuail, 1992: 183). Objectivity, and the related concepts of impartiality and balance, became the means by which to assess the provision of news, particularly in broadcasting where it was enshrined into legislation. As a result journalists are 'encouraged to assume the existence of an external world which could be known and reported on with accuracy' (Gunter, 1997: 9–10). The absence of objectivity came to be equated with bias. The problem for the news media is how to attain objectivity in practice. Journalists have identified a range of criteria to put objectivity into practice, including even-handedness in presenting different sides of an issue, accuracy, presentation of all the main points, separation of fact and opinion, minimising the influence of the personal views of the practitioners and avoiding slant (McQuail, 1992: 184). Each of these attempts to operationalise objectivity is problematic. Take even-handedness, how does the journalist identify what are the different sides of an issue? Aren't there more than two sides to any issue? If so, how many and whose views are to be reported? Similarly separating fact from opinion is not clear-cut. What is a fact? Facts cannot be pointed out in the way trees or flowers can. They are 'shaky sorts of objects' and the journalist's search for 'hard facts' is fraught with difficulties (see Romano, 1986). Furthermore facts by themselves are meaningless, simply a list of dates, names, places and so on. The playwright Pirandello compared facts to a sack. A sack won't stand up unless there is something in it and facts without interpretation are empty of meaning. To be given meaning they require interpretation.

Broken eggs

Whitaker (1981) provides a simple example to illustrate the problem of distinguishing between fact and comment. He takes an everyday occurrence, an egg lying broken on the floor, with a man – who is called Joe – standing next to it. He shows how several witnesses can describe what happened in a number of different ways:

- the egg is broken
- Joe broke the egg
- the egg fell
- Joe dropped the egg
- Joe dropped the egg and broke it
- Joe dropped the egg and it broke
- the egg fell and broke
- the egg rolled from Joe's hand and broke
- the egg hit the floor and broke.

Whitaker points outs all the accounts are objective in that they contain only facts not openly expressed opinion. But, he states, they are not pure description in that they are all interpretations.

Matters are further complicated by claims the news media should not always be objective. In certain circumstances it is deemed acceptable for the media to be partial. For example, at times of war the failure of the media to support the war effort of their own country is thought by some to be inappropriate (Gunter, 1997: 16; Williams, 1992). A former Director General of the BBC accepted the Corporation is 'biased in favour of parliamentary democracy' (Curran, 1979: 106). Opinions or views that clash with the so-called national interest or public interest are often not treated objectively. Socially unacceptable beliefs and actions, such as those of the paedophile, are not treated in an even-handed, balanced or fair manner. Similarly on morally dubious or controversial matters broadcasters have tended to shy away from an impartial or objective approach to the subject matter.

Not all news is intended to be objective. There are forms of news reportage that traditionally have deviated from the 'objective model'. McQuail (1992: 189–91) identifies 'some older versions of news' such as the 'human interest, partisanship and the investigative' functions of news that are seen as legitimate parts of the practice of journalism, but each of which contradicts in some way what is expected of objective journalism. The human interest tradition is often associated with the pejorative notion of sensationalism, which exaggerates appeals to emotion at the expense of elucidation and information. Advocacy or partisan journalism is defended by and expected of certain media or certain media practitioners in certain circumstances. During elections the partisan stance of newspapers is accepted, while individual journalists – such as John Pilger in Britain – have built their reputations upon advocacy of the powerless and the exploited in society (see Pilger, 1992; 1998). The investigative tradition of journalism, which underpins the role of the media as 'the fourth estate', the public's watchdog over the exercise of power in society exposing scandal, corruption, incompetence and venality, cannot easily be reconciled with objectivity.

Some argue objectivity itself is a form of bias. Schudson (1978: 160) describes how objectivity became a term of abuse, and objective reporting was looked on as 'the most insidious bias of all' as it 'reproduced a vision of social reality which refused to examine the basic structures of power and privilege' and 'represented collusion with institutions whose legitimacy was in dispute'. For post-modern scholars such as Fiske (1989a) so-called objective facts 'always support a particular point of view and their "objectivity" can exist only as part of the play of power'. One of the major failures of 'objective reporting' was the period of McCarthyism in the United States when reporters simply reported objectively what McCarthy claimed without questioning or challenging the veracity of the claims, many of which were untrue and they knew to be untrue (Bayley, 1981; Aronson, 1970). Hence they would often report propaganda as facts, sometimes knowing what was claimed was not necessarily true. Objective reporting was reduced to presenting 'competing truth claims' in a detached manner without making any assessment of their truthfulness nor questioning the assumptions on which they rested. For Glasser (1985: 52) objectivity in American journalism is biased against the media's fourth estate role, independent thinking and individual responsibility. Objective reporting encourages journalists to view the day's news as something they are *compelled* to report, thereby negating any responsibility they have for what is reported and how. By placing individuals in the position of detached and disinterested spectators it emasculates their intellect and militates against 'the need ... to develop a critical perspective from which to assess the events, issues, the personalities he or she is assigned to cover'. It is also seen as favouring the 'status quo' by focusing on the statements or claims of prominent members of society. Such reporting is not 'true journalism', which is to 'look behind the screens erected by established authority and to decode the language of power which, as George Orwell wrote, "is designed to make lies sound truthful and murder respectable, and to give an appearance of solidity to pure wind"' (quoted in Pilger, 1995).

Objective reporting is also seen as producing a simplified picture of events and issues. Epstein (1974: 266) argues balance in television news, with its requirement to present 'conflicts as disputes between no more than two equally matched sides tends to reduce complex issues, which may have a multitude of dimensions, to a simple conflict'. For Hall (1974: 22) balance leads broadcasters 'into the impasse of a false symmetry' of oppositions, which 'has little or no relevance to the quite unequal relative weights of the case for each side in the real world'. Thus balance might ensure the broadcasters' commitment to impartiality but 'hardly advances the truth'. Hall concludes objectivity is an 'operational fiction'. Others point to the range of external and internal pressures that makes objectivity impossible in practice. The commercial imperatives, such as the drive for ratings in television, can work against the detached and balanced approach demanded by objective journalism. The whole logistics of television production, like the choice to film this aspect of an event rather than that aspect, means 'all filmed accounts of reality are selective ... impregnated with values, viewpoints, implicit theorising, common sense assumptions' (Hall, 1974: 23). Whether objectivity is possible to achieve in day-to-day reporting is, then, debatable.

Research has consistently cast doubt over the possibility of genuine neutrality and objectivity in reporting (see McQuail, 1992: 184). Media studies is replete with examples of how discrepancies, inconsistencies and gaps exist in the media's handling of a range of issues and events in the news. Tunstall (1983: Chapter 10) documents the bias found against trades unions and in favour of management, against women and in favour of 'traditional male chauvinist values', against ethnic minorities and against the old and young. He is critical of such research, accusing 'academic studies from the political left' of exhibiting their own bias in approaching the question of media bias. Tunstall draws attention to the problem of assessing and measuring bias in the news. Bias can be seen as an accusation levelled at something we simply disagree with. In other words, bias is in the eye of the beholder. Anderson and Sharrock (1979) argue media researchers' criticism of news reporting is not grounded in showing how a report has distorted reality *per se* but rather in indicating it has diverged from the way in which researchers have defined reality. McQuail (1992) points to three distinctive criteria used in media research to assess the bias or otherwise of the news: factualness, accuracy and completeness. Factualness relates to distinguishing between fact and opinion, accuracy refers to making judgements as to whether the report is a reliable version of reality, while completeness assesses the fullness of an account of an event or issue (McQuail, 1992: 197). Each of these measurements, while amenable to empirical research is open to the charge of relativism. McQuail (1992: 192) points out 'it is hard ... to see how objectivity can ever be more than relative – a position taken in relation to other positions'. Thus any assessment of factualness, accuracy and completeness of news has to be made against something else, another point of reference or checklist. This is a matter of controversy between the media and their critics. Broadcasting organisations point to the research carried out by regulatory bodies, which shows over a long period of time two-thirds or more of the viewers and listeners to generally believe broadcast news and current affairs is 'fair' and 'unbiased' (Watts, 1997: 67).

This does not mean the coverage is not biased as it could simply reflect the basic values and actual sympathies of the majority of people. Evaluations based on other criteria – the views of sources of information, eyewitnesses to events or parties to the issues – might produce different results.

Further problems in using the concept of bias derive from the variety of ways in which it can appear in the media. McQuail (1992: 193–5) distinguishes between different kinds of bias on the grounds of 'explicitness' and 'intention'. Certain bias is openly expressed. take newspapers whose pages contain editorial articles, opinion columns, letters to the editor and paid-for advertisements that promote partisanship of one form or another. Other kinds of bias are hidden, often part of the propaganda efforts of sources of information and appearing in the form of objective news. Disinformation can be supplied to the news media by spokespeople, PR consultants, interest or pressure groups, political parties and so on, and 'pseudo-events' can be created or staged in order to attract publicity (McQuail, 1992: 194). Bias can also be 'unwitting' or 'unconscious' in that choices made in deciding what to cover in the limited space or time available to the news media rest on certain assessments about the importance of people, events and issues. Such bias is detected in the examination of the ways in which newsrooms work (see Chapter 4). More difficult to detect is 'hidden and unintended' bias, which is embedded in the way in which news stories are told. The hidden assumptions and the value judgements implicit in the story-telling process can only be unravelled by a 'close reading of the text', a detailed examination of the content to reveal the 'ideological framework' on which the news is predicated (see Chapter 6). Bias can also be defined in other ways. For example, Birt and Jay (1975) talk of a 'bias against understanding' in television journalism emerging from practices that inhibit public knowledge and comprehension by presenting narrow and limited accounts of events and issues. Street (2001: 22) examines the ways in which bias poses method-ological problems for media researchers. How do we detect bias that is 'submerged' in the content of the media? How do we know bias is intended? He cites the example of the American rap singer Eminem who expresses aggressive and violent attitudes to women in his lyrics. Some argue the singer is being ironic, parodying male attitudes while others say he really means it. How can we know? The difficulties in defining bias and identifying methods to detect it have led a growing number of scholars in the social sciences and humanities to question its usefulness in making sense of media content.

STEREOTYPING

The stereotype is an important concept in media analysis and the effects of stereotyping have long been of concern (Pickering, 2001). The modern concept of stereotyping was developed by Walter Lippmann (1922) who is credited with introducing the term into the social sciences (Pickering, 2001: 17). Lippmann was interested in the reliability of public knowledge, which he saw as ill served by the inadequate provision of information by the media. He used the concept of the stereotype to explain the media's misleading and manipulated representation of the world. Rejecting the view the media deliberately distort what is happening, he argued stereotypes are necessary to make sense of our environment and social relationships. For Lippmann (1965: 60):

> Modern life is hurried and multifarious, above all physical distance separates men [sic] who are often in vital contact with each other, such as employer and employee, official and voter. There is neither time nor opportunity for intimate acquaintance. Instead we notice a trait which marks a well known type, and fill in the rest of the picture by means of the stereotypes which we carry about in our heads.

Stereotypes are essential in order to process the vast array of information flowing around modern society. An individual cannot personally experience the vast majority of events in which they might be interested and thus must rely on their own mental maps in order to make sense of what is going on. These mental maps – the 'pictures in our heads of the world outside' – are composed of different kinds of categories and 'we need categories to group things that are similar in order to study them and to communicate about them' (Lippmann, 1965). Stereotyping is the process of categorisation and Lippmann points out 'we have stereotypes about many categories including mothers, fathers, teenagers, communists, Republicans, school teachers, farmers, construction workers, miners, politicians, Mormons and Italians'. His list is not exhaustive but the point is clear: stereotypes are not only necessary for an individual to understand their environment but central to our ability to communicate with one another.

While stressing the role of the stereotype in the process of communication, Lippmann recognised the limitations of the concept. He regarded stereotyping as 'inadequate and biased, as endorsing the interests of those who use them, as obstacles to rational assessment, and as resistant to social change' (Pickering, 2001: 18). While stereotypes 'may contain some useful and accurate information about a member of a category', Lippmann (1965) recognised that 'each member of any category will have many characteristics that are not suggested by the stereotypes and may even have some characteristics that run counter to some of the stereotypes'. Stereotypes are thus neither neutral nor fair, preventing the examination of differences within groups. This means 'the loss of individualised understanding of other people ... outside our situated experience' (Pickering, 2001: 18). Lippmann's discussion of stereotypes highlights the contradiction between the need to use stereotypes to understand the world and the restrictive view they present of the world. This contradiction is at the heart of using the concept to explore the nature of media representations.

Lippmann's conceptualisation of the stereotype has been widely adopted by social scientists, media researchers and lay people. The importance of the concept to media representation is seen as being accentuated by the rise of television and the growing pressure to fill more and more hours with material. Theodor Adorno, a member of the Frankfurt School, noted in the 1950s how the technology of television and the development of standardised formulas for TV drama and entertainment programmes was producing more and more stereotypical characters on the screen. He believed standardisation 'automatically produces a number of stereotypes' and that 'the technology of television production makes stereotypes almost inevitable' as 'the short time available for the preparation for scripts and the vast material continuously to be produced calls for certain formulas' and 'since stereotypes are an indispensable element of the organisation and anticipation of experience, preventing us from falling into mental disorganisation and chaos, no art can entirely dispense with them' (Adorno, 1957). Stereotypes came to be seen as an unavoidable part of media representations. Early silent films laid down the pattern of stereotypical representation with its need to resort to simple visual representations to communicate effectively with its mainly illiterate and multi-ethnic audience (Branston and Stafford, 1996: 91–2). Such representations emphasised that stereotypes are simple and only open to fixed interpretation. The danger of such representations is that 'people may not only lose true insight into reality, but ultimately their capacity for life experience might be dulled' (Adorno, 1957).

Armed with the concept of the stereotype the media have been criticised for the generalised, partial and selective way in which they have represented different groups, emphasising easily identifiable, unchanging and often negative characteristics (O'Sullivan and Jewkes, 1997: 73). In a world of complexity and ambiguity, media stereotypes may simplify and help us to make sense of the 'confusion of everyday reality', but they can also further misunderstanding and prejudice. Research identifies stereotyping in the media as occurring in three distinct ways. First, the media distorts the 'real' presence or prevalence of a group in society. This can be done by one or more ways. There can be an *under-representation* of a group in the media. An example would be the limited presence of women. Research in 1995 found men outnumber women three to one on prime-time television in the United States (www.media-awareness.ca) The media can *over-represent* by associating a group with one particular kind of activity – for example, the over-reporting of black people in crime news. The media can *misrepresent* by equating a group with a particular activity, such as trades unionists with strikes (see Beharrel and Philo, 1977; Glasgow Media Group, 1976; 1980; 1982). The second kind of media stereotyping is the *narrow and fixed representation* of a whole group of people. Thus media stereotyping occurs when the roles, behaviour or personal characteristics of a particular group are portrayed in a limited fashion. The stereotyping of women in the media occurs when their role in society is represented as either housewives or mothers or sexual objects (Tuchman, 1978: 175). Young black men are stereotyped by linking their behaviour with violent or criminal activity, while gay men have been stereotyped by their portrayal as camp. The final form of media stereotyping is the delegitimising of a group by *comparison with idealised images of how people ought to behave.* Thus a group of people can be marginalised by their portrayal as an unrepresentative minority or denigrated by being presented as abnormal and peculiar, or excluded by only appearing in the media when they present a problem.

Media stereotyping provides false impressions of certain groups and people. Stereotypes are 'less real, more perfect or imperfect and more predictable than their real life counterparts' (www.media-awareness.ca). For example, male stereotyping can narrow perception of what men can and cannot do, can and cannot be, as well as shaping women's and children's expectations of men and men's view of themselves and how they should behave. Viewers, listeners and readers can make erroneous judgements about entire groups, peoples and nations. The stereotyping of children in the media has been a matter of academic research and political concern. Criticism of the media for their perpetuation of stereotypes has resulted in media professionals becoming more sensitive to their portrayal of certain groups. But in media theory it has led some to question the whole notion of the stereotype.

Children and media stereotyping

A number of organisations of different political persuasions have documented their concerns about the media's representation of children and have sought to influence media practitioners to change their practices. In America Children Now and Alliance for Child and Television and in Europe Children's Express have complained about the media stereotyping of children. In a conference organised by Children's Express in 1998 a survey of over 400 stories about children in the British press identified 'seven deadly stereotypes' (www.media-awareness.ca). Nearly a third of the stories portrayed children as victims while a quarter 'used cute kids to sell the story'. Kids were also represented as 'little devils', 'accessories' and 'brave little angels'. The 'kids these days' stories — for example, children corrupted by computers — seemed designed to cause adults to mutter 'it wasn't like that in my day'.

Nearly half the stories portrayed children negatively, more than a tenth demonised them. But even positive stories caused problems. 'Kids are brilliant' stories — those concentrating on kids as precocious over-achievers — were seen by some children as having an impact on their self-esteem. Journalists present at the conference acknowledged some of the criticisms made. An associate editor of the Independent newspaper spoke of the 'sin of omission' he committed in doing a big story about parents trying to get their children into good state schools

– he wrote the story without talking to a single child. Similar findings emerge from a report on American television commissioned by Children Now (www.childrennow.org).

Children called for the media to change the ways in which they report and represent children. Children's Express provided a number of suggestions as to how journalists, for example, could improve their practice and hence their product. They asked journalists to give children a say in the stories, listen to what they say, talk to representatives of children's groups, involve children in setting up interviews and consult children more on a range of issues in society (www.media-awareness.ca). Journalists at the conference responded favourably but pointed out the problems they face from time and space pressures in their work, which could prevent them from doing many of these things.

The vast amount of literature searching out stereotyping in the media rarely if ever bothers to provide any precise definition of the concept itself. The term 'stereotype' is largely seen as unproblematic. It is used to indicate representations that are misleading or offensive; as representations they are frozen or fixed so as to fuel social prejudices, and they delineate the boundaries of acceptable behaviour in the society, marginalising those who do not fully belong (Glover, 1984: 27). Perkins (1979) outlines the commonly held assumptions of the nature and purpose of stereotypes: they are always untrue, pejorative, simple, rigid, about groups we have little or no contact with, about minority or marginalised groups. The most commonly held assumptions about stereotypes can be summed up as they are false or unreal, always derogatory or negative, directed at minority or powerless groups and reinforce prejudices against these groups. However, several scholars have pointed out the limitations of the concept. Some identify shortcomings in the way in which stereotypes are normally believed to operate, challenging the assumptions they are simple, untrue, secondhand and resistant to change (Perkins, 1979), while others go further arguing the stereotype is a 'useless tool for investigating media texts' (Barker, 1989). On closer scrutiny the complexity of the term and its usage becomes more apparent.

Perkins (1979) draws attention to the erroneous claims about stereotypes. She rejects many of the ideas held about stereotypes in academic scholarship and 'everyday' life. She argues stereotypes are not always false or untrue, citing evidence that refutes claims of total inaccuracy of stereotypes. Thus while not all gay men are flamboyant and effeminate, such traits do represent some in the gay community. Similarly some businessmen do wear pinstripe suits and smoke cigars, and many cowboys do wear stetsons and boots. There is a 'kernel of truth' in stereotypes, which provides them with their effectiveness as forms of representation. It is also interesting to speculate whether social groups take on particular stereotypes in order to identify themselves (Goodwin, 1988). Perkins also notes that stereotypes are not always negative. For example, the kindly old family doctor in many television series can be seen as a positive stereotype. The French are stereotyped as 'good cooks' and 'great lovers'. Some stereotypes can be seen as both negative and positive, depending on who is asked. They are also not only about groups we have little contact with but can be held about one's own group and influence one's own behaviour. It is not only marginal or disadvantaged groups that are stereotyped. According to Perkins there are stereotypes of all groups in society: 'there is a male (he-man) stereotype, a White Anglo-Saxon Protestant (WASP) stereotype, a heterosexual stereotype, an upper-class leader stereotype' and so on. Perkins also notes while stereotypes are resistant to change over time they, like all concepts, are not fixed and totally resistant to modification. Thus the camp, effeminate image of a gay man mutated into the macho, leather-clad, moustached gay man. The task is to identify the conditions under which this happens. Perkins' influential analysis emphasises that stereotypes are never simple and straightforward. Her critique of the common-sense approaches to stereotypes led her to offer a far more complex and rich outline of the concept. She defines stereotyping as a group concept, in that it is held by a social group about another social group, which results in a simple structure, that often hides complexity, based on an 'inferior judgement process' that downplays rational assessments (Goodwin, 1988).

Barker (1989) also sees contradictions in the concept. He stresses stereotypes are criticised for both misrepresenting the world and for representing things as they are. Thus the representation of women in the media is condemned for reinforcing false stereotypes such as 'women want sex at any time' but also for showing women in the domestic setting, working in the household, which 'is in fact true that very many do'. To be effective stereotypes either 'have to block our perceiving the world as it really is' or 'to stop us seeing anything but the world as it is'. By seeing stereotypes as inaccurate and a distortion as well as natural and normal, Barker believes the concept is seriously flawed. It also serves to prevent us examining the social conflict and inequality that lie behind media representations. It leads to an argument about the need to replace negative stereotypes with more positive forms of representation, which hides more fundamental questions, such as why are groups and peoples represented in particular ways and who has the power to shape such representations. Barker and Perkins highlight the problematic nature of the concept of the stereotype. It is 'remarkably loose and ill-defined' and, after 60 years of usage in media studies and sociology, remains elusive on definition (Goodwin, 1988). But even if it is possible to produce a commonly agreed definition there are still a number of problems in how we apply the concept.

Much of the examination of stereotypes is steeped in the assumption that it is 'wrong to present people as "representatives of categories"' (Barker, 1989). Yet it is recognised by social sciences that to make sense of the world some form of categorisation or typification is essential. All forms of human communication rely on 'common structures of meaning', that is we all make use of common signs and symbols, spoken, written and visual, in order to communicate with one another and make sense of the environment in which we all live. Such signs and symbols can vary from society to society but shared typifications or categorisation of groups is essential to the process of communication. The media are one of the most important sources of collective representations, and they must habitually mobilise typifications and categorisations in order to communicate. Communication would be impossible if we did not possess some categories and typifications to describe the social world. Some scholars distinguish between the 'normal' form of typification needed for communication and stereotypes. Dyer (1977) makes a distinction between 'stereotype' and 'social type'. A social type is 'any simple, vividly memorable, easily grasped and widely recognised characterisation in which a few traits are fore-grounded and change or "development" is kept to a minimum'. He argues social typing refers to simplified representations of those who belong to society. Stereotypes, on the other hand, are 'exclusionary', marking out those who are different, the 'outsiders' or the 'Other'. By attributing particular characteristics stereotypes are designed to exclude certain groups or people. By laying down boundaries between the normal – us – and the aberrant or deviant – them – stereotypes are part of the exercise of power in society. While typifications or categorisations are essential to communication, stereotypes are part of the perpetuation of social inequalities. The problem is determining the point at which a necessary typification or categorisation becomes a stereotype.

Others argue the concept of stereotyping in media studies often prevents exploration of the deeper causes of representation in the media. Too often media research is satisfied with simply documenting the existence of stereotypes. The causes of stereotyping are taken as self-evident. They are attributed to the prejudices, ignorance or attitudes of media practitioners. The remedy is straightforward. The removal of stereotypes and the provision of more positive representations as well as the employment of more people from these groups in the media and cultural industries is the remedy. Homophobic, racist and sexist representation can be challenged by such measures. Such assumptions, however, are seen as limiting possible explanations for how the media represent the world. They prevent us from engaging with the range of influences on the media production process as well as examining why groups are misrepresented and who has the power to misrepresent them. Simply saying women, the aged and Islam are stereotyped does not enable us to analyse the working of sexism, ageism and Islamophobia in the media. There is a tendency to generalise about media stereotyping, as if stereotypes apply across all media. As media operate in different ways the possibility of stereotypes being constructed in ways specific to particular media must be acknowledged. The press may stereotype Asian people but there may be exceptions. The reasons and explanation as to why some media might stereotype more than others requires examination. The pressure of time, space and deadlines as well as the need to achieve rapid audience recognition make the media particularly prone to the manufacture of stereotypes. The media are highly compressed forms of communication, having limited time or space to convey information. The result is a disposition to caricature everybody and everything so that even powerful people such as politicians may suffer from stereotyping. Research has pointed to the ways in which the conventions and codes of news production, and the nature of news values such as the search for 'extraordinariness' generate stereotypes (see O'Sullivan *et al.*, 1994). The search for the lowest common denominator of meaning for a mass audience also makes the media more likely to produce stereotypes.

The concepts of 'bias' and 'stereotyping' are problematic at a number of levels. Perhaps the most significant question that emerges from attempts to apply these concepts to understanding media content is the nature of the relationship between representation and reality. Both 'bias' and the "stereotype" rest on a theory of knowledge that assumes there is an objective reality out there by which the veracity or truthfulness or accuracy of media representations can be judged (see Lichtenberg, 2000: 239). Critics argue such a theory is not only outmoded and outdated but also untenable. Post-modernists, social constructionists and cultural theorists see objectivity as 'a false and impossible ideal' on the grounds there is 'no "true reality" to which objective knowledge can be faithful' (see Lichtenberg, 2000: 238–9). They reject the view there is an independent truth against which media representations can be assessed, arguing representations should not be seen as reflections of reality but as cultural constructions, produced in the context of social power, with which individuals have to interact in their everyday life, either by realising or resisting them. Allan (1995) argues the yardstick of objectivity does not take us very far, locking media research into a very limited means of accounting for the nature of news messages. On the other hand, Lichtenberg (2000: 256) believes 'we cannot get along without assuming both the possibility and value of objectivity' if we aim to understand the world. This difference has sparked off a debate about the relationship between representation and reality, and whether concepts such as bias and objectivity are completely redundant in any attempt to explain the content of media messages. In the process critics have come up with a number of other concepts to assess the content of the media.

Social construction of reality

Berger and Luckmann (1967) in their classic work, The Social Construction of Reality, state that: 'Reality is social defined. But the definitions are always embodied, that is, concrete individuals and groups of individuals serve as definers of reality. To understand the state of the social constructed universe [of meaning] at any given time, or its change over time, one must understand the social organisation that permits the definers to do their defining. Put a little crudely, it is essential to keep pushing questions about the historically available conceptualisations of reality from the abstract "what?" to the sociologically concrete "says who?".'

GENRE THEORY

Those who emphasise the role of the media in the 'construction' of reality often focus on the practices adopted in the media production process as shaping the nature of representation. Despite apparent diversity, the output of the media can be divided into a number of particular kinds of product. The development of formats and formulas to manage the risks of production is a common feature of the media industries. The media encourage formulas or formats by which products with a good chance of success in the market-place can easily be manufactured (Turow, 1997: 184–6, 218–25). Formulas are 'widely recognised principles for selecting and organising material', which provide media practitioners with 'a patterned approach to content which many parties working in a mass media industry agree contain the elements of success' (Turow, 1997: 218). They encourage organisational continuity and consistency while not necessarily stifling the creative dimension of media work. Creators are provided with comfortable moulds, within which stories can be explored while the essence of characterisation, setting and even patterns of action remain the same (Turow, 1997: 218–9). Formulas, it is argued, 'actively shape content' (Tiffen, 1989: 64). The study of these formulas – labelled as 'genres' from the French word meaning 'type' or 'kind' – has become a central part of contemporary media studies.

Genre analysis in literature has a long tradition. The Greek philosopher Aristotle divided the plays of his time into different types, such as tragedy, comedy, drama, epic and lyric, in order to assess whether performances adhered to the conventions of their type. His categorisation became the standard means of assessing classical value in European art (Branston and Stafford, 1996: 57). It was only introduced into the study of media representation in the 1960s as part of film studies (see Neale, 2000). The cinema industry very early on organised film-making around a combination of predictable elements and familiar formats in order to standardise the production and marketing of films and to guide audiences in their viewing of them (see Maltby, 1995). Hollywood developed formulas for producing blockbuster films, such as the western, gangster film, the musical, the horror film, the romance, the melodrama and the comedy. These different film genres utilised an 'easily recognisable repertoire of conventions running across visual imagery, plot, character, setting, modes of narrative development, music and stars', which 'enabled the industry to predict audience expectation' (Cook, 1987: 58). However, genres are able to provide audiences with something different from previous films because they are flexible enough to accommodate variation. According to Maltby (1995: 113) genres offer 'durable frames of reference but they also accommodate change: the variations in plot, characterisation or setting in each imitation inflect the audiences' generic expectations by introducing new elements or transgressing old ones'. Genres fulfil the need for repetition and difference, which became central to the development of the Hollywood studio system.

Genre analysis in film criticism lagged behind the development of such conventions in the film production process (Cook, 1987: 58). Early film criticism and theory had an 'overly individualistic emphasis' (Taylor and Willis, 1999: 61). Referred to as 'auteur theory', the focus was on individual artists, in particular the directors, whose work was discussed in the same way as the 'great masters' of painting and literature. There was growing dissatisfaction with auteur analysis of film products for its tendency 'to treat popular art as if it were 'high culture'' (Ryall, 1975: 28). The lag is also attributable to intellectual hostility to the study of popular art forms such as the cinema. Genre criticism allows the analysis of film texts by the exploration of the 'patterns/forms/styles/structures which transcend the individual films and which supervise both their construction by the film-maker, and their reading by an audience' (Ryall, 1975: 28). As a means of studying content, genre analysis focuses on the interaction between the text, the producer of the text and the audience – in other words between artist, film and audience (Abercrombie, 1996: Chapter 3). The industrial context within which film artists work, as well as the need to respond to audience expectations and collaborate with colleagues, distinguishes genre study from auteur criticism. Crucially the particular rules, codes and conventions of each film genre are seen as determinants of the content of films and the meaning we attach to them.

Meaning in film genres is generated through a number of devices, including setting, plot, character, themes and iconography. Genre analysis emphasises the importance of understanding film as a visual medium. It is through what is seen on the screen that people's understanding of what films are about is shaped. Iconography refers to 'the visual motifs that allow audiences to identify certain films as belonging to particular genres' (Taylor and Willis, 1999: 61). Viewers obtain understanding and information about characters, narratives, action, plots and what is going on from visual signs in the form of costumes, physical attributes, deportment, clothes, sets, familiar objects and so on. They know what to expect when they see particular icons or signs. Thus the western can be identified as a result of a number of basic visual codes such as cowboy hats, guns, saloons, saloon brawls, card games, stage coaches, horses, jails, bank robberies, dusty or windy dirt streets, gunfights, rifles, saddlebags, posses, sheriffs, chases, so-called Red Indians and so on, from which our expectations are that certain conflicts, characters, storylines and outcomes will result. It is also argued that there is an underlying structure of values that can be recognised in particular genres. Thus the western is often about 'the conflict between nature and culture, embodied in competing images of eastern and western life' (Grossberg *et al.*, 1998: 161) or the struggle between individual and community or wilderness and civilisation or good and evil. Genre analysis is about identifying the codes and conventions of a genre and examining how a particular example of that genre 'embodies the features of the genre as well as how it reshapes them, how it defines its own individuality and uniqueness within that genre and even how it transforms that genre itself' (Grossberg *et al.*, 1998: 161).

Genre analysis is associated with the study of moving images (Hansen *et al.*, 1998: Chapter 7) but has increasingly been applied to other media forms. News is seen as constructed around a particular formula, which is implicitly part of the working assumptions of all news producers (see Bell, 1991; Fowler, 1991). The conventions of the news story, its ordering and presentation, its narrative structure, have been shown to shape not only what becomes news but also how it is presented (see Gans, 1979; Schudson, 1995). Formulas also exist for the popular romantic novel, so successfully captured by Mills and Boon, the pornographic movie, the popular song, as well as other media products. Negus (1999: 4) explores 'the way in which musical categories and systems of classification shape the music we might play and listen to, mediating both the experience of music and its formal organisation by an entertainment industry'. From his experience of being a musician he found that failure to conform to the codes, expectations and boundaries of musical genres resulted in gigs not being booked and tapes not being listened to. His audiences or fans also judged his music in terms of the category they believed it fell into. He concludes most musical production involves musicians working within relatively stable musical genres in which creative practice is less about 'sudden bursts of innovation' and more about the 'continual production of familiarity' (Negus, 1999: 25). The task of analysis is to identify and delineate the rules – creative, behavioural, economic and social – that shape the activity of musicians and their audiences. Television in particular is regarded as a medium that operates generically (see Abercrombie, 1996). Soaps, serials, news, current affairs, police series, sitcoms, talk shows, documentaries and quiz or game shows are amongst the formats that can be seen as constituting television genres. The boundaries between these genres are apparently secure and the expectations of the TV audience are satisfied as they become used to seeing particular kinds of programmes. For critics this makes TV an uncreative medium. The emphasis on repetition outweighs that of difference. TV practitioners are seen as choosing to work within these structures that emphasise security over innovation and creativity. However, many writers, directors and actors in television see the strict set of rules guiding TV genres as allowing them the opportunity to develop their talents (Abercrombie, 1996: 43).

Genre analysis can take place at a number of levels. From her study of television genres, Feuer (1987: 119) identifies three distinct approaches to genre study – the aesthetic, the ritual and the ideological. The aesthetic approach examines genres in terms of the degree of artistic expression they allow and whether the work of individual authors or practitioners transcends its genre. The ritual approach sees genres as exchanges between industry and audience, which involves the negotiation of shared beliefs and values. Genres are analysed as forms of cultural expression, how society speaks to itself through the negotiation of the commercial and production needs of industry and the wants and desires of the audience. Popular genres are seen as reflecting the moods, sentiments and values of the society (see Strinati, 2000). The ideological approach analyses genres as vehicles for the reproduction of dominant ideologies such as capitalism, nationalism, individualism, sexism, racism and class structure (Hansen *et al.*, 1998: 183). Thus meaning is constrained within genres by what is acceptable in ideological terms (see Chapter 6). Each of these approaches wrestles with the problem of establishing the boundaries between different genres. Abercrombie (1996) highlights the fluidity of genres. The conventions of genres change over time. He contrasts TV police series of the 1950s with those of today; if *Dixon of Dock Green* struggled with criminals, the heroes of *Between the Lines* battle against bureaucracy, political corruption and their colleagues. More recently ITV's *The Bill* and American series such as *Hill Street Blues* and *NYPD Blue* have put the private and personal world of police officers at the centre of their story-lines. This seems to blur the distinction between police series and soap operas, which are supposed to focus on the private, the domestic and the personal. The rigid distinction between factual and fictional programming is also seen as breaking down as TV news and documentaries have adopted mechanisms from fictional formats to present and report the news and current affairs.

There is a problem of identifying and recognising particular genres. Some scholars see the existence of genres as being self-evident whereas others draw attention to the difficulty of distinguishing between them. Tudor (1974) argues it is far from easy to determine where one film genre stops and another begins. As he put it:

> . . . most writers tend to assume that there is some body of films we can safely call the western and then move on to the real work – the analysis of the crucial characteristics of the already recognised genre . . . these writers and almost all writers using the term genre are caught in a dilemma. They are defining a western on the basis of analysing a body of films that cannot possibly be said to be westerns until after the analysis . . . to take a genre such as the western, analyse it and list its principal characteristics is to beg the question that we must first isolate the body of films that are westerns.

If it is not possible to precisely define what constitutes a genre and the demarcation between genres is unclear then there are questions as to whether it is possible to identify precise codes and conventions governing particular genres. Addressing the problem of delineating individual film genres Neale (1980) suggests we should not concentrate on genres as collections of texts with common features but explore them in the broader context of 'the social process of cinema as a whole' (Cook, 1987: 63). He is more interested in exploring how and why genres change in relation to what audiences want and will accept, and what the industry is prepared to provide. Rather than concentrate on the texts themselves Neale draws our attention to innovation and difference in genres and the exchange between those involved in the process of media-making.

NARRATIVE THEORY

Narrative theory examines the ways in which storytelling frames the content and meaning of media messages. Storytelling – narrative – is central to how people communicate their understanding of the world, and stories are seen as the primary means by which we construct meaning about the world around us. For subscribers to narrative theory, storytelling is at the heart of all human interaction. We tell stories about what has happened to explain events and issues. We tell stories about ourselves and even without an audience we organise in our heads narratives to help interpret and impose some kind of order on the multitude of things we see and hear. The media, like any other form of communication, organise their products around narratives – whether it is in the lyrics of popular songs, the talk of talk shows or the stories in newspapers. While particular media may tell their stories in different ways, all media, factual and fictional, are involved in constructing narratives. Thus the news is as much a process of storytelling as any fictional media form. Journalists are always looking for the 'story' to package information about the issues and events of the day. 'Storytelling ... is a key way which unites journalism and popular culture' (Dahlgren and Sparks, 1992: 14) If storytelling is ubiquitous in media and society, narrative theory suggests that stories, whoever tells them, are governed by certain features. Studying the devices that underpin the organisation of the story is central to narrative analysis.

Much of the theorising of the structure and organisation of stories and how they shape the nature of meaning is rooted in the work of a Russian folklorist Vladimir Propp in the 1920s. He examined hundreds of folk tales to see if they shared any similarities in their structures. He found that in spite of the differences in the tales and their events, certain kinds of characters and occurrences appeared regularly. He identified 31 devices or 'functions', which were used in different ways to move the story along in a predictable order, and eight character roles – or 'spheres of action' as he called them – that were common to all narrative to perform these functions. Propp reduced 'the apparent complexity of a great number of stories to a simple set of underlying narrative elements that could be combined in a strictly limited number of ways' (Lorimer, 1994: 191). While Propp's work may seem somewhat dated today – for example, in the gender assumptions of his hero – his attempt to expose the underlying structures of the most popular stories of his day are still pertinent. Fiske's examination of popular TV formats found they closely adhered to Propp's functions and spheres of action (Fiske, 1987). Other theorists developed Propp's work. The anthropologist Claude Lévi-Strauss identified the importance of opposition in the development of narrative structures. He argues stories move from one stage to another by positing a conflict between two opposing elements or qualities that characters have to resolve. This clash of 'binary oppositions' organises the narrative. The *Guardian* (23 January 1991) provided examples of how such binary oppositions shaped the whole reporting of the Gulf War in the British press in 1991. The West was represented as 'good' and the Iraqis as 'evil'. While the West had 'reporting guidelines' and 'press briefings', Iraq

141

had 'censorship' and 'propaganda'. The West's weapons caused 'collateral damage' while Iraq's weapons resulted in 'civilian casualties'. In this case the binary oppositions were used to structure a narrative that privileged the West not Iraq. The same oppositions were seen in the NATO bombing of Serbia in 1999 and the destruction of the World Trade Center in New York and the subsequent US incursion into Afghanistan in 2001.

Propp's spheres of action

Propp, in his book Morphology of the Folk Tale (1928), identified a group of characters common to the narratives of the folk tales he examined who perform certain functions essential to the development of the story. They are: the hero/subject whose function is the seeker; the villain who opposes the hero; the donor who provides an object to assist the seeker in his quest; the dispatcher who provides information to launch the hero on his journey; the false hero who is mistaken for the hero as the person to solve the problem; the helper who assists the hero; the princess who is the reward for the hero and the object of the villain's evil plans; and finally the father who rewards the hero.

Barthes sees narrative working with different kinds of codes, which direct the reader in making sense of the story. Todorov (1977) argues that narrative is all about the disruption of an equilibrium and the consequences of that disruption for a range of characters until a new equilibrium is constituted. Meaning emerges from how the equilibrium is set up, that is the conditions making up the status quo, the nature of the events or actions that disrupt the status quo, who is responsible for the changes and what has changed and what is lost or gained with the establishment of a new equilibrium. All these theorists – albeit in different ways – believe it is possible not only to unravel all the ties and threads that hold narratives together but also to identify the patterns of meaning that are produced. While different media will tell stories in different ways, often to do with the material of the particular medium – for example, sound, drawings, photographs, image and sound, and words alone result in the narrative being constructed differently – there are basic structures that 'seem to govern all story making and all story telling' (see Branston and Strafford, 1996: Chapter 3). The construction of a narrative involves 'processes of selection and organisation which structure and order the material narrated so that it can be invested with significance and meaning' (Alvarado *et al.*, 1987: 120). The purpose of narrative analysis is, then, to unpick how the narrative is constructed to identify the meaning of the event or story.

Barthes codes

Barthes, in his book S/Z, proposed the meaning of particular texts is produced through five 'codes of intelligibility'. The hermeneutic code is the sets of cues that initiate, develop and resolve the narrative. When we want to know what happens next, we are responding to this code. The proairetic code – or code of action – consists of the range of actions that move the narrative forward, from entering a room to our hero being chased by the baddies. The cultural code – sometimes called the referential code – relates to our common-sense, which provides the narrative with plausibility. The semic code organises all the cues that relate to character and place in the narrative. The use of language and physical appearance, as well as lighting and camera angles play their part in this process. Finally there is the symbolic code, which organises the binary oppositions that are deemed important in any particular culture. Barthes identified these codes from a detailed analysis of a short novel by the French writer Balzac. (See Fiske, 1987: 142–3; Cook, 1987: 160; Watson, 1998: 138–40 for details of Barthes' narrative codes.)

Narrative theory – as well as genre theory – is anchored in structuralism, which assumes there are key structures that underpin all social phenomena and social activities. These 'deep structures' are seen to operate in all cultures and apply whatever the medium. These structures are seen as constraining the author in what he or she can say. Media texts – as narrative and genre theorists label the content of the media – are thus not the product of the author but a reflection of the structures and devices that underpin the process of story-telling and the nature of the genre. For them the objective is to discover the underlying pattern of single texts as well as genres. Some structuralists proclaim the 'death of the author'. Barthes argues that texts only become meaningful in the process of consumption. The meaning of texts is not to be found in identifying what the author intends but in what readers, viewers and listeners bring to the text. The empowerment of audiences (see Chapter 8) became a feature of this approach to media representation. Media texts came to be seen as open to a range of different meanings. The term 'polysemic' refers to the notion that any message can have a variety of interpretations – or in the language of narrative and genre analysis, can have a range of possible 'readings'. However, it is open to question whether texts have limitless meaning as it is argued there are 'preferred' readings incorporated into the text. Analysis of media content as a result became a matter of understanding not only how things are told but also how they are interpreted. This is a long way from the approach of social science and its attempts to assess the truth or otherwise of media representation. It is not surprising scholars involved in this approach come primarily from the disciplines of literature and the humanities. Their focus is on texts and their readers, which contrasts with social scientists who locate their analysis of media content within the broader context of how messages are formed and transmitted (Lorimer, 1994: Chapter 8). Genre and narrative analysis are concerned not with objective reality but with the subjective world of readers and texts. By casting what is seen as a narrower net they often ignore the social world.

SUMMARY

This chapter has examined some of the different theoretical approaches to understanding and assessing the nature of media content. Two distinct ways of understanding the picture of the world represented in the media are identified. Concepts such as 'bias' and 'stereotyping' are based on measuring what appears in the media against the yardstick of 'reality'. Often the discussion can be couched in terms of whether the media are 'telling the truth' or 'accurately' reflecting what is going on, or presenting a realistic picture of events. However, claiming the real is seen as problematic. Not all media seek to portray what is going on. Drama, film and cartoons, for example, are media that ask us to suspend our sense of the 'real' and enter the world of the imagination, even though such media forms can be and are used to comment on contemporary issues and situations. What is the 'real'? How are we to assess what constitutes the 'real world'? Some argue that no representation of reality can ever be real. All representations are the product of processes of selection, which include some aspects of reality and exclude others. Others argue 'social facts' do exist by which we can make judgements about media representations. Increasingly those who reject the existence of an objective reality are being heard in the analysis of media content. Reality is a social construction, and representation should be seen as the process by which reality is constructed. In other words, representation is reality. Concepts such as genre and narrative enable us to examine how media messages are constructed or manufactured, and the factors that shape the production of meaning.

Chapter Six

WAYS OF MAKING YOU THINK: ▢ THEORIES OF IDEOLOGY AND MEANING

Media theory has speculated about the extent to which a coherent and unified view of the world emerges from the content of the media. To what extent does the range of meanings incorporated into media representations constitute a particular way of seeing the world? Is there an underlying and coherent set of values and beliefs that characterise media representations of the world? Do the media prescribe particular ways of thinking about social problems and their solutions? Do the media articulate appropriate ways of thinking and behaving? Is there a consistent pattern to the bias and stereotyping observed in the media's coverage of events? Do the media construct specific meaning through genres and narratives? Are the media vehicles for carrying and conveying ideas of one group of people rather than others? Such questions are tied up in the concept of ideology. Examining the role of the media in the reproduction of ideology is an attempt to uncover the values, beliefs and interests underlying media representation. Despite the concept of 'ideology' being a matter of considerable debate and dispute (see Van Dijk, 1998) and a 'decidely complicated term with different implications' (Croteau and Hoynes, 1997: 163) it has become centrally important to the study of the media. Media scholars have, for example, examined whether the media represent a particular view of men and women, gay and straight, workers and managers, young and old, rich and poor, politicians and voters, and whose interests are served by this view.

Efforts to identify the ideological role of the media throw up a number of problems. Perhaps the most important is that of meaning. How do we make sense of what is in the media? People are often in dispute over the meaning of the messages transmitted by the media. Often communication in everyday life breaks down because people have not understood what they have heard or seen. Individuals can interpret the meaning of issues, events, and even objects and symbols differently. They can make their own meaning out of what they see, hear and read. But how free are they to make any meaning they want? To what extent are they constrained by cultural and social factors? History, tradition, ways of life, and language are a few of the limitations placed on people in their efforts to find meaning. The media are centrally concerned with the production of meaning. Their attempts to provide meaning are located within a broader cultural context and any enquiry into whether they perform an ideological role must address this. The intellectual

tensions and arguments around meaning in the media have led to new ways of conceptualising the ideological power of the media, in particular the development of the notion of
'discourse', as well as debates between scholars over the most appropriate method to
analyse what is in the media.

DEFINING IDEOLOGY

The concept of ideology is a matter of much debate amongst social scientists (see
Eagleton, 1991). The French philosopher, Destutt de Tracy, first used the term in the
eighteenth century to describe the systematic study or science of ideas (Van Dijk,
1998: 1). Confusion has arisen from how the term has been politically and popularly
used since this time (Thompson, 1990). Many employ ideology as a pejorative term to
label what they see as the erroneous and misguided views of their opponents (see
Larrain, 1979). The term is taken to mean, 'a system of wrong, false, distorted or
otherwise misguided beliefs, typically associated with our social or political opponents'
(Van Dijk, 1998: 2). During the Cold War America and the Soviet Union described
each other's views as ideological. Marxism was the ideology that justified the power of
the Kremlin while free enterprise upheld the business and military interests exercising
power in the American system. Ideology is often used as a term of abuse, applied to
views considered dangerous and a threat to people's well-being. More recently ideology has been used to suggest a 'strong emotional or psychological attachment to
biased ideas' as in the case of religious fundamentalism, which is seen as being
'beyond the reach of any reasoned challenge' (O'Connor and Downing, 1995: 18).
The assumption made in such usage is that ideologies are false and self-serving, and if
they were removed the people who adhere to them would see the truth or reality of
situations. Ideology is a difficult concept to deal with because of the strong, negative
association the term has for many people.

As a neutral concept ideology is supposed to describe 'systems of thought' or 'systems of
belief' or 'symbolic systems' pertaining to social action or political practice. As a result ideology is seen as being 'present in every political programme and is a feature of every
organised political movement' and the task of the analyst is to 'delineate and describe the
major systems of thought or belief which animate social and political action'. Such inquiry
leads into a world of 'isms' – such as conservatism, liberalism, communism, materialism,
capitalism, Thatcherism, Reaganism or even Blairism. Such 'isms', or systems of thought
or belief or values, are seen as open to categorisation. They can be unpacked into their
distinctive constituent parts without making any pejorative judgement about the view of
the world they put forward. The word 'system' is crucial to delineating ideology. Not all
ideas or beliefs can be considered as ideology. McLennan (1991a) argues that in order for
a set of ideas or beliefs to be 'ideological' they need to be shared by a significant number
of people, form a coherent system and must connect to the use of power in society. The
problem is how do we recognise ideology in practice.

Ideology is centrally concerned with the notion of power between people and groups. Some people and groups are seen as having the power to impose their view or understanding of the world on others. They use their ideological power – their ability to represent the world in a given way – to prevent other individuals and groups from obtaining a true picture of the world. This is how Marx used the term in developing his notion of false consciousness (see Chapter 1). He explained the inability of working people to recognise the true conditions of their existence by their adoption of the beliefs and values of the dominant class in society, the bourgeoisie. Marx referred to the creation of false needs to divert people's attention from the exploitative nature of capitalism. Advertising, for example, persuades people they need the products manufactured by capitalism. He used the term 'fetishism' to describe the cultivation of people's need for commodities. Such a state of affairs explains why many working people do not support political ideas or causes that promise an improvement in their conditions of existence. Classical – or vulgar as it is sometimes called – Marxism views ideology as the product of class. The ruling or dominant ideas in society are those of the bourgeoisie, serving their economic and class interests. The emphasis on individualism and the free market in bourgeois ideology is the result of their economic interests. Ideology is deliberately and consciously produced by this class and passed on to other classes through the media and other social institutions (see Chapter 3). The implication is clear: ideology is manufactured by those at the top of society and distributed to the rest of society who are presented with a false picture of the world. For Marx the media are willing vehicles in the reproduction of the dominant ideology.

Media theory increasingly focused on the role of the media in promoting, elevating or legitimating the dominant ideology in the late 1960s and 1970s. However, it was in the context of a more critical approach to the Marxist concept of false consciousness. The notion of false consciousness was found wanting by a variety of commentators on a number of grounds. It does not include any possibility for groups to resist and produce counter-ideologies. Subgroups and subcultures in society have throughout history resisted the voice of the powerful and often reacted spontaneously against the dominant ideology. Working-class people's attitudes are often based on contradictory beliefs and values. Marxism itself is a coherent ideology that runs counter to the ideology of the bourgeoisie. How did Marxism develop if the media and other social institutions simply reproduced the views and values of the bourgeoisie? Marx is also criticised for portraying the dominant ideology of the bourgeoisie as a unitary and coherent set of ideas. Such a view ignores the fact that struggles and contradictions occur within the bourgeoisie and within the dominant ideology. Capitalists quarrel amongst themselves – competition is in fact inherent in the system – and the ruling class is composed of different groups, with different economic interests and political beliefs. Hence different positions can be found on topics such as education, welfare and trade within the ruling class. There is also concern about the pre-eminent role attached to 'class' in shaping and accounting for human behaviour. Other factors can be seen as equally important, if not more important, than class in influencing how people see themselves and their position in the world – factors such as age, gender, ethnicity, religion, race and nationality. The neo-Marxist perspective on media theory in the 1960s and 1970s was based on a re-evaluation of the concept of ideology. This was a reaction to the deterministic and totalising nature of the classical Marxist notion of ideology, which reduced everything in society to its economic base. Two key thinkers in this process of re-evaluation were Gramsci and Althusser.

IDEOLOGICAL STATE APPARATUSES

Gramsci and Althusser took issue with Marx's view that social and political institutions, including the state, and their interactions, as well as the ideas, values and beliefs of a society, are solely determined by the economic organisation of society (see Chapter 2). They both argue that the superstructure of society has some degree of autonomy from its economic base and the relationship between ideas and economic and class interests is not straightforward. The institutions charged with the task of imparting ideology, such as the media, the education system and the Church, have relative independence in how they operate. In fact this independence plays a crucial role in their ability to gain popular acceptance or consent for the dominant values of society. Althusser drew attention to how the media and other ideological state apparatuses work to reproduce the dominant ideology and the part ideology played in people's everyday lives. He was interested in understanding the mechanisms and means by which the ruling class ruled as well as how the dominant ideology shaped people's perceptions of the world.

Althusser defined ideology as the 'representation of the imaginary relationship of individuals with the real conditions of their existence'. The media manufacture an imaginary picture of the real conditions of capitalism for their audiences thereby hiding the true nature of their exploitation. Unlike Marx he did not see ideology as 'false' but something that structured people's 'lived experience'. Ideology has real consequences for people; it plays a part in their everyday lives. It is not just about ideas or a mental state but something tangible and material in that it is carried out by groups and individuals, and inscribed in the practices and rituals of various institutions or apparatuses. He argued that ideological state apparatuses are responsible for constructing the themes and representations through which men and women engage with the real world. This is how they 'play a key part in governing individuals in the interests of the ruling class' (Taylor and Willis, 1999: 31). Repressive state apparatuses such as the police and army who utilise coercive force to maintain the power of the ruling class support them but it is the ideological state apparatuses that are at the forefront of the long-term efforts to maintain power. The main way in which ideological state apparatuses position individuals within society is the process of 'interpellation'. From a very early age individuals are subject to the material practices of ideological state apparatuses, starting with the family, which interpellate or call them into certain positions as to how they should act, behave and think. The output of the media should not be seen as entertainment or news or information but as producing particular forms of consciousness by making available a range of positions to understand the world. This is done in a way that conceals the part the media play in the promotion of these norms and values to ensure they are seen as natural. As Curran *et al.* (1982: 24) put it, 'the effectivity of the media lies not in an imposed false consciousness, nor in a change in attitudes, but in the unconscious categories through which conditions are represented and experienced'. Influenced by Althusser's work scholars attempted to examine how certain ideas, views and beliefs were made 'real' or legitimised by their representation in the media. This has not always been easy. Althusser's concepts are criticised for being 'extremely abstract and impossible to apply in practice' and the charge is made that Althusserian theory had 'little to say about anything but ideology' (McDonnell and Robins, 1980: 156). As a result his work, which dominated discussion of ideology in the late 1960s and early 1970s, has fallen out of fashion. It is Gramsci's concept of hegemony – which Althusser drew on heavily in developing his thinking – that has come to exert more influence over the contemporary approach to ideology and the media.

Interpellation

Althusser does not believe that the individual is a self-conscious, autonomous being whose actions can be explained by personal beliefs, intentions, preferences and so on. Rather he sees individuals as subjects constituted as a result of pre-given structures. He introduces the concept of 'interpellation' to describe the process by which individuals are constituted as subjects. Ideology operates to do this. Individuals are interpellated (have social identities conferred on them) through ideological state apparatuses from which people gain their sense of identity as well as their understanding of reality. Like all structuralists Althusser sees the human being as determined by pre-given structures such as language, family relations, cultural conventions and other social forces. Althusser did not concede that the individuals could resist the process of interpellation.

Source: adapted from Althusser, 1971: 162; Chandler, www.aber.ac.uk/media/Documents/marxism; Lapsey and Westlake, 1988

HEGEMONY

Gramsci was troubled by the impression created by classical Marxism that, in crude terms, people are being 'brainwashed' by the dominant class. His theory of hegemony rejects the view of people as passive recipients of the dominant, class ideology of the bourgeoisie. Dominance is not obtained through the simple imposition of the will of the ruling class but by the ability of the ruling class to present itself as the group best equipped to fulfil the interests and goals of other classes, and as a result for society as a whole. Consent has to be earned from the subordinate classes and this involves a continuous process of negotiation to accommodate their views and interests. This means making compromises and granting concessions in order to win legitimacy and maintain equilibrium within the existing fundamental structures of society. However, at 'moments of crisis' when these fundamental structures are severely threatened, Gramsci accepts the dominant class will resort to the use of force to discipline those who do not or will not accept their will. Consent nevertheless is a more effective means of controlling society in the long run than coercion. This chimed with Gramsci's own view of political struggle, which placed emphasis on political education as the means by which people would be able to free themselves from the shackles of oppression. For Gramsci ideology is not something injected into passive subjects who then simply live out the ideas and beliefs assigned to them. Rather it is an area of debate and struggle between dominant and subordinate groups in society. Hegemony 'suggests that subordinate groups accept the ideas, values and leadership of the dominant group not because they are physically or mentally induced to do so, nor because they are ideologically indoctrinated, but because they have reason of their own' (Strinati, 1995: 166). The dominant or ruling group has to work continuously to gain acceptance for its ideology from all members of society, a process that is described as the exercise of moral and cultural leadership.

Like Althusser, Gramsci sees the mobilisation of consent – or the exercise of leadership – taking place through the institutions of civil society: education, church, family and media. As hegemony is constantly fought over to be maintained and secured, such institutions are sites of struggle between hegemonic and counter-hegemonic ideas. They are where consent is won, reproduced and maintained. The media, therefore, do not simply reproduce the views and beliefs of the ruling class but are crucial sites for struggle between competing ideas and beliefs, between rival worldviews and ideologies. By identifying the media as a site of struggle between dominant and subordinate views, Gramsci's theory of hegemony provides a more dynamic view of the institutions, role and practices of the media than Althusser's ideological state apparatus. Unlike Althusser, he emphasises the notion of struggle. More crucially, he departs from Althusser's conceptualisation of the dominant ideology as permanent and unalterable by seeing it as having to be reformulated in changing circumstances. Hegemony offers an insight into how change in society can be brought about and the key role of the media – and other social and cultural institutions – in the transformation.

Gramsci's conceptualisation of hegemony, with its stress on individuals always interacting and responding to the society and culture they live in, offers a more pluralistic and complex model of ideology than that put forward by Marx. Hegemony allows for people's experiences of life to lead them to question, and even resist, the dominant views of society and provides for the possibility of opposing or contrary views becoming part of the dominant ideology. Hegemony must be 'flexible, responsive to changing conditions, adaptive – the same old ideas and procedures, in a situation of change will fail to wield the same hegemony' (O'Connor and Downing, 1995: 16). However, this is not to say that all views and values carry the same weight. Hegemony still operates within the confines of the inequality in the distribution of economic and political power. The bourgeoisie still have the advantages of economic domination and intellectual and moral leadership, and their authority enables them to exercise a disproportionate influence over what is the dominant and generally accepted way of understanding the world.

A CRISIS OF HEGEMONY?

Hall *et al.* (1978) attempted to apply Gramsci's concept of hegemony as well as Althusser's notion of ideology to the economic and political crisis that was apparently unfolding in Britain – as elsewhere – in the late 1960s and early 1970s. Revolution hung in the air as political and social upheaval seemed to pose a threat to the powers that be. In Gramscian terms these events represented a 'crisis of hegemony'. Hall and his colleagues (1978) examined how the ruling class, to win popular consent for more repressive legislation and action, and to establish stronger state control, used the media. They documented the success of those in power in manipulating the media to present their view of the world and marginalise other interpretations of what was happening. They were able to do this because of the preferential access the media affords to the powerful. While the media exercise relative autonomy from the dominant class they naturally turn to those in power to interpret and make sense of events, especially at times of crisis. The representatives of the dominant class were the primary definers of the crisis, not the media who had a secondary role.

Policing the Crisis

The book, Policing the Crisis, published in 1978, examined the role of the news media in promoting ideological representations of law and order in the early 1970s. The authors showed how the media created public anxiety over the crime of 'mugging', student protests and picketing. Together the media represented the increase in violence and disorder as a threat to law and order in society. There was no evidence to show that any increase had taken place – in the period the book examines the incidence of crimes of violence had actually fallen. The coverage, however, called for and in turn precipitated longer sentencing policy, tougher policing and attempts to introduce new legislation to control industrial disputes. The media's reporting and interpretation of these 'moral panics' was shaped by the degree of access they provide to people in power, the spokespersons for the government and other 'agencies of control' such as the police and courts. These spokespersons were the 'primary definers' of what was happening (see Chapter 4). In

151

the midst of the 'crisis of hegemony' the media was able to pave the way for more consent for measures that led to stronger state control. The focus in particular on the 'new' crime of mugging – the old offence of street crime with a long history in Britain but now associated with a marginal group in society, young black men – created the impression of a disordered and troubled society threatened by a new threat. By amplifying this 'threat' by a regular supply of stories, together with more and more editorial or expert comment calling for action, a climate was orchestrated to support the introduction of repressive measures thereby supporting the interests of the ruling class in a time of crisis and assisting the maintenance of its hegemonic control.

The media, according to Hall (1977), perform the 'ideological work' of the ruling class. While they do not act as mouthpieces for the dominant class, and present competing definitions of reality, media institutions frame reality in a way that serves the interests of the dominant class. This, for Hall (1977: 332–3), is the hegemonic effect of the media. The dominant class strives and succeeds in 'framing all competing definitions of reality within their range and bringing all alternatives within their horizon of thought'. The result is that 'they set the limits – mental and structural – within which subordinate classes 'live' and make sense of their subordination in such a way as to sustain the dominance of those ruling over them'. Hall spoke of the media producing a 'preferred reading' of what is happening. While the preferred interpretation of events exists alongside other meanings, there is the chance that hegemonic control can be lost and as a result the ruling class must continuously struggle to ensure the production of the preferred meaning of events.

Hall (1980) also introduces struggle into the way in which people understand the output of the media. He argues that audiences can respond to the preferred message in a number of ways. Hall's theoretical work was drawn up into his 'encoding-decoding' model, which was influential in shaping how research into the production and reception of media messages was subsequently conducted (see Chapter 8). He argued the media and their audiences play a part in the process of producing ideological meaning. By drawing on Gramsci's work the model provided a more sophisticated conceptual tool for understanding and analysing how the media reproduce the dominant ideology than traditional Marxist theory. It introduced the notion of the media being a site of struggle over the production of meaning. The media's main role may be the promotion of dominant ideologies but it could also, albeit less often, undermine and challenge such ideologies.

A CRITIQUE OF THE DOMINANT IDEOLOGY

Althusser and Gramsci's critique of Marx's notion of 'false consciousness' undermined the view that a single 'dominant ideology' determines the culture of capitalist societies (see Abercrombie *et al.*, 1980). They question whether it is possible to see the content of the media as a coherent and unified set of ideas, beliefs and practices. They allow us to see the media as containing contradictory messages, some articulating the 'dominant ideology' of the bourgeoisie but others to a greater or lesser extent challenging the dominant worldview. Behind this difference of approach is a disagreement over the relationship between ideology and the 'real' world. Marx held to a realistic theory of ideology in that he argues the bourgeoisie deliberately and intentionally misrepresents the world through the media. The notion of 'false consciousness' assumes a true knowledge of the world exists and it is possible to distinguish between truth and falsity. However, Marx's critics in their different ways argue against there being a truth or reality against which ideology can be measured. Neo-Marxist and structural theorists increasingly came to accept that there is no 'unmediated (non-ideological) experience of the world that can serve as a ... yardstick against which to judge specific ideologies' (Grossberg *et al.*, 1998: 191). Individuals live in a world in which there is nothing outside their existence that enables them to assess the truth or otherwise of their statements, beliefs or actions. All they have is their experience, and ideologies can be seen as different systems of meaning people attached to the world through their experience of it. This approach creates more space to discuss different kinds of ideologies tied to gender, ethnicity, sexuality, race and so on, as well as the notion of the dominant ideology as a site of struggle.

While all the theorists mentioned above share the basic belief that the media possess ideological power, they differ over how that power is exercised. Classical Marxists – usually associated with the political economy approach – argue the process of ideological reproduction cannot be understood without analysis of the economic context within which it takes place and of the pressures and determinations this context exerts (Murdock and Golding, 1977: 19). People with economic and political power use ideology to maintain their privileged positions. Thus media owners shape the messages the media reproduce. Neo-Marxists – such as Althusser and Gramsci – argue that ideology in the media is influenced but not determined by the material basis of production. While those with economic and political power exercise considerable say over what appears in the media it is but part of the wider cultural contests over meaning. Rather than a single ideology dominating the media and culture in general, there are a number of competing ideologies different groups seek to defend or promote through the media and other institutions. In winning and maintaining hegemonic consent for dominant ideas importance is attached to the process of making these ideas seem natural, part of common-sense and emerging from human nature. For example, particular forms of behaviour associated with men and women are not the product of patriarchal ideology but a natural and inevitable expression of human nature. Barthes' work provides insights into how ideological representations come to be accepted as common-sense and the part played by the media in this process.

Barthes and myth

Barthes was reflecting on the 'myths of French daily life' in the 1950s and 'impatient at the sight of the "naturalness" with which newspapers, art and common sense constantly dress up a reality, which, even though it is the one we live in, is undoubtedly determined by history' (2000: 11). He used the term 'myth' to describe the situation where latent or hidden meaning was accepted as 'natural' and 'normal' in helping us to make sense of the world. However, myths while appearing as universal truths embedded in common-sense are cultural constructions serving particular interests. For Barthes, myth makes particular worldviews natural and unchallengeable. In modern society, he argues, myths primarily serve the interests of capitalism and bourgeois ideology, promoting the ideology as obvious, taken for granted and inevitable. Something that is ideological is made into common-sense through the process of mythic representation. As mythic representation is seen as self-evident it is seldom questioned.

Barthes' most-often- quoted example of the work of myth is the cover of the French photo magazine *Paris Match*, which featured a picture of a young black soldier in French military uniform saluting the French flag, the tricolour. (See Figure 6.1) The soldier's eyes are looking upwards at the flag. At the manifest level the picture *denotes* a black soldier saluting the flag. But at another level – the level of *connotation* – the picture can be interpreted in a different way, a more ideological way. It can be seen as suggesting the loyalty of black French subjects to the French flag, thereby rejecting criticism of French colonial activity. As Barthes puts it the picture signifies to him 'that France is a great Empire, that all her sons without colour discrimination, faithfully serve under the flag and that there is no better answer to the detractors of an alleged colonialism than the zeal shown by this Negro in serving his so called oppressors' (Barthes, 2000: 116). He proceeds in the rest of his book, in what his translator calls a highly poetic and idiosyncratic style, to discuss the 'hidden meaning' of a wide range of images in the media and popular culture, ranging from wrestling and red wine to soap powder and tourist guides. Barthes' work can be seen as specific to a particular period. France's colonial war in North Africa, particularly Algeria, was one of the formative political backdrops to his work and hence can explain his particular interpretation of the *Paris Match* cover. However, his belief that the media are more than the 'transparent bearers of meaning' and that ideological meaning in the media, and any kind of popular culture, can be uncovered by means of reading the 'signs' had a profound impact.

In identifying the myths in the media and popular culture Barthes applied the concepts and procedures of semiology to media content. Semiology was developed by the Swiss linguist Ferdinand de Saussure to explore the relationship between words on a page and the concepts and ideas the reader has inside her head. His work coincided with that of Charles

Figure 6.1

Peirce (see Chapter 1) who, unknown to Saussure, was developing a similar approach to the study of language on the other side of the Atlantic, which he labelled semiotics. Semiology – or semiotics as it is more commonly referred to nowadays – examines how meanings in texts are constructed through the arrangement of signs and the use of cultural codes. Barthes drew attention to the part the media play in disseminating an ideological view of the world through their ability to make signs and images work in a particular way. Signs convey deeper, mythical meaning than the surface images signify. Barthes attaches importance to the latent – the connotative – meaning of media messages. It is as a result of the process of signification at this level being invisible to the individual that ideology is seen as simply 'the way things are' and not in terms of the dominant values of the bourgeoisie. All signifying practices are imbued with the ideas and values of the bourgeoisie but this is not apparent to the individual.

Semiology/semiotics

Semiotics argues that language and communication in general is structured according to certain rules, which are commonly understood in a culture. In order to communicate, these rules have to be learned. For de Saussure language is a system of 'signs'. The sign, which conveys meaning, is divided into two components: the signifier and the signified. The signifier is manifest in the form of a printed word, a picture or a sound, which is perceived by our physical senses. The signified is the meaning that cultural convention determines we attach to the signifier. While the signifier is what we perceive, such as 'the marks on the paper or the sounds in the air', the signified 'is the mental concept to which it refers' and 'is broadly common to all members of the same culture who share the same language' (Fiske, 1982).

Peirce distinguished between signs that contain a direct reference to what they represent and others that do not. He identified three different kinds of relationship between a sign and what it refers to.

> In an icon the sign resembles its object in some way: it looks or sounds like it. In an index there is a direct link between a sign and its object, the two are actually connected. In a symbol there is no connection or resemblance between sign and object: a symbol communicates only because people agree that it shall stand for what it does. A photograph is an icon, smoke is an index of fire and a word is a symbol.
>
> (Fiske, 1982: 50)

At the level of the symbol the relationship between the sign and what it stands for is 'arbitrary'; there is no inherent connection between what it looks or sounds like and what it represents. For example, there is no link between the word cat and a feline four-legged creature other than we agree this should be so. It is a standardised representation accepted in our culture.

Barthes – and others including Umberto Eco (1966) who used semiotics to understand popular literature such as James Bond novels – applied the ideas of Saussure and Peirce about language to contemporary culture. He identified how signs were organised into particular systems or codes, which provided them with meaning. These codes are central to any culture, and learning them is essential for communication in society. However, at the same time they are not neutral or value free, incorporating particular assumptions, ideas and meaning. These are the 'myths' that can be drawn out by analysis of the connotative meaning of a message.

Barthes' approach to ideological meaning in the media emphasises the importance of the symbolic nature of representation. As a structuralist he sees meaning as constructed according to the rules and conventions of language and culture. Using semiotics he argues that the latent meaning of the communication can be prised out, revealing how what we communicate is framed by a set of values. The crucial question is whether these values form a cohesive ideology. Barthes initially assumed they did but was later to agree that images – or signs – are capable of more than one set of meanings. The limitations in Barthes' work can be attributed to the method he uses. While semiotics is underpinned by linguistics for its methodological rigour, often the process of identifying what a sign means is highly intuitive and subjective. The sign often simply means what the semiotician wants it to mean rather than conveys how most people understand it. McQuail (1987: 189) points out that semiotics 'offers no way of knowing whether or not its findings are representative'. The examples chosen for analysis – such as Barthes' front cover of *Paris Match* – are not selected systematically. Thus what may be claimed in the reading of a single advert, photograph or film may not be true for all similar adverts, photographs and films. Critics also argue that semiotics confines itself to the study of media content, ignoring the intentions of the communicator and the interpretations of the audience. While showing the output of the media is permeated and saturated by bourgeois ideology, many argue Barthes fails to demonstrate how this ideological domination is created and sustained (Golding and Murdock, 1978: 70). He is seen as failing to grapple with the issue of how ideology is actually reproduced through the activities of media workers and the reception of media messages by their consumers.

STRUGGLES OVER MEANING

Barthes' work highlights one of the difficulties of ideological approaches to the media. Theories of ideology are often formulated in abstract and generalised ways. Trying to apply them to make sense of the content of the media is not easy. Barthes' use of semiotics was a response to frustrations with the quantitative methods used to analyse media content in the 1950s and 1960s. Content analysis emerged from the American mass communications tradition. It sought to provide 'the objective, systematic and quantitative description of the manifest content of communication' (Berelson, 1952). While there are practical problems of content analysis as a method, it is the theoretical assumptions it rests on that concern critics. By focusing on what is overt and manifest in the media, it is seen as a superficial mode of analysis. Counting categories of things is a very limited way of conveying the meaning of media messages (Woollacott, 1982). It ignores covert or latent meanings. Burgelin (1972: 319) points out that content analysis assumes the item that appears most frequently is the most important and significant. He argues that the content of the media is 'a structured whole, and the place occupied by different elements is more important than the number of times they recur'. Content analysis ignores the broader context within which communication takes place and therefore is only able to deal with what is on the surface. It does not take account of the structures crucial to the meaning of messages. For example, in examining the language of the media, content analysis as a method of research can only classify and count words, neglecting the ways in which stories or programmes are linguistically constructed. For critics this ignores the essential component of communication in the determination of meaning.

Content analysis

> Content analysis is essentially a counting exercise. Usually certain conceptual categories are established and then quantitatively assessed against their presence or absence in the content of the media. Thus the Glasgow Media Group (1976) in a case study of the reporting of industrial stoppages examined the content of British TV news bulletins over a six-month period in the early 1970s to ascertain their frequency and how they were explained. They found a discrepancy between how much attention was paid to the issue by TV news and the number of stoppages officially recorded. TV news exaggerated their importance. They also found that stoppages were attributed much more to trades unionists than employers, and concluded TV news constructed a particular picture of the world of work to serve the interest of employers rather than workers.
>
> Critics of content analysis argue that the method is not as objective as it claims. They draw attention to the practical problems of defining the topic for investigation, selecting the sample and units of analysis, choosing the categories and making judgements about how to implement them. The six-month period of the Media Group's study has been criticised for being atypical, in that the number of industrial stoppages in this period was abnormally high. The researchers have been criticised for developing categories and units of analysis to serve their own purposes, and counting material according to their subjective perspectives. Subjectivity is seen as determining choices at every stage of content analysis. (See Barrat, 1986: 102–7, for a simple and brief overview, and Fiske, 1982: 119–29, for critical account.)

The media, like all other forms of communication, can only communicate through the shared acceptance of commonly agreed rules for the senders and receivers of messages. These codes, as semiotics refers to them, organise the variety of signs that comprise communication to produce meaning. People understand these codes because they have lived with them for such a long time they are part of them. They enable us to understand media messages. While codes are multi-layered and complex, they are not neutral – as Barthes points out. They are ideologically loaded. Content analysis does not enable us to identify the codes and the ideological messages they carry. Semiotics does address the complexity of communication as well as assist us in penetrating the surface of what is communicated to get at the hidden meaning. However, semiology has increasingly been found wanting in unpicking meaning and identifying ideology. The limitations of research methods to grapple with meaning have corresponded with a re-evaluation of the concept of ideology as a result of the debate over how meaning is produced. Drawing on the work of Michel Foucault (see Chapter 2) discourse theory has resulted in a re-thinking of the relationship between meaning and social structures.

FOUCAULT'S DISCOURSE

If ideology was the concept that dominated efforts to analyse media content in the 1970s, by the 1980s Foucauldian discourse theory became the dominant paradigm (Tolson, 1996: Chapter 7). Theories of ideology in the 1970s explored how systems of dominant meaning are imposed through the media — and other ideological apparatuses – and the means by which individuals accept or resist the dominant ideology. The emphasis was on an external social power – in simple Marxist terms, the ruling class – or in more complex terms the broader social system. In the 1980s the structuralist revolution had shifted discussion of ideology to explore how meaning is made by social institutions such as the media. This has implications for the role of the media in the reproduction of ideology, summed up most clearly by Stuart Hall (1982). He describes the media as being part of the 'politics of signification' in that they are involved in giving meaning to events that happen in the world around them. He argues the media do not reflect reality but are engaged in defining reality. Rather than 'transmitting already-existing meaning' the media through the 'active work of selecting and presenting, of structuring and shaping' are 'making things mean' (Hall, 1982: 64). This is the essence of representation. It is the practice and production of meaning, which is now commonly described in the literature as 'signifying practice'. As there are multiple meanings of reality the power of the media rests in how they decide to signify events. Ideology is not imposed on the media but is something the media play a role in creating and constructing. The intimate link between meaning and social practice/signification is central to discourse theory as developed by Foucault.

Foucault's work explored how discourses were used to control the sick, the mentally ill and the criminal throughout history, highlighting how they had changed to adapt to new social conditions. He began by describing how science and the scientific method as it developed from the eighteenth century established, through the process of observation, what was deemed 'normal' in relation to health and sexuality. Those who deviated from what science deemed normal were seen as requiring correction, treatment or discipline. He also used the concept of surveillance to describe the ways in which people were subject to regular examination in order to find out whether they were healthy or not. Thus for Foucault new forms of knowledge result in new forms of power and control. Instead of the visible exercise of power that characterised traditional societies and was embodied in the form of the monarch or sovereign, modern institutions seek to hide their power. They do so by concentrating on those who are the subjects of discipline, observation and judgement (Stevenson, 1995: 138). His work on prisons and punishment outlined how control over the convicted criminal changed from the exercise of physical punishment of the body to moulding the prisoner to conform to normal behaviour through the process of punishment and surveillance. He then proceeds to generalise that punishment and surveillance are part of social life. We all exist in a disciplined society in which we are subjected to surveillance and control.

Discourse

Following the work of Foucault a discourse can be defined as a systematically organised set of statements that gives expression to the meanings and values of an institution. It describes, delimits and defines what it is possible to say and to do and not possible to say and to do with respect to an area of concern of that institution. A discourse provides a set of possible statements about a given area, and organises and gives structure to the manner in which a particular topic, object, process is to be talked about. And as a result it provides descriptions, rules, permissions and prohibitions of social and individual actions.

Source: adapted from Kress, 1985: 6–7

Foucault's work has been used in media studies to suggest the media are mechanisms or arrangements through which discursive power is exercised. The media are means of exercising surveillance and control. Tolson (1996: 192–3) discusses the ideology of sex and sexuality that features in women's magazines such as *Cosmopolitan*. While traditional ideology theory would regard the amount of space devoted to sexual technique and sexual problems as a 'massive distraction or displacement', Foucault would argue it performs a useful controlling or what he calls 'governmental' function. The talk about sex 'polices' the audience by presenting a particular discourse around sex and sexuality. The discursive power of women's magazines and the media in general is the production of certain kinds of statements or talk, which position its participants in a particular relationship to power. Stevenson (1995) argues the tabloid press in Britain often utilises disciplinary forms of power, pointing out that many of the stories in the British tabloids such as the *Sun* have to do with the normalising surveillance of the private lives of ordinary people. Stories often are 'individualised cases of moral transgression for wider disapproval' and as such are an 'attempt to impose regularised norms of behaviour on the populace by providing clear cases of deviant activity' (Stevenson, 1995: 140). Regularised forms of behaviour for the populace are provided by discourses in the media that document deviant behaviour and action, and what happens if norms are transgressed. However, Foucault's theorising of power does not lead to a search for sources of power or structures of power but rather to an acceptance that power is 'pervasive, ubiquitous, anonymous' (Ferguson, 1998: 62). Thus power relations are embodied in forms of language, types of news stories, kinds of buildings, ways of seeing and understanding and so on that constitute discourses rather than in individuals or organisations.

This has, according to Curran (1990: 140), reduced the role of media to a series of reader–text encounters in the context of a society in which power is diffuse and invisible. Foucault's failure to offer any explanation for why certain kinds of discourse emerge at certain points in history or why particular discourses are adopted and others are not has led to the consideration of discourses at the expense of the question of who 'produces' these discourses and how they produce them. There is no sense of 'agency' in his work. The implication is that discourses are constructed by people unaware of what they are doing. Thus media texts are considered in isolation from their construction in Foucauldian media theory.

Structure and agency

The concepts of structure and agency are central to discussion of social relations and the media. Structure refers to constraints on human actions while agency indicates independent human action. All social relationships are characterised by tensions between structure and agency. Structures such as the family, education system, work etc. limit individual action and behaviour. These structures are, however, simply recurring patterns of behaviour and only continue as long as people continue to conform to them. Daily activities help to reproduce social structures as well as possess the potential to change them. Agency is intentional and undetermined human action. Individuals have the capacity to behave in ways that reject the norms and conventions laid down by social structures. In relation to the media there are a number of levels at which the tension between structure and agency operates. We have already discussed these tensions in media organisation (see Chapter 4). But it also exists around media representation – how far are media workers and organisations able to produce meaning and to what extent are they constrained by cultural, linguistic and discursive structures? Foucault's discourse theory dispenses with human agency altogether, seeing meaning being constructed through the myriad interactions and networks of everyday life.

Source: adapted from Croteau and Hoynes, 1997: 20–4

161

Foucauldian notions of the role of the media in the regulation of human behaviour and the establishment of the parameters of normal activity can be contrasted to early work done on the media's representation of deviancy. Stanley Cohen in his examination of media representations of youth in the 1960s introduced the concept of the 'moral panic', which not only became part of media theory but also has entered into the public domain.

MORAL PANICS AND FOLK DEVILS

Not a day seems to pass by without some newspaper, politician or public body warning of the new and potentially calamitous dangers of this behaviour or that action. Whether it is the MMR jab, alco-pops, CJD, football hooligans, New Age travellers, ecstasy, crack-cocaine or paedophiles, contemporary society has been subject to a series of panics about the consequences of certain activities or groups. The term 'moral panic' was first used by the criminologist Jock Young in 1971 to describe public concern about the seemingly rapid increase in drug abuse in the UK, leading to the establishment of police drug squads throughout the country and a rise in drug-related arrests (Thompson, 1998: 7). The concept was developed by Cohen in 1973 to examine the response of the media, public and agencies of social control such as the police and judiciary to the seaside fights between mods and rockers in 1960s Britain. Cohen (1987: 9) defines a moral panic as follows:

> A condition, episode, person or group of persons emerges to become defined as a threat to societal values and interests; its nature is presented in a stylised and stereotypical fashion by the mass media; the moral barricades are manned by editors, bishops, politicians and other right-thinking people; socially credited experts pronounce their diagnoses and solutions; ways of coping are evolved or (more often) resorted to; the condition then disappears, submerges or deteriorates and becomes more visible.

Cohen identifies several stages to a moral panic. It begins with the definition of a threat or the emergence of a problem or concern; this is represented in the media; there is a rapid build-up of public anxieties and calls for something to be done; the authorities respond and finally the panic recedes or changes in the law or social behaviour result. In his study Cohen argued the media labelled mods and rockers in a stereotyped and negative way, thereby creating 'folk devils'. He saw the media as playing a crucial role in amplifying the problem, creating a social reaction against mods and rockers. They did this by exaggerating the nature and extent of the problem, galvanising public concern and police activity as well as leading the courts to take tough action against offenders. A spiral effect of reaction and action is set in motion by the media's over-reporting, exaggerating or distorting the extent of the original events. Cohen draws attention to the power of the media to define a situation as real with corresponding real consequences. What happened on the beaches of Clacton was neither as serious nor as threatening as suggested by the media accounts of the time (Eldridge *et al.*, 1997: 62–3). In fact he suggests that mods and rockers never really saw each other as enemies until the media created an imaginary rivalry that many young people came to see as real. Cohen's work highlighted how particular definitions of social reality come into play and the role of the media in the process. His focus on the control culture leads Cohen to emphasise the role of the media in the exercise of social control. *Policing the Crisis* places even more stress on the media as an agency of social control in the moral panic over mugging. However, it is equally possible to argue the agencies of social control create more deviance through moral panic. Redhead (1993) shows how the moral panic over raves, which resulted in legislation introducing heavier fines for organising illegal raves, provided publicity that increased the popularity of such events and alerted criminals to their profitability.

Cohen's notion of a moral panic has been subject to criticism. Goode and Ben-Yehuda (1994) reject the model of moral panics based on stages. From their study of a range of case studies, beginning with the Prohibition movement in the early 1900s, they argue moral panics 'make up an extremely diverse collection of events' which do not 'go through specific stages, predetermined stages, with a beginning, a middle and a predictable end' (Goode and Ben-Yehuda, 1994: 226). They identify certain elements that distinguish moral panics: a level of *concern* about a problem or group; *hostility* to objectionable behaviour, which can be identified with a group; some degree of *consensus* in society that there is a real threat caused by such behaviour; the reaction to such behaviour is *disproportional* and that moral panics are volatile, in that they erupt suddenly and subside equally abruptly. Goode and Ben-Yehuda (1994) are critical of the elite-engineered version of moral panics exemplified as they see it in *Policing the Crisis*. They do not see the state as using the media and other social institutions to maintain social control by whipping up moral panics but prefer to emphasise the role of professional organisations, the police, moral entrepreneurs and other interest groups in bringing issues to the fore, by alerting legislators, using the media, demanding new laws or instituting new practices. Others (see Taylor, 1997: 156) criticise the moral panic theory for its lack of clarity as to why certain groups or events are selected for media attention. The implication is that the subjects of moral panics are by and large harmless and the threat they pose exaggerated. Some deviant behaviour, such as joy-riding, can lead to death and destruction. It is also the case that agencies of social control and the media prevent the amplification of some problems – for example, the moral panic over HIV/AIDS in the late 1980s was dampened down by the state.

SUMMARY

This chapter has discussed different theoretical approaches to understanding the role of the media in the reproduction of particular ways of thinking. Classical Marxist theory see the media as representing the world according to the ideology of the ruling class. As a result they present a partial view of the world, misreporting and misrepresenting the views of other classes. Neo-Marxist theories see the media as a site of struggle between dominant and subordinate ideologies. However, the dominant ideology has particular advantages in what is an unequal competition to shape the media agenda. Structuralists see ideology and meaning as not imposed on the media from outside by a class or system but stress the role of the media in the construction of meaning. The media do not reflect the world but manufacture reality. This has changed the ways in which we understand and analyse ideology in the media. Traditional forms of analysis, such as content analysis, are found wanting, unable to extrapolate the hidden latent meaning of media messages. Semiotics is seen as enabling the scholar to dig out the underlying meaning of what appears in the media. More significantly it has moved many theorists away from what they see as the mechanical nature of ideology with its connotations of the imposition of values to the more fluid and ubiquitous concept of discourse; the main difference being the conceptualisation of power and how it is exercised. The Foucauldian view of a web of power woven without any directing hand is contrasted with traditional notions of ideological power exercised by groups in society and exemplified through the part the media play in the process of moral panics.

Section 4
Theories of media effects and audiences

The study of the audience and effects of the media is the most active and well-supported area of investigation in media studies. It has generated the most continuous and cumulative mass of data. However, claims and counter-claims about the media's potential to influence people mark the interpretation of this data. The history of media effects research is characterised by a debate between two different camps: one emphasising the effects the media have on their audiences, the other stressing the variety of ways in which different audiences make use of media output.

Common-sense leads many to believe the media has a strong influence on people's attitudes and behaviour. Why else would companies spend millions of pounds on advertising? Why else would political parties and politicians devote so much time, money and resources to the presentation of their message and image in the media? Why else would radio and television stations be amongst the first institutions to be seized during coups? Examination of academic theorising about media effects has to be set in the context of popular understanding and attitudes. Perhaps in no other area of media studies is there such a gap between popular perceptions and social science theory. The media themselves are full of stories about the possible impact of their output on individuals. Pressure groups warn of the dangers of watching too much television or allowing children to see violent films. Concern about the harmful consequences of the media has been expressed throughout the twentieth century. The early film industry generated this concern and each new media of mass communication ever since has been subject to similar charges. While many people adhere to the idea of the media having the power to influence, they see themselves as immune to such manipulation (Kitzinger, 1997). The media industries are keen to play down the power of the media. It is in this politically charged environment that much theorising has taken place and, as a result, it has not escaped the politics of the debate.

The vast array of research into the potential links between the content of the media and audience thinking and behaviour has thrown up a range of different and often contradictory findings. Historically, thinking about the impact of the media has gone through different stages. Early theorising tended to assume people are easily influenced. The 'hypodermic model' assumed media effects were simple and direct, a causal connection existing between what people see, hear and read in the media and their knowledge, attitudes and behaviour. The failure of successive research to provide conclusive empirical support for the hypodermic model led to challenges from other schools of thought. Media effects theory increasingly began to 'assert the independence and autonomy of media audiences and dispel the notion people are easily led' (Curran, 1990: 146). Dismissing the direct effects theory as unsophisticated and unsociological, Katz and Lazarsfeld (1955) put forward their 'two step model', which advances the view the media by themselves are not very powerful in influencing people, arguing people are more influenced by members of their family, friends, neighbours and fellow workers. They stressed the role of personal influence in shaping people's attitudes. One group of people, however, were singled out as exerting particular influence, what the authors referred to as 'opinion leaders'. These were 'individuals whose views and ideas were respected and deemed important in the voter's immediate social circle' (Glover, 1984: 5). These opinion leaders absorbed information from the media and then passed it on to the less active sections of the population – hence the two-step flow of information. The importance of the media in this process was deemed limited.

The two-step model shifted the focus away from the individual as being the 'passive' dupe of the media implicit in hypodermic theory. Subsequent research moved beyond opinion leaders to the general population to assess how the media are used by different groups of people. The 'uses and gratifications' approach argued the audience brought its own needs and desires to the process of message reception, which structured the way in which the message is received. Researchers identified a variety of needs and desires (McQuail *et al.*, 1972; Blumler and Katz, 1974). This approach is a reversal of the hypodermic model; the media now have no effect on their audience. Rather they are at the 'beck and call' of their audiences, with power resting with individuals who determine what part the media play in their lives. Increasingly effects theory invested more power in the audience. The 'active audience' tradition located the audience as 'active participants in the creation of meaning' (Kitzinger, 1997). Reception studies began to document how audiences could challenge the messages from the media by reading the output in a number of ways. The active viewer could appropriate unexpected pleasures from his or her reading of the mainstream media. The capacity of the audience to produce diverse interpretations of what they see, hear and read came to be celebrated in some quarters as evidence of the freedom of the audience to resist the media. Thus even if the media produce a dominant ideology or discourse, the audience can resist this. The active audience paradigm quickly established itself in the field of media studies but today is under challenge. Critics question the extent to which people differ in their readings of media messages, and argue the desire to document variations in how people read media messages neglects the more fundamental questions of what people believe.

The shift to greater engagement with the audience was also the result of some scholars becoming increasingly frustrated with the efforts to assess the effects of the media on the individual. They saw this approach as too narrowly psychological. Distinctions were also made between short-run immediate effects and the long-term, cumulative impact of the media. The 'cultural effects' approach addressed these concerns, examining the broader role of the media in performing what Hall *et al.* (1978) labelled the 'orchestration of public opinion' as a result of the 'slow cumulative build-up of beliefs and values through which we understand the world' (Glover, 1984: 10). The new question is 'how do the media affect the way in which we collectively think'. Academics tend to present the range of approaches documented above as mutually exclusive. However, there are considerable overlaps between the approaches and over time a common set of questions has developed around how the audience understands media messages. One underlying problem over the years and across the different approaches is the question of what we mean by an effect.

Chapter Seven

☐ EFFECTS, WHAT EFFECTS? POWER AND INFLUENCE OF THE MEDIA

The question to exercise media theory most is 'What effects do the media have?'. In trying to answer this question the pendulum has swung back and forth over the years from great effects to minimal effects. The power of the media has concerned society since the birth of mass communication. Pearson (1984) documents a long tradition of complaint against the influence of popular media and entertainment forms in Britain. The birth of every new media of mass communication has been accompanied by fears about its corrupting influence on the audience. Not surprisingly theorising media effects, especially relating to sex and violence, is shaped by a highly charged popular debate and sometimes slanted by attempts to blame the media for society's ills. Often it is difficult to untangle perceptions of audience responses from actual facts (Watson, 1998: 61). The early history of media effects research was infused by deeply ingrained assumptions about the negative and anti-social effects of exposure to the media. However, the development of effects research has seen a shift from perspectives stressing the impact of the media on people to what people do with the media. Tudor (1979) traces the different stages of effects research and the shifting ideas of the relationship between the media and their audiences. Within each stage there have been disagreements between those adhering to the direct effects model and those subscribing to a limited effects model but the trend in thinking about the impact of the media has increasingly moved towards ascribing more power to audiences to understand media messages according to their individual attitudes and opinions, and social backgrounds.

Social concerns of media influence

In the 1950s there was an outpouring of concern about the corrupting and depraving influence of American comic book magazines and rock 'n' roll music. In the 1930s the worries were over the cinema, which according to cultural critic F.R. Leavis, involved the 'surrender, under conditions of hypnotic receptivity, to the cheapest emotional appeals' (quoted in Pearson, 1984: 93). One psychiatrist could assert in 1938 that '70% of all crimes were first conceived in the cinema'. Earlier, at the turn of the century, the music halls were seen as encouraging lawlessness with their glorification of violence and immorality. The 1840s and 1850s witnessed the 'penny gaff' theatres and 'two penny hop' dancing saloons, singled out for peddling immoral and criminal behaviour amongst the young. An editorial in the Edinburgh Review in 1851 stated that

> one powerful agent for the depraving of the boyish classes of our towns and cities is to be found in the cheap shows and theatres, which are so specially opened and arranged for the attraction and ensnaring of the young. When for 3d a boy can procure some hours of vivid enjoyment from exciting scenery, music and acting ... it is not to be wondered that [he] ... then becomes rapidly corrupted and demoralised, and seeks to be the doer of infamies which have interested him as a spectator.

(Quoted in Root, 1986: 19)

At the end of the eighteenth century people talked of the harmful impact of newspapers with the depiction and discussion of villainy and depravity in their columns. The emergence of the first newsbook, or corantos, at the beginning of the seventeenth century was greeted with hostility by dramatists such as Ben Jonson who referred to them as 'a degradation of the proper function of a writer', and references to the 'contemptible trade' were common in Jacobean drama.

Source: Eldridge et al., 1997: 10–11

EARLY MEDIA EFFECTS

The early twentieth century saw the emergence of the widespread belief that the media exerted considerable influence over people and society. This pessimistic view of media effects was shaped by the mass society theory and its attempts to come to terms with the changes wrought by the advent of modernity (see Chapter 1). Early efforts to examine and assess the influence of the media were the outcome of the political lobbying of groups fearful of the media's impact. These fears were directed at the rise of the popular press in the late nineteenth century. The rise of the popular press for intellectuals was accompanied by cultural debasement – for Nietzsche the 'rabble vomit their bile and call it a newspaper', while T.S. Eliot was more restrained in expressing his view that the effect of Sunday and daily newspapers on their readers was 'to affirm them as a complacent, prejudiced and unthinking mass' (quoted in Carey, 1992: 7). It was the rise of the film industry that turned the concerns of moral entrepreneurs into political action. One of the first enquiries into media effects was conducted in 1917 by the National Council for Public Morals, which represented all of Britain's moral reform groups, from a variety of backgrounds and political persuasions.

The Council set up an enquiry into the harmful impact of the cinema on the young. Held by a commission including figures such as Lord Baden-Powell, the founder of the Boy Scout movement, and Marie Stopes, the campaigner for contraceptive birth control, the enquiry took evidence directly from nearly 50 witnesses, including doctors, policemen, social workers and probation officers, as well as representatives of the film industry and the British Board of Film Censors, and received written submissions from many others (Dewe-Mathews, 1994: 27). The evidence was collated in a 400-page document, comprising nearly a quarter of a million words detailing the views of the witnesses on topics ranging from the educational value of cinema to something ominously referred to as 'the moral dangers of darkness' (Pearson, 1984: 95). Some witnesses expressed their concern about the display of the enlarged view of the face, which emphasised pain, lust, hate and grief (Pearson, 1984: 96). Others linked the rapid spread of the cinema with rising lawlessness and juvenile delinquency. Much of the evidence was anecdotal and for every chief constable who took the opinion that the cinema caused copycat crime, there was another that disagreed. Particularly telling seems to have been the evidence from those who worked in deprived areas with young people. One probation officer from London's East End told the inquiry that the cinema made his job easier by taking children off the street. In his view they learned more about crime at home than they ever did by spending a few hours in the cinema. Such evidence – as well as police statements denying any link between crime and the cinema – led the Council to reject calls for the banning of children from picture houses. The Council concluded on the topic of juvenile crime that 'the problem is far too complex to be solved by laying stress on only one factor and that probably a subordinate one, among all the contributing conditions' (quoted in Dewe-Mathews, 1994: 29). It also stated the cinema does not cause imitative behaviour but 'suggests the form of activity rather than provides the impulse to it'. However, ever since the publication of the Council's report, the finding that the cinema does not have a harmful impact on its audience has been contested.

The findings of the National Council's enquiry were not based on any social-scientific evidence. They represented the impressions and speculations of those directly involved with the problems of juvenile delinquency. Speculation fuelled debate about the impact of the media on the young and 'impressionable'. The view the masses could be manipulated by the media acquired more support as a result of the effects of Allied propaganda in the First World War, and Soviet and Fascist propaganda in the 1930s. The Frankfurt School's argument that mass popular culture pumped out by the media and cultural industries caused a loss of individual freedom and creative thinking was shaped by its members' experience of the rise of the Nazis to power in Germany. It was in the 1930s that the first social-scientific efforts to investigate the possible effects of the media were undertaken. In 1933 the Payne Fund published the findings of its examination of the effects of film on children. The research found watching films could disturb children's sleep patterns, lead to substantial emotional arousal, and contribute to delinquency and criminality. These findings were qualified by the conclusion the same film would affect children differently depending on their age, sex, predispositions, perceptions and social environment, past experiences and parental influences (Grossberg, 1998: 279), a similar conclusion to that reached by many of the audience reception studies today. Nevertheless the climate of the times focused on findings that supported the media having a strong influence on their audiences. A similar response happened with the research into the impact of Orson Welles' *War of the Worlds* broadcast (see Chapter 1). Such research projects could not sway the general belief in the great power of the media that emerged in the inter-war years as a result of the apparent success of propaganda.

DIRECT EFFECTS THEORIES

While never formulated into any systematic theory during the period, the earliest theoretical perspective on media effects has been described as the 'hypodermic needle' theory – it has also been called the 'magic bullet' and 'transmission belt' theory (De Fleur and Ball-Rokeach, 1989: 164). Whatever its label, the basic idea is simple: 'media messages are received in a uniform way by every member of the audience and that immediate and direct responses are triggered by such stimuli' (1989: 164). Lasswell (1927) and Hovland *et al.* (1953), in their studies of the effectiveness of propaganda and communication, both subscribe to the view the media could – under the right circumstance – stimulate specific behaviour amongst a target group of people. Today this theory is seen as crude, simplistic and naive. Yet the view of an omnipotent media rested on an understanding of human behaviour common at the time. An individual's behaviour was seen as conditioned by inherited biological mechanisms that were fairly uniform from one person to another. The emotional nature of these mechanisms – as opposed to the rational nature – was stressed and it was only through social pressures that individual behaviour could be shaped. The breakdown of traditional society was seen as weakening these pressures. This view is rooted in behavioural psychology, which gained prominence in the first part of the twentieth century. Behaviourism takes the view that human behaviour is a more sophisticated version of animal behaviour. Human learning is no different in principle from animal learning in that it responds to the stimuli of rewards and punishment. The stimuli-response model is an essential component of the hypodermic needle theory. Curran and Seaton (1997: 262) conclude that 'all of the terms used to describe what the media do have a behaviourist bias, in which a single and external force – the media – have an impact on a single subject – the person'.

The hypodermic needle theory in its pure form no longer survives. Weaknesses in the theory are apparent. It does not address the influences that intervene between the messages from the media and the opinions and attitudes people hold. It also denies the audience any capacity to interpret, discount or distort the media messages they receive, ignoring that people engage with media messages from their own ideas, prejudices and preconceptions. The theory presents people as passive recipients of media messages, with little or no say in how they interpret them. The message is simply 'injected into' the subject who responds in a simple and observable way. These deficiencies led to serious re-assessment of media effects, which has all but discredited the theory, although contemporary discussion of media effects is haunted by the ghosts of past theories, and the potency of the hypodermic needle theory is apparent today, particularly in political circles and popular culture (Glover, 1984: 4). For example, a junior government minister stated in the British House of Commons in the early 1980s that 'violent films can give way to violent imitative behaviour' (quoted in Root, 1986: 13). Adherence to the view that the media generate copycat behaviour is also implicit in the work of a number of pressure groups that lobby against too much sex and violence on television and in the cinema. The image of the television viewer in popular culture is of a zombie or couch potato glued to his or her television screen while the press continually carry stories about the negative and detrimental impact of television and film on children (see Root, 1986). Contemporary concern with direct effects is largely associated with television and film, and their impact on children – although similar concerns about the advertising industry were voiced in the 1950s and 1960s (see Packard, 1957).

The direct effects theory has not entirely disappeared from the social sciences. Over the years efforts have gone into elaborating and correcting this model (Grossberg *et al.*, 1998: 286). Since its demise in the late 1940s the stimulus-response theory has reappeared albeit in a more sophisticated form, particularly in the field of psychology. Since the early part of the twentieth century psychology has moved away from a simplistic notion of human behaviour. Behaviourists have come to accept that people do not respond in 'a more or less uniform way' to external stimuli (De Fleur and Ball-Rokeach, 1989: 165). Social factors are now seen as important determinants of individuals' responses to media messages as mass society theorists' view of society as comprised of isolated, vulnerable individuals with few strong ties was increasingly rejected by social scientists. However, this has not prevented scholars from postulating explanations as to how the media influence behaviour. One such theory is that of social learning, which argues people can learn new behaviour through their observations of the behaviour of others (Grossberg *et al.*, 1998: 287). First articulated in the early 1940s social learning theory postulated imitative behaviour occurs when people are motivated to learn and when such behaviour is reinforced. Early social learning theorists stressed the importance of reinforcement, the rewards associated with performing the learned behaviour, and never applied their ideas to individual actions. The three main ways in which people can learn from observation are through personal experience, interpersonal exchanges and the media. How much and what kind of behaviour people learn from the media became a matter of debate.

In the early 1960s Albert Bandura developed social learning theory to understand media effects. He argued the actors in the media are powerful role models whose actions provide the information on which individuals base their own behaviour (Bandura, 1965). He believed the media were the most efficient means of teaching new ways of behaving, particularly to children and young people. People could learn new behaviour and the solutions to problems more quickly and with less cost through the media than in everyday personal interactions. He stressed the importance of imitative behaviour, which he demonstrated through a number of controlled laboratory experiments. Bandura's Bobo doll studies sought to establish if observing a filmed behaviour could teach children that behaviour and motivate them to be like the film model (Grossberg, 1998: 288). He concluded from his research that new patterns of behaviour could be learned by simply watching filmed portrayals of them. Seeing a film model being punished for exhibiting certain behaviour was found to decrease the chances of that behaviour being imitated, and depictions of a model being rewarded for prohibited behaviour increased the chances of that behaviour being copied. What Bandura labelled inhibitory and disinhibitory effects qualified the capacity of social learning through media representations. Bandura's experiment is considered a classic piece of media research, establishing that behaviour can be learned from the media. Subsequent research has applied his work to testing whether filmed violence results in more aggression in viewers (see Buss, 1961; Berkowitz and Rawlings, 1963). Their laboratory experiments found that certain forms of film violence are imitated and aggression is aroused by the viewing of certain kinds of violence (Newburn and Hagell, 1995). However, such research is heavily contested on the grounds of its methods (see below) and its neglect of the broader social context within which learning takes place.

Bobo doll studies

> Bandura's experiment began by showing a group of children between the ages of three and six years of age a film scene in which a man walked up to an adult-size plastic Bobo doll and told it to move aside. After glaring at the non-compliant doll, the man then began a series of physical and verbal assaults on the doll, including putting it on its side, sitting on it and punching its nose while shouting 'Pow, right in the nose, boom, boom', and bashing it on the head with a mallet while saying 'Sockeroo . . . stay down.' This scene was then repeated. For one group of children the film ended there. For another the film went on to show the man being rewarded with soft drinks and sweets for hitting the doll and being told he was a 'champion'. A third group saw a film in which the man was told off by another who told him he was a 'big bully' and should 'quit picking on' the doll.

After the viewing each group was taken into a room with various toys including a Bobo doll like the one in the film, balls, a mallet and other toys children liked to play with. These toys offered the opportunity for the children either to imitate the aggressive behaviour they had seen in the film or start playing with other toys in a non-imitative way. Each child was left alone in this room while they were observed by the researchers from behind a two-way mirror.

The researchers found imitation occurred with those children who had seen the film with no consequences or with the actor being rewarded for his aggressive actions. Boys were more likely to imitate the actor's behaviour than girls. Children who had seen the actor punished were less likely to imitate but when offered a reward for doing so they did.

Source: adapted from Grossberg et al., 1998: 288–9

LIMITED EFFECTS THEORIES

The direct effects theory was superseded by the 'limited effects paradigm', which dominated audience research in the 1960s and 1970s (Gitlin, 1978: 207). Rejecting hypodermic needle theory as unsophisticated and unscientific, the origins of this new way of thinking about media effects lay in the empirical work into attitude change and persuasion undertaken in America during the Second World War. In an attempt to assess different sorts of propaganda on American service personnel, the experiments of researchers such as Hovland and Lasswell gradually eroded the direct effects theory to which they had subscribed. The outcome of these experiments was the recognition that the effect of a particular item or image was not a simple linear consequence of the content of that item or image (Tudor, 1979). Rather perceptions were conditioned by the predispositions of audience members. People were not the passive, isolated and impressionable entities of mass society theory but individuals who could 'interpret what they saw and heard in line with their own already established beliefs' (Tudor, 1979). Above all people exist within groups and their immediate set of social relations was seen as an important determinant of their understanding of media messages.

TWO-STEP MODEL

Research by Paul Lazarsfeld and colleagues into the impact of the media on people's voting behaviour presented the most serious challenge to the hypodermic needle model. In their study, *The People's Choice*, of a presidential election they found the media did not play a significant part in influencing how people voted (Lazarsfeld *et al.*, 1948). Social characterisitics such as religion and class were seen as more important factors in determining voting behaviour, with the media reinforcing existing beliefs rather than changing them. They argued personal influence is significant in changing people's opinions. Some people, however, are more influential than others. They are the 'opinion leaders' whose knowledge and views were particularly respected by voters. They pay more attention to the media and transmit what they learn to others whom they can influence through personal contact. They spend more time consuming the media but the effects of their exposure are not straightforward. The 'two-step flow' of information and influence is from the media to opinion leaders and then from opinion leaders to their less interested friends, workmates and neighbours. Opinion leaders have strong political beliefs, hence they pay closer attention to the media, and are less likely to be influenced by media messages.

Katz and Lazarsfeld (1955) developed the notion of opinion leaders in subsequent work on how women made decisions about politics, consumer products, films and fashion. Opinion leaders exercised influence within their narrow spheres of expertise, some only for fashion with others only for kitchen appliances. While the opinion leaders were different for each type of activity what they had in common was a great deal of influence over their peers, playing a critical role in the dissemination of ideas and attitudes from the media to less active or involved sections of the population. These opinion formers are located at many levels of society – some of high status, others of low status. Thus the process of social mediation of media messages was not solely determined by wealth, power or status (see Curran et al., 1982). Such a theory contradicted the view mass society theorists had of people as an 'atomised mass of isolated individuals' (Glover, 1984: 5). The two-step model re-asserted the primacy of group life in shaping social attitudes, emphasising the importance of social relations within the audience in determining responses to media messages.

As a view of media effects the two-step model emphasised the minimal or limited part the media play in shaping individual's decisions about the choices they make, from how to vote to what washing powder to buy. The media's influence, if it had any, was in reinforcing existing attitudes and opinions. The model reinforces a pluralist view of society by identifying opinion leaders as not necessarily being of high status or economically advantaged but as individuals from all walks of life who exercise influence because of their knowledge and the respect they have attained on a particular matter. The strength of the two-step model is to locate media effects in a broader social context. The media were conceptualised as having no direct effect on the audience but as operating within established social relations that shaped not only people's opinions, attitudes and beliefs but also the attention they paid to and use they made of the media. Such thinking had practical consequences in the 1960s when it was applied to the process of modernisation (see Chapter 9). Social scientists became interested in how 'innovations' such as means of birth control or more efficient farming methods could be spread within society. The role of opinion leaders in the diffusion of innovation was identified as being crucial.

Diffusion theory argues innovations in whatever sector of society will spread through a series of stages before being adopted (Rogers, 1962). Initially people will become aware of the innovation through means such as the media. Some – the early adopters – will take up the innovation but will be small in number. Their efforts will lead opinion leaders to try the innovation for themselves and, if they find it produces results, they will encourage their friends and associates to adopt it, and eventually many more people will make the change. The media are assigned a limited role in the diffusion of innovation (see Baran and Davies, 1995: 171–3). Such a theory is a more sophisticated version of the two-step model. The theory became part of the training manual for efforts to get rural communities in the USA and peasants in the developing world to adopt certain agricultural innovations. However, the failure to bring about change in the real world led to a re-evaluation of the basic assumptions of the two-step model. The model was seen as simplifying the process of communication and how influence is exercised. By conceiving influence as the power of one individual over another, the model ignores the power of political and economic institutions, such as big business and government, to exercise influence over the flow of information in society. It also negates the control over ideas – ideological power — that shapes interaction between opinion leaders and others. The nature of interaction between opinion leaders and their followers is unclear. The assumption made is that the choice of a film, a product, a fashion or a political candidate is the outcome of the same process. But is it? Perhaps the media play a more significant role in some decisions than others? The model provides no basis for establishing why some people are opinion leaders – how do people assess the knowledge of opinion leaders and why do they accord these individuals respect? And why is it that only opinion leaders are active? The majority of individuals in the two-step model are still passive, but only now other people directly influence them. There is also no reason why there should not be more than two steps in the flow of information. The model's emphasis on the media reinforcing pre-existing attitudes can also be seen as according with the functionalist perspective of those who held to this theory that society was orderly, unchanging and working for the good of all.

While there is dispute over the nature and impact of the findings and theoretical implications of the work of Lazarsfeld and his colleagues on media research (McLeod *et al.*, 1991: 240–1) the two-step model opened the way for a more complex understanding of media effects. For some it represented the end of the notion of an all-powerful media. As Klapper (1960: 8) concluded, 'mass communications does not ordinarily serve as a necessary or sufficent cause of audience effects, but rather functions through a nexus of mediating factors'. Media influence only operates through a range of other factors including personality characteristics, social situations and the general climate of opinion and culture (Grossberg *et al.*, 1998: 277). Media research and theory became increasingly interested in unravelling the countervailing pressures on the audience and explaining the ways in which people select, reject and assess media information. The limited effects tradition came to underpin the development of media effects research and thinking. The model spawned 'uses and gratifications' theory, which emphasises the range of purposes an individual uses the media for.

USES AND GRATIFICATIONS

Limited effects research in the 1960s abandoned the focus on opinion leaders and concentrated on the uses made by people in general of the media. The uses and gratifications approach to media effects assumed the audience brought their own needs and desires to the process of making sense of media messages. Needs and desires structured how messages are received and understood by the audience. The focus shifted from what the media do to people to what people do with the media. Katz (1959, quoted in McQuail, 1984) provides a mission statement for the approach:

> Such an approach assumes that even the most potent of mass media content
> cannot ordinarily influence an individual who has no 'use' for it in the social
> and psychological context in which he lives. The 'uses' approach assumes
> that people's values, their interests, their associations, their social roles, are
> pre-potent and that people selectively fashion what they see and hear to
> these interests.

While there are several versions of the uses and gratifications model, it is possible to identify three basic assumptions on which the approach rests. First, people actively use the media for their own purposes; second, people know what these purposes are and can articulate them, and third, despite the variations between individuals in their use of the media, it is possible to identify some basic patterns in uses and gratifications. Researchers attempted to identify the uses people made of the media in their lives, and in particular how and why different media forms appeal to their audience.

The roots of such research can again be traced back to the war years. Herzog (1944) wanted to know why so many women listened to radio soaps, what were their motivations and what satisfactions did they derive. Drawing on interviews with 100 listeners, Herzog's study went well beyond the categories of being informed, educated and entertained to include the promotion of a sense of belonging, acquiring insight into self and others, providing the opportunity for wishful thinking and experiencing emotional release (Curran, 1996: 127). Nearly three decades later, McQuail, Blumler and Brown (1972) argued soap operas such as *Coronation Street* fulfilled the social need some people had for companionship. From their examination of five types of programme – a radio serial, and from television a soap, a quiz show, the news and two adventure series – they concluded there were four types of uses and gratifications (1972: 155–61). First, the media provide *diversion*. They are able to do this in different ways. They allow people to escape from the constraints of routine that make up everyday life. They can help people to escape from their worries and personal problems, and they can provide emotional release. Second, the media provide *personal relationships* for some people in the form of companionship. McQuail *et al.* (1972: 157) argue 'the characters may become virtually real, knowable and cherished individuals, and their voices are more than just a comforting background which breaks the silence of an empty house'. The content of the media can also be used as a source of conversational material in people's lives – what the authors label as a 'social utility' for viewers and listeners. Third, the media play a part in the development of *personal identity*. They can act as points of personal reference for individuals, to reflect on aspects of their own lives or personal situations. The content of programmes can provide people with information to develop ideas about the problems they are facing in their lives – a process of 'reality exploration' – as well as reinforce their views and values. Finally, the media offer the opportunity for *surveillance* of what is going on in the world, to keep abreast of issues and events.

Researchers in the years between these studies identified numerous different uses of the media (see McQuail, 1984). They also noted that different programmes or media forms are used in different ways depending on the individual. Ostensibly trivial programmes can be used for serious purposes, for example quiz shows could be used to improve general knowledge and serious programmes can be used for 'unserious' reasons – for example, being interested in what a newscaster is wearing. One of the major findings of this research is the unpredictability of uses and gratifications as people may use a programme in a number of quite unexpected ways. Such research generated a very different picture of media effects. No longer did the media manipulate the public but now viewers, listeners and readers could do what they wanted with the media. The passive dupes of the hypodermic needle model were replaced by 'a new, confident breed who knew what they wanted and how to get it' (Ruddock, 2001: 69).

The strength of the uses and gratifications theory is its focus on the role of individuals in making sense of media messages previously neglected or ignored. Critics, however, argue the approach suffers from a number of serious flaws (see Elliott, 1974; Ang, 1995). The first is the focus on the individual as the unit of analysis. By concentrating on the individual psychological make-up of audience members the approach tends to lose sight of the social dimension altogether. Consuming the media, such as television viewing, can be social activity undertaken with others, such as family members, and making sense of media content is often done in conversation with friends, family and workmates. There is also doubt as to whether it is possible to do no more than speculate about the audience's basic needs. Research has produced a long list of such needs, highlighting there is little agreement over them. To explain the basis of such needs requires a fairly deep, complex and thorough understanding of human experience, which is not evident in the research (Howitt, 1982: 13–14). The model also assumes individuals act with purpose in their viewing, listening and reading but often activities such as watching television are casual and unplanned, and the motive for watching can be due to the reputation of the programme or a lack of sufficient choice rather than the result of any specific need of the individual (Glover, 1984: 8). One way of summing up these criticisms is to say the uses and gratifications model is narrowly psychological and fails to locate the message or the audience in a wider social context. Some say this represents a retreat from the two-step flow approach.

CULTURAL EFFECTS THEORIES

Dissatisfaction with limited effects theories grew out of their focus on the individual psychology of the audience and their failure to locate discussion of media effects in a broader social context. Cultural effects theories started with the social context and worked into understanding the media. While accepting the media have an effect on their audience, these effects are not immediate but the product of a 'cumulative build up of beliefs and values over a long period of time' (Glover, 1984: 10). The 'cultural effects model' is usually seen as Marxist in orientation. In its Marxist version it rests on a number of assumptions: that capitalism creates a class society in which inequality is endemic; that the ruling or dominant class maintains its power through coercion and ideology, and that the media are central to the exercise of power through ideology, helping to win popular consent for their rule (see Chapter 1). However, not all cultural effects theory rests on Marxist assumptions. Early attempts to locate effects within a broader cultural context emerged from within the empirical tradition of American mass communications research.

CULTIVATION ANALYSIS

One of the most influential theories about the cumulative impact of the media is cultivation theory developed by the researcher George Gerbner. Based on empirical research over 20 years Gerbner and his colleagues argue television 'cultivates' a particular view of the world in the minds of the viewers. Regular usage of television over a long period of time can influence people's beliefs and their conduct. According to Gerbner (1992: 100) television viewing 'cultivates a commonality of perspective among otherwise different groups with respect to overarching themes and patterns found in many programmes'. Heavy television viewing over time was found to bring people's views of the world closer to one another. Their exposure results in them internalising the political and social picture of the world presented by television. Television plays a 'homogenising' role by its tendency to erode traditional differences amongst divergent social groups. Gerbner and his colleagues labelled this 'muting' of differences as 'mainstreaming' (Croteau and Hoynes, 1997: 212).

Gerbner's initial work was in the area of TV violence (see below). Those who viewed a great deal of television were found to be more likely to be concerned about crime and violence as the medium tended to report and represent this much more often than it happens in real life. Subsequent work refined and extended this work into many other areas of 'cultivation'. Research found far fewer old people on television than in society and heavy television viewers tended to underestimate the number of old people in society. Not only did they 'misrecognise facts' but extrapolated these facts into a set of beliefs about the powerlessness of older people (Ruddock, 2001: 102). It is also argued television cultivation tended to push political beliefs in a more conservative direction (Gerbner *et al.*, 1982; 1984). Later writers took up the theme of cultivation in the area of political opinion, arguing media coverage of politics is responsible for the growing cynicism, alienation and apathy amongst the American electorate. Postman (1985: 144) believes television alienates viewers from the political process by presenting 'information in a form that renders it simplistic, non-substantive, non-historical and non-contextual'. He also argues the medium has a detrimental impact on viewers' education by reducing their attention span, emphasising entertainment over information and by inhibiting people's ability and capacity to read. For Postman (1985: 155) 'television viewing does not significantly increase learning' and 'is inferior to and less likely than print to cultivate higher-order inferential thinking'. Others have referred to the consumerist logic of television whereby corporate power and television images cultivate the view that the more individuals consume the happier they will be (Morgan, 1989).

The strength of cultivation analysis is the emphasis on continued exposure to the content of television over a long period rather than the selective exposure to individual programmes or films. The approach rejects behaviourism but does not argue the effects of the media are limited or minimal. Gerbner and his colleagues draw attention to the role of media messages in the maintenance of social structures over time. The aim of media messages is not to change beliefs and behaviours but 'to ensure the longevity of an existing social structure based on a particular set of beliefs and values' (Ruddock, 2001: 106). It is the cultivation of particular beliefs about the real world that is crucial. Cultivation analysis is interested in the ideological effects of the media and seeks to develop empirical means to assess them. Critics argue cultivation analysis fails to move beyond the 'conventional wisdom' of the direct effects paradigm. The viewer is still the passive dupe, unable and incapable of resisting media messages (see Gauntlett, 1998; Wober, 1998). They criticise the assumption in cultivation analysis that there is homogeneity in how people watch television and how they respond to the picture of the world it promotes. Viewing patterns and the meanings people take from television can vary. Barker (1998) comes to the defence of the 'heavy viewer' who is seen in cultivation analysis as 'accumulating deposits of message fat', which eventually submerge him or her in the media's worldview. From his work on comic and sci-fi fans Barker argues heavy viewers are more involved in the process of media consumption and more likely to critically engage with media content than the casual viewer, listener or reader. They are more inclined to express their views about media messages. Other critics express misgivings about the methods employed by Gerbner and his colleagues, which fail to establish clear categories for what constitutes heavy, moderate and light viewing (Ruddock, 2001: 108). Attempts to replicate the research have not generated data to support the claim television shapes people's perceptions of the world around them (De Fleur and Ball-Rokeach, 1989: 263). Limitations of method – as well as the failure to explain how cultivation occurs – cast doubt over the theory but in spite of these controversies cultivation analysis helped to broaden the debate about media effects.

AGENDA SETTING

The problem of assessing the effects of the media on people and society led some scholars to emphasise the media's power to determine what people should think about. Cohen (1963: 13) in a study of the media and foreign policy in the United States claimed the news 'may not be successful in telling people what to think but it is stunningly successful in telling them what to think about'. The power to push people into thinking about certain kinds of issues became known as 'agenda setting'. Agenda setting research was a response to growing disenchantment amongst American scholars 'with attitudes and opinions as dependent variables and with the limited effects model as an adequate intellectual summary' (McCombs, 1981: 121). It was another attempt to 'overcome the limited effects findings' by questioning the 'prevailing wisdom that the media have little, if any, influence on voters' (quoted in Rogers and Dearing, 1988: 560). McCombs and Shaw (1972) developed the hypothesis in researchable form in their examination of the news coverage of the 1968 US presidential election campaign. They examined the content of the political news of the campaign in the press, news magazines and on television, and conducted a survey of people's views of the importance of particular issues covered in the media. They found a 'high level of correspondence between the amount of attention given to a particular issue in the media and the level of importance assigned to that issue by people in the community who were exposed to the media' (De Fleur and Ball-Rokeach, 1989: 264). While there was a strong correlation between the issues that appeared on the media's agenda and the salience and importance attached to issues by voters, it was not clear whether the media influences the public or the public sets the media's agenda. McCombs and Shaw initially assumed the media influenced their audiences, but others argue the media simply respond to the public, including many working in the media who see themselves as giving the people what they want. Subsequent agenda setting research has tried to resolve in which direction influence operates.

The struggle to set the agenda in elections across the world, as well as in relation to a number of issues, has concerned scholars (see Iyengar and Reeves, 1997: Part IV). One crucial piece of work by Iyengar and Kinder (1987) attempted to overcome the limitations of earlier research through a series of experiments (see also Iyengar et al., 1982). They sought to test whether the issues that gained prominence in the national news became the problems the viewing public regarded as the nation's most important. Under laboratory conditions individuals were asked to view newscasts over a period of a week, some of which were altered to place more emphasis on certain issues. At the beginning of the week they were asked to rank in order of importance a number of issues, an activity they repeated at the end of the week. They found people shown television broadcasts doctored to focus attention on a particular problem assigned greater importance to that problem. These people attached more importance than they did before the experiment as well as in comparison to people in control groups in which other, different problems were emphasised (Iyengar and Kinder, 1987: 112). Iyengar and Kinder (1987: 114) introduced the concept of 'priming' to describe how the media could go beyond telling people what to think about and shape the criteria used by individuals to judge the merits of their political leaders and the pressing political issues. Priming presumes that when evaluating political phenomena, people do not take into account all they know – even if they wanted to, time often prevents them. Instead people rely on what comes to mind, 'those bits and pieces of political memory that are accessible'. Iyengar and Kinder found evidence to support the claim that 'television news was a powerful determinant of what springs to mind and what is forgotten or ignored'. It helps to shape the standards by which the performance of politicians are measured and by which political choices are made. For Iyengar and Kinder (1987: 117) the power of the media does not rest in persuasion but in 'commanding the public's attention (agenda setting) and defining criteria underlying the public's judgements (priming)'.

Despite the flourishing of agenda setting research, the concept is criticised for a number of shortcomings (Perry 1996: 151). Lang and Lang (1981) draw attention to the problem of identifying what an issue is. They argue 'without a clear definition, the concept of agenda-setting becomes so all embracing as to be rendered practically meaningless' (1981: 450). Agenda setting research has focused on a range of 'issues' from general topics such as inflation to more specific events such as natural disasters. The confusion between happenings constrained by time and place and broader cumulative happenings is further confused by the media locating particular events within a broader category (Rogers and Dearing, 1988: 566). As Rogers and Dearing (1988: 567) point out, different issues may influence the agenda setting process in different ways. It is possible to distinguish between 'rapid onset news events' such as the US bombing of Libya in 1986 and 'slow onset' items such as the 1984–85 famine in Ethiopia, as well as a 'high salience, short duration' issue such as the hijacking of a TWA airline in 1985 and a 'low salience' issue such as the rise and fall of US employment figures. While agenda setting research shows a correlation between the media agenda and the policy and public agendas, there is limited conceptualisation of how and why this might happen. Despite all the research we do not have a clear understanding of the process of agenda setting, of what happens when the issues of importance on the media's agenda are transferred to the minds of the public or policy makers. Is this a short-run or long-run process? Research into how long it takes for the public to take up the media's agenda has generated different and inconclusive answers (Severin and Tankard, 1988: 278–9). To what extent is agenda setting a conscious or unconscious process? How far do certain cues (such as headlines, visuals or position of item in a newscast) suggest the importance of an issue? How do people store information about the importance of an issue? These – and other – questions about the processing of information from the media's agenda are largely ignored in agenda setting research. Only in recent years have researchers acknowledged that the media's agenda is shaped by others. Research into who sets the media's agenda has highlighted the interplay between interest groups, government officials, citizens and politicians amongst others in trying to influence what the media reports as important. The complexity of the process by which issues become important in policy-making circles and public debate led the Langs (1983) to develop the notion of 'agenda building', which suggests the process of putting an issue on to the public and policy-making agenda takes time and goes through several stages. From their study of the media's reporting of the Watergate crisis they identified a number of key variables in determining whether an issue is taken up. The language the media use to describe the importance of an issue, the way in which the media frame the issue, and the role of credible, well-known people in articulating the importance of an issue are deemed crucial (see Severin and Tankard, 1988: 279–80). While agenda setting has been 'one of the major concepts in media effects theory since the 1970s' (Severin and Tankard, 1988: 282) – particularly in the area of political effects – there are doubts about the exact nature of the impact on the public of the media's agenda.

MEDIA AND VIOLENCE

The issue of television and violence has dominated the media effects debate. In popular circles watching violent television and films is a cause of violence in society. Children, as young, impressionable and innocent, are seen as especially vulnerable. High-profile murder cases have evoked the power of the visual media to explain the behaviour of offenders. In the 1993 trial of the two young boys who killed the infant James Bulger the judge stated his belief that 'exposure to violent films may in part be an explanation' (quoted in Jones, 1997). In America defence lawyers in some cases have argued viewing violent films influenced the actions of their young clients. Supporting evidence for the 'copycat' violence being learned from the media is provided by a number of official government reports. In 1972 the US Surgeon General concluded from his interpretation of a vast amount of data put before him that 'a causal relationship has been shown between violence viewing and aggression' (quoted in Schorr, 1985: 160). In Britain the Newson Report in 1994 came to the same conclusion on less evidence (see Barker, 2001). The outcome has been legislation restricting access to violent material, one of the most recent being the introduction of the V-chip into television sets, which allows parents to censor what appears on their screens. Such actions have not curtailed the debate about media violence as more recently concerns have been expressed about children and teenagers downloading violent images from the Internet (see Craig and Petley, 2001).

This highly charged debate about media violence provides a case study for examining the issues and problems that have beset theoretical approaches to understanding media effects. In examining media violence there is a clear problem of distinguishing *what kind* of effect of *what* on *whom*. Effects research is often confused by bracketing together different kinds of behaviour. The media violence debate puts sex and violence together as if they are a natural couplet (see Root, 1986). Moral guardians such as the late Mrs Whitehouse in Britain, and her pressure group the National Viewers' and Listeners' Association (NVLA), lump media representation of sex and violence together because of their moral disapproval of both. Some feminist scholars associate pornography with 'violence against women'. Andrea Dworkin (1981) sees pornography as the cause of rape in society. There may be an occasional convergence between sex and violence in the media, with some of the more distasteful forms of pornography involving violence, but there is no reason to assume sexual behaviour and violent behaviour is the same. Different kinds of behaviour can be seen as similar if we accept the stimulus-response model. However, as we have seen, there are limitations with this model, and the attempt to generalise about behaviour across a range of walks of life is problematic.

The media violence debate is also clouded by a conception of the audience that focuses primarily on young people and children. Barker and Petley (1997: 5) argue media effects studies generally are biased in their understanding of whom the media is supposed to effect – they do not usually examine 'the "educated" and "cultured" middle classes, who either don't watch such rubbish, or else are fully able to deal with it if they do'. It is, for example, the young, the uneducated, the 'heavy viewer' and the working class who are seen as susceptible (Gauntlett, 2001: 57). There is also the question of what is meant by 'violence' both on the screen and in the behaviour of audience members. Research and popular debate do not provide a clear-cut definition of violence. Media portrayals of violence range from violent behaviour in cartoons to news footage from the world's war zones. It can

> encompass anything from cartoons (ten-ton blocks dropped on Tom's head by Jerry, Wily Coyote plummeting down yet another mile-deep canyon); children's action adventure films (the dinosaurs of Jurassic Park alongside playground scuffles from Grange Hill and the last-reel shoot-outs in westerns); news footage from Rwanda and Bosnia; documentary footage showing the police attacking Rodney King in Los Angeles . . . etc. etc.

which, for Barker (2001: 42), represents a 'useless conflation of wholly different things'. Violence in real life can vary enormously, from anti-social behaviour to aggressive actions and, in certain contexts, aggressive behaviour can be deemed acceptable or at worst understandable. There is, then, a basic difficulty of defining violence. Thus what appears an obvious discussion requires careful consideration and clear definitions.

The direct, limited and cultural effects models have been applied to the question of media violence in different ways. The direct effects approach has basically sought to measure how behaviour is influenced by exposure to violence on film and television screens. Experiments have been the primary way in which such research is conducted. While there is a variety of ways in which laboratory experiments on media violence have been done, it is possible to identify the same basic design (see Murdock and McCron, 1978). Researchers usually select a violent episode from the content of the media and show it to a group of subjects. These subjects are then frustrated in a particular way and provided with an opportunity to act out their response to the film and the experience of frustration. These responses are observed and measured, and then compared with those of a control group who did not see the extract. Both groups are usually selected to have the same basic composition – whether it is to include an equal number of women and men or introverts and extroverts. If those in the group who saw the extract react more violently or aggressively, this can be attributed to the effect of the media. A range of techniques has been used to assess the effects, from charting physiological change during viewing (such as an increase in blood pressure or sweating) or by observing whether social behaviour has changed afterwards. The main conclusion of such laboratory research is that exposure to violent media material can cause violent responses. Thus certain forms of filmed violence are seen as imitative and aggression can be aroused by the viewing of certain types of violent episode (Newburn and Hagell, 1995). Bandura's work is seen as a typical example of the laboratory experiments on media violence. Such work has the aura of 'scientific authenticity'. The laboratory is central to popular conceptions of science as the place where discoveries are made and hypotheses are subjected to rigorous testing (Murdock, 2001: 164). For others they are places staffed by 'mad scientists and numerical charlatans' in which the researcher's 'myopic allegiance to experimental methodologies' produces findings that are 'hopelessly divorced' from reality (Ruddock, 2001: 38).

Laboratory experiments into media violence are criticised for 'taking place under extremely artificial conditions which are unlikely to occur very frequently in other circumstances' (Newburn and Hagell, 1995). It is doubtful as to how much a subject's behaviour in a laboratory can be applied to the outside world. Other factors in the 'real' world, such as peer group pressure or family environment, militate against certain forms of action or behaviour being taken. There is also a problem of distinguishing the media from the range of other factors or stimuli that could account for violent behaviour. Producing the controlled experiment that makes it possible to identify one single stimulus to account for a person's behaviour is problematic. Subjects in laboratory experiments often provide responses they believe the researcher wants. The stimuli in such experiments – the film extract – often only reflect the researchers' interests and are viewed by subjects in highly contrived conditions. Samples are often seen as unsatisfactory as they do not represent the population at large. Thus laboratory experiments that take people out of their social context are seen as producing artificial behaviour in strange, atypical surroundings and providing little concrete evidence to judge what real people would do in the real world.

Dissatisfaction with method – as well as reservations about the simplistic conception of human behaviour – led to attempts to understand the effects of media violence in their 'natural' environment. As one researcher put it: 'do we want to know with certainty what will happen in a highly specific set of circumstances, or do we want to know what is more or less likely to happen when media violence is seen in "natural everyday viewing situations"?' (Noble, 1975: 153). Researchers observe and question people in their natural habitat by means of the field study. For example, Noble (1975) examined teenage boys in an Irish boarding school. He argued there are too many variables in the process of watching television for us to be certain an effect can be attributed to the medium. He also suggested that some media violence may be cathartic, a release mechanism for aggressive impulses that could otherwise be acted out in real life. Such a finding is reinforced by other field studies, in particular that of Feshbach and Singer (1971) who examined teenage boys in American private and care homes. Noble's conclusions were that the effects of media violence depend on the degree to which viewers recognise or identify with the perpetrators or victims of the violence. In other words, they are limited or mediated by the disposition or attitudes of the audience. This is in keeping with the uses and gratifications approach. Noble also distinguished between factual and fictional violence, arguing the boys he studied were more disturbed by 'real' violence on the news than by violence in the context of fictional programming.

Halloran *et al.* (1970) stressed the role of the audience in an examination of television and juvenile delinquency. The viewing habits of delinquent children were compared with those of non-delinquents. The former watched slightly more television overall and a few more 'violent' programmes. Halloran *et al.* concluded children did not become delinquent because they watched a lot of television but they watched a lot of television because they were delinquent. The heavier viewing was attributed to the deprived backgrounds from which such children generally came. Deprivation resulted in increased television viewing because such children lived in families where the TV set was always on, in neighbourhoods in which alternative leisure activities were absent and they found personal relationship difficult, and television became a substitute. Halloran *et al.* (1970: 178) concluded

> the whole weight of research and theory in the juvenile delinquency field
> would suggest that the mass media, except just possibly in the case of a very
> small number of pathological individuals, are never the sole cause of
> delinquent behaviour. At most they play a contributory role and that a minor
> one.

Both Noble and Halloran avoid the problems of direct effects research and its emphasis on laboratory experiments and simplistic learning models. They recognise and examine different styles of violence, noting the importance of how violence is presented in the media. However, their focus on the nature of media violence and the way in which the audience uses it ignores or downplays the cultural context within which media violence operates. At the simplest level a number of variables such as age, sex and ethnicity are neglected in uses and gratifications approaches to media violence.

The cultural effects model is less concerned with the impact of media violence on the individual than with how media violence affects society's ideas and views of violence. For Murdock (1982b) effects theories usually start from the wrong point. Instead of asking whether the media causes violence we should ask what causes violence and then examine the role the media play. Murdock's starting point is society, not the media. He points out that research into delinquent subcultures provides a good deal of material about the social background and attitudes of delinquent teenagers, their schooling, work and unemployment, group behaviour and social attitudes. The real problem is delinquency, which is the product of a set of social circumstances and can result in violence. By focusing on television, Murdock argues, we are using the medium as a scapegoat for our social problems and blinding us to other more deep-rooted social causes. Gerbner (1992) argues the obsession with the effects of television on violent behaviour has distracted from more important questions about the impact of television violence on how dangerous and violent audiences believe society is. He tested his belief that television affects people's feeling about violence in society by surveying a group of students, first ascertaining their viewing habits then asking them a number of questions about violence in society. Students who were heavy television viewers saw society, the streets and the police as more violent and people less trustworthy than light viewers. People who believe the world is more violent than it is and who are more fearful of becoming victims are more likely to favour law and order policies. This is the cultural effect of television on society.

Cultural effects theories do locate media violence in a wider cultural context, drawing attention to questions other theories marginalise as well as the political dimension of the debate. They also raise questions about how we define and think about the problem of violence in the media. Murdock (1982b: 87) states, 'it is not enough to provide different answers to the dominant questions, we need to ask other kinds of questions and to work our way towards more plausible answers'. However, as with other theories, the empirical evidence to support the cultural effects model is far from clear-cut. Gerbner's studies can be criticised on several grounds. Using students is problematic, as they do not represent a cross-section of the population. People's views of violence in society are shaped not only by television viewing but also by other variables, including their social circumstance such as where they live, their age and gender. There is also the possibility that people watch a lot of television because they are afraid of going out. Demonstrating the cultural effects of media violence is problematic.

The debate on media violence highlights the more general limitations of the thinking about media effects. Conclusions as to the impact of media violence on behaviour are extremely weak. There is little empirical evidence to support the views that the media has a powerful or a marginal impact on people's behaviour. There is also little support for the position that the media foster particular views of violence in society. Often the debate about media violence rests on moral and aesthetic considerations rather than any solid evidence. What is clear is that discussion of media violence often isolates the media from other social factors. The media are one factor in explaining violence in society. Other factors are as, if not more, important. For example, most acts of violence are committed by men so perhaps we should focus our attention on masculinity rather than television or the media. Focusing on the effects of media violence on behaviour prevents us from understanding either violence in society or the media in society.

SUMMARY

The history of understanding media effects is characterised by a number of key periods in which the conceptualisation of media effects has been distinctive. Early effects theory and research was shaped by ideas, which highlighted the negative and anti-social impact of the media on those who consumed them. Notions of an all-powerful media with simple and straightforward effects on their audiences prevailed. The process of mass communication was 'a one-way hypodermic injection in to the veins of the body politic. Whoever they were, wherever they were, the media of mass communication affected all its uncritical consumers equally' (Tudor, 1979: 176). Gradually the all-embracing view of direct and clear-cut media effects gave way to a notion of selective perception, whereby individuals interpreted what they saw, heard and read in the media according to their own pre-dispositions. The two-step model of media effects emphasised that people were not simply 'faces in the crowd', individuals isolated from society, but part of groups and networks that enabled them to make sense of media messages. The variety of ways in which people use the media to gratify their particular needs came to dominate media effects research. The emphasis now was on what people do with the media rather than on what the media do to them. The context within which individuals consume the media became important as the pendulum swung toward understanding of media effects as minimal or limited. However, the focus on individuals and their social context was increasingly seen as a narrow way of understanding the effects of the media. For many researchers traditional effects approaches were asking the wrong questions (see, for example, Murdock, 1982a). Cultural effects theories seek to understand the broader impact of the media, on what we think about, how we understand society and how we collectively think. This represents a shift from examining the media as sources of individual effects to understanding them as 'articulators of our cultures' (Tudor, 1979).

The outcome of this history is far from conclusive. Four decades of media effects research have delivered inconsistent and contradictory results. Which model of media effects – direct, limited or cultural – is the most viable is a matter of conjecture. Academic debate throughout these decades has tended to see each model as being mutually exclusive. Social scientists are a disputatious community and prefer one model, seeing it as incompatible with others. This has been reinforced by a difference between scholars as to what is meant by an 'effect'. There are today signs of a growing convergence between the different model of media effects as researchers start to ask similar questions as a result of a more sophisticated conceptualisation of the audience, which is the subject of the next chapter.

Chapter Eight

☐ THE AUDIENCE STRIKES BACK: NEW AUDIENCE AND RECEPTION THEORY

The previous chapter examined the main schools of thought that have shaped our understanding of media effects. Contemporary media scholarship has moved away from examining how particular messages influence people, to exploring the nature of media audiences. Building from the cultural approach, media researchers are more interested in what audiences say about the influence of the media in their lives. Media theory now concentrates on how audiences generate meaning, and enquiry into media effects has been replaced by examination of the creativity of audiences in the generation of meaning. Audiences interpret media messages and their ability to do this is determined by a range of individual, social and cultural factors. They are no longer seen as an undifferentiated mass of passive recipients of messages but a multitude of different groups with their own histories, habits and social interactions. Specific audiences exist for particular media products. The notion of a captive audience forced to digest a daily dose of what media practitioners think is good for them has been superseded by a more promiscuous and powerful audience who can decide what they want to consume and when. What audiences think and what they do is more central to understanding the influence of the media. Scholars increasingly focus on the contexts within which the reception of media messages takes place.

The change in thinking about media audiences coincided with the technological advances that have enabled the media to cater for more specialised audiences. The emergence of 'narrowcasting' has seen the growth of channels on cable and/or satellite dedicated to the delivery of specific kinds of output such as history programmes or comedy shows or sport. Audiences are defined by contemporary scholarship in a number of different ways: by a particular product such as a newspaper or film or TV programme, or by specific types of product such as women's magazines, film genres such as westerns or action movies, television formats such as soaps, quiz shows and news programmes, or specific types of music such as rap or hip-hop, or by social or geographical type such as age, gender, sexuality, nation, ethnicity, political allegiance, education, religion, urban and rural, and so on. Scholars have sought to examine the nature of these specialised audiences, attempting to identify the factors that shape their interpretations and understanding of the output. They have also sought to examine how different groups of people interpret and make sense of messages in different ways. In doing so they have moved away from the notion that the media have direct power to determine the interpretation and understanding people have of media messages. The discovery of the ability of audiences to make meaning has produced 'active audience theory', which has established itself as the new orthodoxy in media studies.

The 'new audience research' is seen as beginning, at least in the United Kingdom, with David Morley and Charlotte Brunsdon's study of the audience for BBC TV news magazine *Nationwide* in 1978. Their approach was influenced by Hall's encoding-decoding, which Morley (1980) applied to an empirical investigation of the *Nationwide* audience. A detailed textual analysis of the programme was completed to identify the 'preferred readings' in the text (Morley and Brunsdon, 1978) and Morley examined the context of media consumption to determine the meaning people took from their interaction with the programme. Morley concluded that meaning is not solely inscribed in the messages produced by the media but is the outcome of the interaction between the audience and the text. His findings also showed people from the same socio-economic background could generate different interpretations of the output. This led him to examine the 'everyday lived arenas' in which people made sense of what they see, hear and read. He placed emphasis on the family and home – as well as the workplace – as where meaning had to be negotiated (Morley, 1986). In the 1980s numerous pieces of research examined how audiences made sense of a variety of media texts according to the social and cultural backgrounds and experiences that influence their understanding. Such research stressed the capacity of audiences to appropriate and resist the dominant meaning encoded in media texts. Post-modernism encouraged this perspective by claiming that cultural identities can be freely selected by individuals from a wide variety of choices available in the media. Critics such as Curran (1990) argue such work ignores the constraints, which limit people's ability to interpret media messages. This led to a debate about the 'new audience research' (see Curran, 1996; Morley, 1996; Ang, 1996), which ultimately centred on the extent to which audiences are free to interpret messages.

DESPERATELY SEEKING AUDIENCES

An impetus for the new audience theory came from the frustrations many scholars had about the hold the media industries had over thinking about the nature of audiences. In their attempts to reach as many people as possible the media had developed techniques to discover information about their audiences. The British press began to audit its circulation figures in the 1920s and newspapers started to employ agencies to survey their readers in order to package their products more effectively (Curran, 1980). In 1936 the BBC established the Listeners Research Department to gain more information about who was tuning in to the different kinds of programmes it was broadcasting (Williams, 1998: 106). Since the end of the Second World War audience data has come to play a crucial role in the success or failure of media products, especially in broadcasting. In Britain the British

Audience Research Board (BARB) and in the USA Nielsen Media Research produce indicators of the relative popularity of television shows. Known as the 'ratings' such indicators are compiled by the installation of 'people meters' to monitor what is watched in a cross-section of households in the country as well as diaries people keep of their viewing activity. Ratings enable broadcasters to determine how many people are watching a programme; the size of the audience for any programme is crucial as it effectively determines how much advertisers can be charged. Even broadcasters such as the BBC, a public service organisation, which does not carry adverts, need to justify their licence fee by attracting large audiences. This had led some scholars to describe media audiences as commodities waiting to be sold to advertisers (Smythe, 1977). Viewers, listeners and readers are potential 'consumers' for media products who can be offered for sale to advertisers. Other scholars describe audiences as 'invisible fictions that are produced institutionally in order for various institutions to take charge of the mechanisms of their own survival' (Hartley, 1992). Media institutions have no real intention of knowing their audiences but seek to produce data about audiences for the purpose of economic or institutional benefit.

The institutional view of the media was complemented in early effects research by the conceptualisation of media audiences as 'masses'. Scholars emphasised their large size and saw them as being made up of isolated and defenceless individuals. The notion of the 'masses' reinforced a particular image of media audiences as passive dupes – or couch potatoes – who are easily manipulated. The undifferentiated and anonymous conception of media audiences does not provide 'any understanding of the worlds of media audiences themselves' (Ang, 1995: 211). Raymond Williams (1961) argued there are no masses but 'only ways of seeing people as masses' and drew attention to how the media construct their audiences to serve their own needs. New audience research challenges the institutional view of media audiences. The approach shows how audiences are more complex, diverse and problematic than is assumed by the media industries and effects scholars. Ang (1991) in her study of ratings documents how the methods and devices used by broadcasters to measure audiences are not only subject to error but contain huge inaccuracies and sometimes outright fictions. She highlights we need to know more about audiences than who they are and their size. Above all we need to know more about how they interact with and respond to what they see, hear and read if we are to make any judgements about the power and influence of the media. Ratings are criticised for simply reflecting the views of those 'hooked' on television. The new audience research for scholars such as Ang was a response to the scant academic understanding of the practices and experiences people bring to their consumption of television. It was also a challenge to 'our knowledge of television audiencehood which has been colonized by ... the institutional point of view' (1991: 2), which reduces 'the dispersed realities of television audiencehood' to 'a single, unitary concept of "television audience"' (1991: 8). The new audience research is regarded as providing greater insight into the nature of media audiences and liberating scholars from the dominant discourse of the media industries and early effects research.

ACTIVE AUDIENCES

New audience research focuses on how audience members generate meaning from the media in the broader context of the exercise of power in society. Like the uses and gratifications model the approach is interested in what audiences do with the media. However, the new audience research is more interested in understanding how audiences actively engage in the process of generating meaning and the factors outside the media that shape the sense they make of media messages. This line of research is attractive to many scholars as it emphasises the intelligence and capacity of people to make decisions for themselves. People are not the pawns of the media industries; they have some power and freedom in their use of media (Croteau and Hoynes, 1997: 230–1). Audiences are seen as being active at the individual, social and political level. In order to explore how people participate in the creation of meaning from media texts scholars adopted the method of ethnographic research. Unlike previous effects research, which relied on survey, questionnaires and laboratory experiments, ethnography draws on people's personal accounts of their involvement with the media through in-depth interviews about their media consumption habits. It could lead to researchers spending time with a particular group to observe at first hand their media preferences.

Ethnography

Ethnography as a research method plays an important role in media research. Although it can take a number of forms it is usually associated with participant observation. Researchers spend time in 'real' situations with the group of people they are studying, observing and sometimes sharing their experiences. Production studies (see Chapter 4) have seen researchers observing the activities of media workers in their places of work – for example, Schlesinger's study of the BBC TV newsroom.

Ethnography is now associated with new audience research. Participant observation is only one form of ethnographic method used by new audience researchers, and rarely used at that. Audience understanding and interaction with media messages is more often examined by textual analysis of transcribed interview material, produced through group discussion or individual conversation, or other forms of written communication such as letters. To what extent such methods reflect the natural settings within which people consume media products is a matter of debate. See Machin (2002) and Ruddock (2001: 128–46).

The move back to speaking with real-life audience members, which previously exemplified uses and gratifications research, is associated with the work of the Birmingham Centre for Contemporary Cultural Studies (BCCCS) in the 1970s. Its empirical work with audiences contrasted with the approach that emerged from the development of structuralism, and particularly the work of Althusser. Structuralists argue the content of the media is organised in particular patterns that position audiences and determine the meanings people take. This process of interpellation is the primary means by which capitalism and the dominant class won acquiescence for their ideology (see Chapter 6). Audience members are subjects and as such forced to accept the ideological prescribed position laid out for them by the media. This relationship between the media and their audiences was most clearly articulated in the pages of the film journal *Screen*. Writers from the *Screen* theory perspective such as Stephen Heath and Laura Mulvey analysed how films position the audience as subjects and force them to take on the identity and ideology pre-ordained by the film's text. Heath (1981) argues the audience is positioned in the narrative of a film by a number of cinematic techniques. For example, the camera often shoots from the perspective of the protagonist and what he and/or she is looking at, thereby offering the audience the fictional character's purchase on the world. The realism of the way in which mainstream film represents the world is seen as encouraging the viewer to see the camera's view as real and not as an ideological construction. Hollywood cinema with its high production values and pronounced realistic style was seen as exerting a powerful influence over its audience.

Screen theory offered an analytical means to engage with the media. By examining the structure of the film through the use of camera angles, editing devices and other techniques it was seen as possible to identify the ideological version offered by the text. Mulvey (1975) shows how mainstream Hollywood cinema encourages the viewer to identify with the male protagonist and the 'male gaze'. In a very influential piece of work, which has been extended to the analysis of a variety of forms of visual culture, Mulvey contends that spectatorship is constructed as a male activity. From analysis of the camera angles she found that films 'tend to construct masculine subject positions' (Eldridge *et al.*, 1997: 128). In mainstream Hollywood women act as erotic objects for the male audience and for the male protagonists with whom the male audience can identify (Van Zoonen, 1994: 89). For example, rape scenes are shot from the perpetrator's, not the victim's, point of view therefore underpinning the male gaze in film spectatorship. Cinema may provide escapism but it is also shaped by a social reality structured in patriarchy. For Mulvey the link between cinematic practices and patriarchy is clear: 'film reflects, reveals and even plays on the straight, socially established interpretations of sexual difference which controls images, erotic ways of looking and spectacle' (quoted in Van Zoonen, 1994: 90). Mulvey's work and that of *Screen* theory in general was challenged by theorists at BCCCS for its failure to explore the relationship between actual audiences and media content.

Screen theory presents audience members as passive recipients of the ideological meaning of media texts and ignores the possibility of differences between audience members in making sense of media messages. Mulvey's work, for example, has been challenged for neglecting differences in sexual identity amongst audiences and for emphasising gender at the expense of other differences such as race (Eldridge *et al.*, 1997: 129). BCCCS researchers argued *Screen* theory fails to acknowledge that audience members come to the media with their own views, perspectives and identities, and took issue with the view that film texts or any media texts construct one clear ideological position. The basis for their alternative approach to media audiences was the encoding-decoding model articulated by Stuart Hall.

ENCODING AND DECODING

The encoding-decoding model is the starting point of the active audience approach (Cruz and Lewis, 1994). Hall (1980; 1982) was critical of traditional effects theories because of their narrow conception of effects, focusing on the influence of A on B's behaviour and on changes of behaviour such as a switch between political candidates or advertised consumer goods. For Hall this ignored 'larger historical shifts, questions of political process and formation before and beyond the ballot box, issues of social and political power, of social structure and economic relations' which were 'simply absent, not by chance, but because they were theoretically outside the frame of reference' (Hall, 1982: 59). He attributed the traditional approach of effects studies to the pluralist views of effects researchers (see Chapter 2). Hall rejected pluralism, arguing certain groups had the power to impose their values on society and the media played a central role in this process. For him research should be concerned with the 'ideological effects' of the media; on how the media are used to promote or reinforce a particular set of dominant values and how successful they are in doing this.

Conceiving of ideology in hegemonic terms (see Chapter 6), Hall developed his encoding-decoding model. This is not the easiest theoretical formulation to understand, not least because it went through a number of versions (see Hall, 1973; 1975; 1980) and was presented as a 'polemical thrust' to the existing state of media research in the 1970s (see Gray, 1999: 26–7). Hall's model adopts the cultural effects approach, focusing on the mass communication process in its totality, and suggests that any understanding of modern media culture must focus on 'the fit between the discursive construction of the message and the interpretative understanding of the audience' (Stevenson, 1995: 42). The content of the media is *encoded* ideologically. The meaning of what appears in the media is determined by the nature of the production process, which operates according to institutional constraints and professional codes and practices to produce a preferred meaning in media messages for the audience to understand. Recognising struggles can and do occur within the production process, Hall acknowledges that a number of messages could be encoded in media texts. However, he argues there is one dominant message coming from the media's tendency, consciously or unconsciously, to reproduce the meaning preferred by the most powerful groups in society (see Chapter 6). On the audience side the process of under-standing or *decoding* the messages is open to a degree of interpretation. The content of the media, described as media texts, is open to a range of interpretations as it is polysemic. Audiences are involved in 'semiotic work' in decoding the meaning of media texts. However, the ability of the individual to interpret media texts is shaped by the specific social circumstances or situations in which he or she is located. Hall emphasises social factors, in particular class, rather than individual inclinations or preferences as determi-nants of the decoding process. He distinguishes three possible kinds of decodings or read-ings of media content: *dominant, negotiated* and *oppositional.* The dominant – or hegemonic – reading accepts the preferred meaning encoded in the text. The oppositional reading occurs when people understand the preferred reading, reject it and decode meaning according to their own values and attitudes, and a negotiated reading is where people adapt rather than completely reject the preferred reading.

Hall's model represented a shift in the effects debate by making the influence of media dependent on people's interpretations and thought processes. It 'moves away from a behaviouristic stimulus-response model to an interpretive framework where all effects depend on an interpretation of media messages' (Alasuutari, 1999: 3). He provides a more dynamic understanding of how the media constructs meaning and how people make sense of what they see, hear and read. The model emphasises the interaction between the audi-ence and texts as well as the social context within which such interaction happens. Meaning cannot simply be read off from media texts. Hall's work moved audience research on by speculating on the different and contradictory interpretations that could be made of media content. Unlike the uses and gratifications model he did not focus nar-rowly on the individual's uses of the media but rather on how different social contexts and backgrounds influence individual interpretations. Perception was not conceived in per-sonal or psychological terms but social. People were part of 'interpretive communities' who made common interpretations of media messages. However, Hall's model resided solely at the hypothetical level and was not based on any empirical evidence to support the claims made about the ways in which people 'read' media messages. The first effort to test Hall's model was a pioneering study of the *Nationwide* audience.

THE NATIONWIDE STUDY

Nationwide was a 1970s news magazine programme broadcast by the BBC after the early evening news. The programme was a round-up of news from the different nations and regions of the United Kingdom and focused on human interest stories and the stories behind the main events of the day. Morley and Brunsdon (1978) examined the content of the programme to identify the main messages that producers sought to get across and then interviewed groups of people from different social, cultural and educational backgrounds to see how they interpreted what they had seen in the programmes they were shown.

Morley (1980) discovered that different groups made sense of the messages in different ways. His examination of how different groups decoded the 'preferred meaning' encoded by the makers of *Nationwide* found that dominant readings were, for example, common amongst bank managers, negotiated readings amongst trades union officials and university students, and oppositional readings amongst black students and trades union activists. The group of bank managers, while objecting to the tone and style of the programme, dismissing it as 'teatime stuff' or 'undemanding entertainment', accepted the content and assumptions behind it. They saw the preferred reading as common-sense, which therefore prevented them from seeing the constructed nature of the text. Trades union activists approved of the 'populist' style of the programme but were highly critical of the whole framework, seeing *Nationwide* as trying to wrap up contentious issues in a particular way, which worked against the interests of working people. Their perspective led them to reject the preferred reading. Black students also provided an oppositional reading but their reaction to the programme differed from that of the activists. *Nationwide* was irrelevant to them and their lives. Their opposition came from the black, working-class, inner city experience simply not being accounted for in the *Nationwide* programme (Morley, 1980: 122). Theirs was a 'critique of silence' as they had nothing to say about something so distant from their experience. Morley's research also showed that many people across the groups understood the preferred reading of the programme but this awareness did not lead them to reject the message put forward (1980: 140). To account for this Morley concentrated on the socio-economic background of the groups, and in particular their social class.

Morley's findings underlined that people are not passive, and to understand their interpretations of media messages we must examine both the content of the media and the social background and experience of the audience. However, his findings raised questions about Hall's encoding-decoding model. He discovered that social background and experience did not necessarily determine people's understanding of the content of the media. Social class alone was not an adequate explanation for different audience responses. Respondents who shared a similar class background sometimes produced different responses. For example, working-class people active in trades unions did not respond in the same way to *Nationwide*'s preferred reading as those who were not active. Morley later acknowledged he had 'over-simplified the relationship between someone's class position and the meaning he or she gave to the TV programme' (Lewis, 1991: 59) and suggested other social variables such as age, gender and ethnicity are often as relevant as class background in shaping the way in which people decode media messages. He also argued that people's competence to actively engage in making sense of the media was crucial. Despite the limited cultural resources at their disposal due to their class background, some people still had the capacity to decode media messages in a variety of ways, and in particular in opposition to the preferred reading or dominant message (Morley, 1986: 43). The *Nationwide* study spawned a number of similar studies that examined a programme and analysed its reception among a particular audience.

RECEPTION ANALYSIS

A great number of the reception studies in the 1980s were on popular entertainment forms. If much of the traditional effects research had been done on news, information and 'serious' programming, the new audience research is associated with soap operas, romance novels and women's magazines, previously dismissed as beneath serious critical attention (Eldridge *et al.*, 1997: 144). It also pays much attention to one segment of the audience – women readers, viewers and listeners. Despite Herzog's pioneering work on women radio listeners in the 1940s, there had been an academic neglect of 'mass female culture'. Several feminist authors, such as Hobson (1982), Radway (1984) and Ang (1985), re-dressed this neglect. They were interested in understanding why such large numbers of women consume media products that are predominantly sexist, patriarchal and capitalist in their content. What was behind the popularity of watching soaps such as *Dallas, Dynasty* and *Crossroads*? Why did women, including many who called themselves feminists, enjoy reading Mills and Boon novels and *Woman's Own*? In answering such questions feminist research emphasised the creative abilities and cultural competencies of the female audience to interpret media messages to suit their own needs.

Mulvey (1975) came to the conclusion to liberate women from the 'male gaze' the pleasures of popular cinema had to be eradicated. She advocated the merits of the avant-garde that challenged mainstream cinema at the political and aesthetic level. Her dismissal of popular media and cultural forms was a matter of controversy amongst feminist writers (see Gamman and Marshment, 1988). Modleski (1982) in her discussion of popular media forms for women, such as romance novels and soap operas, argued 'mass produced fantasies for women' could 'speak to the very real problems and tensions in women's lives'. Radway (1984) examined how women readers of romance novels interpret and make sense of what they are reading. To understand the meaning women readers attach to romance novels Radway argues it is more important to study the act of reading than the construction of the text. Despite the patriarchal ideology underlying most romantic fiction, Radway's research found reading such novels allowed women to escape from the constraints of their social existence. By entering the world of the romantic heroine, all of whose emotional needs are satisfied, Radway argues these women were able to shake off their daily routines of wives and mothers and enjoy the pleasures of the stories, which help to satisfy requirements not met by these roles. Romance novels are not 'simply sexist trash that reaffirms cultural restrictions of female behaviour' but are used by women readers to 'critique their own social conditions' and 'compensate for its shortcomings' (Croteau and Hoynes, 1997: 248). For Radway there is an element of empowerment for women in their reading of romantic fiction. Women's reading of romance novels is an example of how subordinate or oppressed groups create meanings for themselves out of 'the very stuff offered to them by the dominant culture as raw materials and appropriating it in ways that suit their own interests' (quoted in Eldridge *et al.*, 1997: 143).

Reception analysis emphasised the ability of audiences to appropriate the meanings they wanted from popular media and cultural forms. The media form that received most attention from active audience researchers was the soap opera. Hobson (1982) showed how women actively engaged in bringing meaning to *Crossroads*, Britain's most popular soap opera in the 1970s, by drawing on their own experiences. *Crossroads* was enjoyed not for its acting or its situations but for its focus on women's everyday lives. The appeal of the soap opera, Hobson (1982: 32–5) postulates, comes from the 'range of strong female characters'. It offers 'women of different ages, class and personality types . . . with whom many members of the female audience can empathise' and is 'primarily about the problems of everyday personal life and personal relationships'. The 'emotional realism' of the soap opera is an appealing quality. She found that *Crossroads* viewers 'make their own readings of what the production sets out to communicate' as they 'work with the text and add their own experience and opinions to the stories in the programme' (1982: 135). This, she argues, is encouraged by the format of the soap opera, which is 'one of the most progressive forms on television because it is a form where the audience is always in control'. Soaps open up discussion of everyday dilemmas over a period of time and whatever the resolution or ending of the storylines put forward by the programme-makers viewers can incorporate their own perspectives and re-interpret endings according to their own opinions. Hobson (1982: 136) emphasised the power of the audience in making sense of *Crossroads*, by stating 'there are as many different *Crossroads* as there are viewers'.

The most cited piece of work on soap operas is the study of the American soap *Dallas* by Dutch academic Ien Ang (1985). The starting point for her research was that 'people actively and creatively make their own meanings and create their own culture, rather than passively absorb pre-given meanings imposed on them' (quoted in Eldridge *et al.*, 1997: 148). She wanted to explore why viewers in The Netherlands, over half of whom were watching the programme in 1982, enjoyed *Dallas*. Like Hobson she draws attention to the nature of soap operas and their emphasis on the representation of ambivalence and contradiction that makes it difficult to produce any ideological consensus. 'The continuing ideological uncertainty creates a certain "freedom" for viewers to construct their own meanings' (Ang, 1985: 120). Like Hobson she argues the appeal of watching the programme rests with its 'emotional realism', stressing the enjoyment the audience, most of whom were women, gained from watching *Dallas* came from the way in which the programme 'facilitated fantasy' (quoted in Eldridge *et al.*, 1997: 149). Ang's watchers of *Dallas* made no assessment as to whether the programme represented an accurate picture of 'reality'; they accepted what they were seeing is fictional and far removed from daily life. What they enjoyed was the ways in which the programme appealed to their emotions. *Dallas* encouraged their 'imaginary participation in the fictional world' (Ang, 1985: 49). Ang did not see this simply as 'escapism' but emphasised the pleasure women experienced from making links between the fictional world of female characters such as Sue Ellen and the situations they found themselves in and their own day-to-day lives. Ang uses the term 'tragic structure of feeling' to describe the ways in which *Dallas* 'plays with the emotions in an endless musical chairs of happiness and misery' (Storey, 2001: 128). The emphasis on feeling is highlighted in the programme by the regular use of close-up facial shots. Ang argues to access and engage with this 'structure of feeling' the viewer must have certain cultural competencies. The viewer has to be able to 'project oneself into i.e. recognise a melodramatic imagination' (Ang, 1985: 79). Such competencies are more likely to be associated with women because femininity in a patriarchal society is constructed around responsibility for personal relations.

The work of feminist scholars such as Ang and Hobson challenged the assumption of the 'crude hypodermic needle model of media effects' that characterised much of the early feminist work on women's media consumption (see Ang and Hermes, 1991: 308–9). More importantly such reception studies introduced the notion of pleasure into the discussion of what audiences obtain from popular media and cultural forms. Ang and Hobson describe the pleasure women gain from soap operas and direct attention to the creative ways in which they do this. Their view of the pleasure differs from that of Adorno and Horkheimer who argue it is a 'false kind of pleasure', which manipulates the masses into accepting the status quo of exploitation and oppression. Ang is critical of traditional Marxists for seeing people's enjoyment of popular culture as a reason for gloom (Ang, 1985: 17). For Ang gaining pleasure from the media and popular culture is actively constructing meanings that subvert reactionary or patriarchal media messages. People are able to circumvent the dominant ideology seeking to shape their knowledge and behaviour. Programme-makers are not able to control or circumscribe people's pleasure. Fantasy, according to Ang (1996: 106), is a place where the 'unimaginable can be imagined'. She argues that consuming fantasies can be 'liberating' as it allows us to 'adopt positions and "try out" those positions without having to worry about their "reality value"' (Ang, 1985: 134).

Research into other kinds of audience in the 1980s showed how other groups actively generated distinctive meanings and pleasures from what they saw, heard and read in the media. Gillespie (1995) found young Punjabis living in London perceived Australian soap operas such as *Neighbours* as offering them a means to construct 'new modes of identity for themselves'. The programme's exploration of tensions between families and friends resonated with their experience of their own communities and provided opportunities to discuss them (Gillespie, 1995: 164). Katz and Liebes (1990) in their study of international audiences for *Dallas* discovered groups from different cultural backgrounds produced different ways of relating to the series and re-telling stories from it (Ruddock, 2001: 142). Shively (1992) shows how some members of a group of Native Americans identified with John Wayne rather than his 'Red Indian' opponents. This came from their commitment to preserving an autonomous way of life, not fully tied to industrial, urban society, which they saw as encapsulated in the cowboy way of life represented by Wayne rather than any feelings about the values of the Old Wild West (Eldridge *et al.*, 1997: 151). Gay men and lesbians came to be seen as particularly skilled practitioners of creative viewing (see Eldridge *et al.*, 1997: 152–3). Studies such as these can be seen as supporting the view that there is a 'repertoire of responses' from audiences to media messages. Some scholars went beyond emphasising the ability of audiences to produce diverse interpretations to argue that the interpretative activity of audiences is politically significant. Having fun, taking pleasure from and indulging in fantasy in the process of media consumption is an act of resistance, a politically progressive stance against the dominant ideology of the established order.

AUDIENCE RESISTANCE

Equating activity with resistance is initially found in the research into 'street culture' where men and boys dominated. Willis (1977) and Hebdige (1979) studied the capacity of various youth groups such as working-class boys, hippies, Rastafarians and punks to make their own meanings from different cultural and media forms such as music, hairstyles and clothes. Music as a medium of communication has been especially associated with young people's resistance to mainstream culture. From rock 'n' roll in the 1950s through punk in the 1970s to rap in the 1990s, music has been appropriated to assert the distinctiveness of a subculture to the dominant social groups of the day. The ability to create new meanings from established artefacts is dubbed 'bricolage'. However, Hebdige, Willis and other writers associated with the BCCCS (for example, Hall and Jefferson, 1976) went beyond talking about the capacity of people to appropriate the content of the media. They argued that activity represents the 'symbolic resistance' of subcultural groups to the dominant messages pumped out by the media. Hebdige (1979) examined punk culture and the way in which it expressed itself through dress, music and body piercing as a form of self-empowerment. Feminist researchers took up popular resistance to dominant media messages. Ang (1985) refers to the ability of women to 'play' with the texts of soap operas such as *Dallas*. Reception studies have increasingly emphasised the power of audiences, emanating from their critical and creative abilities, to resist the media. Some writers, most notably John Fiske (1986; 1987a), stress the pre-eminence of audiences – rather than the media and cultural industries – in the production of media meaning and popular culture.

Fiske's celebration of the power of audiences derives from his view that the media pump out a variety of material open to multiple interpretations and that pleasure is a subversive activity. Fiske (1986) embraces polysemy, arguing an 'excess' of potential meanings exist within any media text. Whether it is a music video, an advertisement, a TV news bulletin or a feature film, the media text is made up of a variety of images and words from which can be chosen a range of meanings. The dominant interpretation, or preferred reading, cannot completely contain all the bits and pieces that compose the text. People can put these bits and pieces together in different ways to produce different versions of the text. The ambiguities and contradictions that permeate media texts create the opportunity for people to exercise their creative and critical interpretative abilities. Fiske argues some interpretations are more pleasurable and enjoyable than others. From his study of television he believes that resistance is more fun. He argues the pleasure people derive comes from their active engagement in interpreting media texts and generating meanings that oppose those of the dominant social, political and cultural order. This is empowering as it allows people who have no power in their daily lives to subvert or counter the dominant ideology. Their ability to make their own meaning out of what they see, hear and read 'may well act as a constant erosive force ... weakening the system from within so that it is more amenable to change' (Fiske, 1989a).

Fiske explores how different media forms are subverted and resisted. One of his examples is the music videos of the pop star Madonna (Fiske, 1987b). He describes how Madonna was seen as a 'major phenomenon of popular culture' in the 1980s and a 'fine example of the capitalist pop industry at work, creating a (possibly short-lived) fashion, exploiting it to the full and making a lot of money from one of the most powerless and exploitable sections of the community – young girls' (1987b: 271). Her performances are 'teaching young female fans to see themselves as men would see them' and Madonna is 'hailing them as feminine subjects within patriarchy, and as such she is an agent of patriarchal hegemony'. Fiske sees this account as 'inadequate', arguing Madonna can be seen as taking on patriarchy by parodying traditional femininity and using her body as a signifier of resistance. His study of Madonna fans found that young girls see Madonna as a strong liberated woman. Her performances offer them the chance to challenge the dominant model for femininity in a patriarchal society. Fiske concludes Madonna videos are a 'site of semiotic struggle between the forces of patriarchy and feminine resistance, of capitalism and the subordinate, of the adult and the young' (1987b: 272). Similarly women viewers told Fiske how much they enjoyed *Charlie's Angels* when it appeared on their TV screens in the 1970s. 'Their pleasure in taking active, controlling roles was so great that it overrode the incorporating devices that worked to recuperate the feminist elements in its content back into patriarchy' (Fiske, 1987a: 39).

For Fiske, audiences have the power and freedom to make sense of television, the media and popular culture in general in any way they wish (see Abercrombie and Longhurst, 1998). As such the media do not have an effect on people. People's power of interpretation is paramount and only subject to the texts they interact with and the social forces that shape their beliefs, attitudes and viewpoints. Thus Fiske (1987a) – like some feminist scholars – distinguishes between men and women in their abilities to engage in 'semiological guerrilla warfare' against the symbolic power of the media. He cites numerous examples of subcultural groups using the media and popular culture for their own interests, seeing television as a plurality of reading practices, a democracy of pleasures and only understandable in its fragments. As he says (1987a: 324), 'It promotes and provokes a network of resistances to its own power whose attempts to homogenise and hegemonise breaks down on the instability and multiplicity of its meanings and pleasures.' Fiske believes the people exercise symbolic power, which enables them to win battles against their oppressors who exercise political, economic and cultural power (Lull, 2000: 168). The media enable people to fight these battles by providing them with the cultural resources out of which they can construct 'tactics of resistance'. Pleasure plays a crucial role as it is disruptive to social structures and cannot be contained by them. He supports the power of pleasure by citing the long history of serious attacks on popular media and cultural forms and activities from the established powers that be. Hence the importance to Fiske of media theory embracing and understanding the subversive power of popular culture and the media.

Fiske's hypothesis on the pleasure of resistance and the power of audiences has generated intense debate (see below). Within the field of active audience research it has led to some divisions. Morley (1992) is critical of what he sees as the excesses of Fiske's version of active audience theory, emphasising the 'dangers of romanticising the role of the reader'. He criticised the 'undocumented presumption that forms of interpretive resistance are more widespread than subordination or the reproduction of dominant meanings' (1992: 20). In response to research that searched out the possibilities for resistance in audience activity Morley (1986) concentrated attention on the 'lived contexts' within which people consume the media. Critical re-assessment of the *Nationwide* study led him to propose more attention should be paid to the factors that shape the decoding of media messages – such as the pleasures of viewing, the leisure patterns of people, and the social and gender arrangements of the place where most people watch television: the home. Examining how people watch television or listen to the radio and how the media are integrated into every-day life became a central component of the new audience research.

MEDIA IN EVERYDAY LIFE

Commentators have long been concerned at the media and in particular television's dominance of the leisure time of most people. In Britain the average amount of time viewers spend in front of their television screens is 26 hours per week, the highest in Europe (cited in Eldridge *et al.*, 1997: 134). This time is seen as consuming energy and time that could be spent on other kinds of activity. Much of this research pre-supposes viewers are passive consumers and TV holds the undivided attention of its audience. Research on viewing habits has found people do not watch television in a single-minded, dedicated way. TV viewing takes place alongside a range of other activities such as washing up, playing cards, ironing, cooking, making love and even sleeping (see, for example, Collett and Lamb, 1986). Rather than 'taking over', watching television is 'integrated into people's day-to-day lives and serves particular purposes in the social organisation of the home' (Eldridge *et al.*, 1997: 135). Much of the research into the part the media play in everyday life focuses on the home. Morley and Silverstone (1990) examined what items of media technology people buy and how they use them, including where they put them in the home. People are active in deciding how to use media technologies and often within the home there are disagreements over what to do with and how to use these technologies; what Cubitt (1985) has referred to as 'the politics of the living room'. It was Morley who pioneered research into the role the media play in the home, focusing on how television acts as a resource for conversation and its usage reflects power relations in family life.

Morley (1986) in his book *Family Television* interviewed 18 working-class families in London to see how the domestic context of family life within which most people watch television influences their interpretations of what they see. For Morley the 'lived contexts' of media consumption and the power relations that structured these contexts are crucial to understanding how people interpret what they see on television. Hobson (1980) in her study of housewives and the media showed how women use the media to structure the lonely, repetitive and monotonous nature of their working day. Radio, for example, acted as an accompaniment to housework and the disc jockeys provided 'the missing company' in the isolation of the home. Hobson argues DJs fulfil the role of a 'sexual fantasy figure' in the sense of being a 'safe though definitely sexually attractive man' (1980: 107). Her analysis suggests the disc jockey's talk in between the music reinforces the dominant ideology of domesticity. However, as the women 'do not have to sit and listen' to what is being said or played due to their housework this does not matter that much. Morley's work also highlights that whatever the ideological content of television, it is the domestic context of family viewing that is important to the medium's consumption. He drew particular attention to the different viewing habits between family members, especially men and women.

Morley's research found decisions to watch particular programmes or formats were not simply based on the pleasure people gained from them or their resonance with the ideological approach. Instead they were the result of family circumstances and power relations within the home. The different roles men and women have in the domestic sphere shape their viewing habits. While men view attentively, women watch television while doing something else. They are distracted. Men also exercise more power over what is watched and when. This is done mainly through their command of the remote control; many of Morley's women and children respondents expressed their frustrations at the device always being in Dad's hand. Gray (1992) also highlights the gendered structure of media usage in the home. She found men were more technically knowledgeable than women when it came to working the video cassette recorder (VCR) and other media technologies in the household. This, she argues, is not because women are technically inept; women are very capable when it comes to operating other domestic machinery such as the washing machine, oven and microwave. Rather women's usage of media technology is due to men's domination of the leisure and domestic sphere. Thus media technology is gendered not because of any innate abilities but by its social and cultural usage. However, Gray also suggests that some women refuse to learn how to use the VCR because it could extend their domestic chores. This she argues could be construed as an act of resistance.

Such findings are not always replicated in other cultural contexts. Lull (2000) contrasts South American families with those in northern Europe and the United States. Research, for example, shows that Venezuelan women 'routinely control the domestic agenda, including choice of television programs and the establishment of desired viewing environments' (Lull, 2000: 45). The uses of media technologies in the family are a cultural matter as well as gender-related.

Research such as that of Morley and Gray began to 'map the intricate social circumstances in which patterns of media consumption are organised in people's day-to-day routines' (Ang, 1995: 218). Moores (1988) extended research into family viewing back into history to show how the introduction of broadcasting in Britain in the 1920s and 1930s was characterised by deep divisions between family members. His study of families' decisions to purchase satellite television also identified struggles within and between families (Moores, 1996). For example, a father and son argue over whether or not a satellite dish on their house is in keeping with their neighbourhood. Some families look down on their neighbours' purchase of a dish as an indication of conspicuous consumption or poor taste. Lull (1990), in his study of around 200 American families, found that television was a catalyst for conflict in the family. The growing body of literature in this area emphasises the centrality of power and interpersonal conflict in the 'lived' context of media consumption. Much of this research focuses on the gender imbalances in the domestic environment, neglecting other kinds of relationships, and concentrates on television, ignoring other media. It is also criticised by political economists as losing sight of the politics of production and distribution (Eldridge *et al.*, 1997: 139). Golding and Murdock (1990) argue this kind of research 'screens out the poor' by failing to address how access to media technology is shaped by people's material resources. However, such work does indicate that people's understanding of and interaction with the media is shaped by their own social and cultural conditions.

RE-APPRAISING THE ACTIVE AUDIENCE

Active audience theory had positioned audience research by the early 1990s. Supporters of the theoretical perspective argue it has opened up 'whole new fields of enquiry and ways of thinking about text–audience relations' (Eldridge *et al.*, 1997: 155). Audiences are no longer passive, gullible entities easily manipulated by the media. The focus on pleasure recognises a more complicated relationship between audiences and the media than previously assumed. It moved away from seeing people's interaction with the media as passive or escapist to stress confrontation and engagement. The attention paid in reception studies to the differences between people in their understanding of media messages, on the basis not only of class but also gender, race, ethnic identity, age, sexual identity, nationality and disability, presents a more complex and differentiated picture of the audience. Active audience theory challenges the notion that what the media say is crucial in determining what people think. People are not simply captive subjects interpellated or positioned by media texts to accept the ideologically dominant message; they have the freedom and interpretative skills to resist and subvert the media. The result is seen as a 'more complex picture of real media uses' (Barker and Brooks, 1998: 103). However, the active audience theory has generated a considerable amount of criticism that argues the approach present a very real and clear danger to the whole enterprise of media studies (see Corner, 1991; Ferguson and Golding, 1997; Philo and Miller, 2001).

Critics argue the active audience perspective is closing down certain lines of enquiry. In particular, the outpouring of a vast number of articles emphasising pleasure, resistance and the politics of consumption is seen as 'revising ideas of media power out of existence' (Eldridge *et al.*, 1997: 156). Active audience theory has led to a complete re-appraisal of the notion of media power. Traditional effects theory emphasises the power of the media to shape the knowledge, understandings and beliefs of their audiences. Active audience theory by stressing the ability of audiences to make their own meanings from what the media pump out, to use media technologies for their own purposes and to take their own pleasures from what they see, hear and read undermines or even invalidates the concept of media power. Fiske's work is the most extreme articulation of this position. While many active audience scholars might see Fiske as overstating the part audiences play in the construction of meaning, they all stress the diversity of interpretation of media messages and the skills of audiences in criticising what they see, hear and read (Abercrombie and Longhurst, 1998: 29). The focus on people's freedom to interpret media messages as they want to, drawing positive meaning and pleasure from the output of the media, even when it is contrary and hostile to their views, leads to the perception that the media lack power to influence people. Critics charge 'the question of an ideological level of media processes, or indeed media power as a political issue at all, has slipped almost entirely off the research agenda' (Corner, 1991: 267). They point to the failure of the approach to engage with many of the key contemporary debates about media power – for example, neglecting the role of the media in the reporting of international events, such as the war in Bosnia and Kosovo, and argue the enthusiasm for documenting audience interpretations and polysemy has militated against discussion of the truth or falsehood of media information (Eldridge *et al.*, 1997: 158).

Gitlin (1991) in his critique of the cultural studies project rejects the view that the resistance to mainstream media messages described by Fiske and other active audience theorists is either significant or political. He is dubious about the extent to which people have the ability to subvert or resist the dominant culture, and critical of the tendency to equate resistance to television programmes with radical political activity. He asks what is resistance or opposition in the context of media consumption, arguing to use such terms to describe 'these not-so-great refusals' is to dignify them beyond their importance (1991: 336). Schiller (1989: 149) observes that in the active audience literature the impacts of resistance and subversion 'on the existing structure of power remain a mystery'. Barker and Brooks (1998: 96) are critical of the assumption that 'having fun with something is per se a political act'. Kitzinger (1999: 19) asks if resistance should be celebrated if people reject the messages of campaigns that encourage safer sex or discourage violence against women. Resisting media messages can be a reactionary as well as progressive activity although the active audience approach focuses almost exclusively on the latter. For Philo and Miller (2001: 57) people's appropriating, borrowing or stealing the symbols of the rich and powerful is not because they are resisting the values of the dominant culture but because they have absorbed them. Several writers take Fiske to task for confusing simple consumer choice with political statement, charging him with 'romanticising consumer sovereignty' (Curran, 1990; see also Philo and Miller, 2001; Seaman, 1992).

The problem of terminological uncertainty is identified in the discussion of active audiences. Barker and Brooks (1998) interrogate what exactly is meant by 'activity'. They point out that actual audiences in some situations could be said to be positively choosing to be passive. They cite examples such as when people decide to curl up with a bad novel or go to a film to have a 'good weep' or be scared. Such examples of passivity, they argue, render meaningless discussion of audience 'activity'. Corner (1991) points to a lack of clarity in the use of the term 'meaning' to describe people's responses to media messages. When examining how people make sense of what the media report or represent, Kitzinger (1999) identifies a difference between how people react or respond to a media text and their interpretation of the meaning of that text. People can agree on the meaning but simply refuse to accept or believe what is conveyed. She concludes, 'diverse response cannot be equated with diversity of "meaning"' (Kitzinger, 1999: 19). Attention has already been drawn to the problem of identifying the 'preferred reading' or 'dominant ideology' encoded in media texts (see Chapter 6). The use of the term 'pleasure' is seen as problematic, ignoring the different – and often contradictory – kinds of pleasure that different groups of people may gain from media messages. The pleasure some women may gain from watching women take controlling roles in *Charlie's Angels* tells us nothing about the pleasure men may take from the same text, which may encourage and amplify sexist attitudes (Seaman, 1992: 308). This can be underscored by Fiske's analysis of Madonna's music videos. While teenage girls may use Madonna's image as a mechanism for resisting dominant ideologies of femininity Fiske ignores the possibility that young boys gain pleasure from the traditional patriarchal image in her performance. Taking such pleasures into real life can have detrimental consequences for young women. Watching Madonna may empower young women but the pleasure men may gain can reinforce sexist attitudes and behaviour.

Finally critics draw attention to what they see as one of the main weaknesses of reception studies, their methods. Stevenson (1995: 100) takes issue with Fiske's methods, arguing he offers limited evidence to support his claims. Much of his analysis is highly subjective, relying on his own interpretations of texts rather than any systematic examination of the audience. He cites as an example the study of Madonna, which 'only briefly engages with the perspectives of her "fans" through the letters page of a teenage magazine', having more to do with the author's 'own skilful reading'. Others are more harsh, noting that one of Fiske's respondents is called Lucy and is 14 years old, the same name and age as his daughter at the time of writing (Booker, 1998: 106). Coincidences aside, claims about audience activity are often based on small, unrepresentative samples of research. Ang's influential study of *Dallas* is based on a sample of 42 letters, varying from a few lines to around ten pages, in response to an advertisement she placed in a Dutch women's magazine (Ang, 1985: 10). These letters form the empirical basis for her research. This is not uncommon with most reception studies, which work with letters or transcriptions of interviews, group or individual. The perusal of such material is compared with 'wrestling with a jellyfish: it squirms in so many different directions simultaneously that it seems impossible to control' (Lewis, 1991: 115). As a result the reader must 'search for what is behind the explicitly written' (Ang, 1985: 11) and such a level of scrutiny becomes 'invariably idiosyncratic' (Lewis, 1991: 115).

Active audience researchers stand accused of reading too much into audience resistance. In their search for progressive interpretations of media texts they create the impression that the media have no power, and the relationship between the media and their audiences is unproblematic as critical readers can use the media to serve their own pleasures, needs and desires. In response the critics are accused of oversimplifying their theoretical models, ignoring the politics and problems of audience research and neglecting the history of audience research (Gray, 1999; see also Morley, 1999). However, this has been a re-appraisal of the theory and attempts to re-assert the concept of media power at the heart of audience research. Livingstone (1998) sees audience research today being at a crossroads. Re-thinking media influence and power is now the matter at hand. Kitzinger (1999) is one example of recent research which acknowledges that audiences are active but also that the media are not without effect. Her work on HIV/AIDS and child sexual abuse identifies both the potential and the limits of people's ability to deconstruct and resist media accounts (Kitzinger, 1999; Kitzinger and Skidmore, 1995). In doing so such work responds to Morley's call to construct a model that is both sensitive to the dimensions of power and ideology, and the way in which the media are inserted into the contexts and practices of everyday life (Morley, 1992: 159).

SUMMARY

The study of the nature of media audiences became central to media studies in the 1980s. The active audience theoretical perspective underpinned most of this research. This approach is distinguished by a number of aspects. It prioritises the issue of pleasure, and the complex ways in which people gain their enjoyment from consuming the media. It challenges the assumption that the viewing, listening or reading public is a homogeneous entity by exploring the difference between groups of people in their understanding and comprehension of media texts. It questions the assumption that the media determine audience responses by showing how the perspectives intended by media practitioners are not automatically accepted by audiences. This represented a shift from traditional effects theory, which emphasised the power of the media to shape their audiences to a perspective that stressed the barriers to the potential effects of the message. Active audience theorists claim that traditional conceptions of media effects are found wanting by the alternative interpretations of audience behaviour put forward in reception studies. The dominant audience has replaced the dominant ideology in understanding media effects. This has resulted in what some have referred to as a crisis in the dominant paradigm of media studies as the notion of media power has been re-assessed. The ensuing debate between active audience theorists and those trying to re-establish the notion of the power of the media to shape people's knowledge, beliefs and attitudes has been intense. The outcome has been to leave the study of audiences at a crossroads with an onus on active audience theorists having to respond to a variety of theoretical, political and methodological criticisms of their approach.

Section 5

Media change and media theory

We are presently living through a communications and information revolution. There is a huge growth in information and communication technology. The 'old' media of television, cinema, radio, music and the press are undergoing considerable change. More significant is the advent of new media, including the Internet, which are changing the face of mass communication. Today there are more media, processing more information and communication more quickly than ever before. The mass media are reaching out and touching someone in nearly every corner of the planet. They are also changing how people interact with each other – technologies such as the Internet combining aspects of mass with face-to-face communication. These developments have implications not only for communication but social relations. The information and communications revolution promises a great leap forward, threatening to radically change society and the way people live as profoundly as the Industrial Revolution did in the eighteenth century. Radical changes in the media landscape have implications for media theory. The possibility of convergence, interactivity and the fragmentation of the audience present a challenge to theorists. How will the new media develop? In what ways will they impact on the process of mass communication? What will be the social and cultural effect of the new media? These – and many other – questions that emerge from the uncertainty around the consequences of new media technology not only exercise the thinking of media scholars but also represent a challenge to media theory (McQuail, 1986; 2000: Chapter 20). Some scholars have speculated as to whether the media theory that has shaped our understanding of mass communication and the media in the twentieth century is adequate to make sense of the new challenges of the new media technologies.

Most of the media theory and research discussed in this book has been built around the 'old media' of film, broadcasting and print, the 'realities' of how they operate and their relationship with society and the individual. The frameworks that have emerged to guide our thinking and the criteria scholars have used to assess the consequences of the media have been shaped by the performance of these media (McQuail, 1986). Some of the existing frameworks will still be able to accommodate the developments in the media and mass communication. Others will seem dated. All will have to make sense of the fundamental changes that are occurring in the media and broader social environment. We have already discussed the impact of new media on the nature of media ownership (Chapter 3) and media work (Chapter 4). In Chapter 9 we examine media theory with respect to some of the key debates and issues about contemporary media developments. These are globalisation, the advent of the 'information society' and the so-called 'dumbing down' debate, focusing on the impact of contemporary media on cultural quality.

Chapter Nine

LIVING IN THE GLOBAL VILLAGE: ☐
NEW MEDIA THEORY

Since the early 1980s there has been an unparalleled growth of global media. Media products are now consumed all over the world. It is not simply that there are more media. New media technologies such as satellite, the Internet and other forms of digital communication are compressing time and space. Put crudely, the world is shrinking. People are increasingly more aware of what is happening elsewhere. As the head of the then world's largest media corporation said in 1990, 'with new technologies, we can bring services and ideas that will help draw even the most remote areas of the world into the international media community' (Ross, quoted in Robins, 1997a). People are no longer restricted by physical distance. Air travel and the transportation of goods and services have lessened the distance between populations. The media reduce the need to travel. Rather than being transported to the other side of the world, television and other media bring the other side of the world to us. There is no longer the need to be in the same place to share in experiencing major events, whether it is the Olympic Games in Sydney, the trial of former US football star O.J. Simpson in Los Angeles or Princess Diana's funeral in London. The electronic media and the new communications technologies make such events instantly accessible to us wherever we are. They are making the world a smaller place than it has ever been.

Global media

The increasingly global reach of the media is widely documented. A few examples are given here to indicate the pervasiveness of the contemporary media. Michael Jackson's music can be heard and bought on every continent, while African music is now available to a global audience (Burnett, 1996). In 1995 the music channel MTV was seen in 320 million households in 90 countries across five continents, fulfilling its slogan of 'One Planet, One Music' (Sturmer, 1993; Burnett, 1996). The magazine **Reader's Digest** as early as 1980 was published in 39 national editions in 17 languages with a global audience estimated at 28 million readers (Scholte, 2000: 76) and by 1996 its worldwide sales revenue was recorded as US$3 billion (Herman and McChesney, 1997: 97). The **International Herald Tribune** is available for purchase in 143 countries and has subscribers in all parts of world. Television programmes such as **Bonanza** and **Hawaii Five-O** have been estimated to reach a global audience of more than three-quarters of a billion people. Wherever you look, whatever sector you examine, the media have become truly global in their reach.

By breaking down the barriers of time and space between people and nations, some argue the media are creating one global family where differences are submerged in favour of what we share, what we have in common. McLuhan coined the term 'global village' to describe this phenomenon (see Chapter 2). He saw the growth in global media and communications technology as positive and beneficial. Electronic communications are producing an environment in which people are 'involved with, and responsible for, each other' (McLuhan and Fiore, 1968: 24). As more people can make their voices heard, international understanding develops and differences are reduced. For McLuhan more information at people's fingertips promotes co-operation, and diminishes conflict and misunderstanding. He sees the global media as a liberating force, fostering equality and acting as an engine for universal democracy. McLuhan's optimism is disputed. Political economists draw attention to the imbalances between global villagers (for example, Schiller, 1969; 1989; Hamelink, 1983; 1995a; Mattelart, 1989; Golding, 1994). There is an unequal distribution of the information hardware and software throughout the global village. For example, 75 per cent of the world's landline telephones are located in nine countries, while less than 10 per cent of the world's telephone, telex and telegram traffic occurs in Africa, Asia and Latin America where two-thirds of the planet's population live (Hamelink, 1995b). There is not an equal exchange of ideas in the global village. Western values, lifestyles and products, in particular those of the United States, prevail. For example, the English language is the lingua franca of the world and US entertainment programmes are most seen on global TV screens. Finally control of the media and communications industries rests in the hands of a small number of firms (see Chapter 3). Thus McLuhan's concept of the global village is subject to the criticisms that not all opinions and voices are equally heard and some values and lifestyles are more accepted. Western countries, in particular the USA, are seen as dominating the global village, controlling the flow of information and entertainment across the planet. The massive growth of global media is uneven and unequal.

The West's domination of the global village is not disputed. What is a matter of contention is the consequence of this influence. The spread of global media as well as their increasing centrality in most people's lives is seen as a problem for local communities. People are trying to preserve their distinctiveness in the face of changes brought about by globalisation. One European in the midst of the GATT trade negotiations over film quotas in the early 1990s spoke for many all over the world when he said: 'We want the

Americans to let us survive. Ours is a struggle for the diversity of European culture, so that our children will be able to hear French and German and Italian spoken in films' (quoted in Robins, 1997a). The debate about the impact of global media revolves around the question of identity – cultural, national and individual. Everybody needs a sense of who they are, a sense of belonging. The primary way in which people have done this in the modern world is through the nation. National identity has been a crucial element in defining who we are. The global media pose a threat to the nation, promising to erode those imaginary boundaries that distinguish one group of people from another.

MODERNISATION THEORY

Initial thinking about the impact of the growth of global media and communication was shaped by modernisation theory. In the 1950s and 1960s a group of theorists examined the role the media could play in the process of economic and social development. The years immediately after the Second World War were a period of de-colonisation. Many countries in Africa and Asia obtained their independence from their former colonial masters. On obtaining their political independence the main goal of these societies was development. They sought to build their economies and the social, cultural and political infrastructures of their nations. It became enshrined in academic theory and research that, to develop, these countries would have to break down the traditional structures and attitudes that characterised their societies and modernise. Africans and Asians were seen as backward and wedded to traditions that held back development. A key barrier to overcome was the traditional personality of people in the so-called Third World. Low esteem, authoritarian values, resistance to innovation, fatalism and non-achievement were seen as the main psychological components of the traditional personality. Psychological and social change could be achieved by imparting modern values. The media played a key role in communicating the modern values, skills, attitudes and structures needed for development. This would be done in a number of ways: for example, the diffusion of skills, producing empathy with new roles or ways of life, and creating symbols that would bind the societies closer together and promote democracy and national integration, thereby giving people a sense of their national identity. Theorists such as Lerner (1958), Rogers (1969) and Schramm (1964) fleshed out the role of the media and communication in the process of modernisation.

Development

Economists argue over the nature of development. For some it is seen as industrialisation and measured in terms of industrial growth and the creation of national wealth through profitable enterprise. Wealth trickles down from successful industries to the rest of society. Others argue that the quality of life is as important as wealth creation in the development process. Thus health care, social provision, housing, sanitation and education are as important indicators of development as national wealth and industrial growth. Many in the newly independent nations of Asia and Africa saw the Marshall Plan in the late 1940s, through which American aid was pumped into Europe to help re-build and reconstruct the continent after the ravages of war, as a model for them. Western government and international institutions did not agree, arguing internal reform and individual effort was required.

The 'Third World'

The post-war world has been divided into three political groupings. The **First World** is the West, the former colonial powers, the rich, industrialised societies of western Europe and North America with the addition of Australia and New Zealand. Japan is sometimes, ambivalently, associated with this grouping. The **Second World** is the communist world, which collapsed in 1989 with the fall of the Berlin Wall. State socialism, a single political party and the Marxist-Leninist ideology characterised this grouping. The **Third World** describes the rest, the poorer former colonies of the West in Asia, Latin America and Africa. Many parts of Africa, Asia and Latin America struggled to gain their independence from the European empires that enslaved them through direct rule in the nineteenth century. Some scholars, political commentators and people living in these countries who use the alternative label of 'global South' have objected to the term. Since the end of the Cold War and the conflict between East and West, this division of the world is no longer appropriate although the labels are still used.

By the mid-1970s the 'dominant paradigm' of modernisation had passed (Sinclair, 1990: 286). Its demise is attributed to the failure of the media to bring about what they promised and the general lack of success in the newly de-colonised nations in achieving sustained economic growth and development. In fact many of these nations went through economic decline in the decades of the 1960s and 1970s. Modernisation theory was criticised for assuming that countries of the South should develop along the same lines as those in the West. The appropriateness of the values, skills and attitudes modernisation was trying to bring to these countries was questioned. As these societies are radically different from western societies don't they need different policies and pathways to develop? The focus on opinion leaders who would pass on their newly acquired skills and knowledge to the rest of society was misdirected. Wealthier farmers often kept innovation to themselves. Finally, the limited reach of traditional media in these parts of the world prevented their use in imparting values to the wider society. Modernisation theory appeared insensitive to the particular problems of the societies of the global South and many Africans and Asians who had previously accepted the theory began to see the dependency of their societies on the West as a reason for their underdevelopment.

THE CULTURAL OR MEDIA IMPERIALISM THESIS

The challenge to modernisation theory first came from researchers in Latin America who sought to account for the increased social inequality, national indebtedness, technological dependency and economic domination of their region by multi-national companies (Sinclair, 1990). They developed 'dependency theory' to explain the gap between the West and the rest of the world. The theory stresses the historical emergence of an unequal global system, arguing countries of the South cannot develop because they continue to be held back by their dependence on the former colonial powers. Despite political independence the institutions and structures of the newly de-colonised nations are still influenced by colonialism. The colonial powers left behind economic structures serving their interests as well as their languages, values and attitudes, political institutions and culture, forms of education and professional training, clothing styles and many other cultural habits that had never previously existed in these parts of the world. This is sometimes described as neo-colonialism. The rapid spread of the media across Latin America is seen as playing a significant part in the perpetuation of neo-colonialism. The media are a 'foreign cultural influence grounded in economic and political domination' (Sinclair, 1990: 287) and according to the first President of Ghana, Kwame Nkrumah, act as a crucial informal means by which the values and structures of neo-colonialism are accepted. If colonialism is a form of imperialism – that is the direct control of one nation by another – neo-colonialism is cultural imperialism, with the media one of the vehicles for the transfer of western values and attitudes. The global television music of MTV, the global news of CNN, the global box office hits of Hollywood films and the global television soap operas shape the cultures of the nations of the global South, ensuring their 'westernisation'. These values conflict with local cultures, often leading to the erosion of local values, and threatening national and cultural identity. The cultural or media imperialism thesis claims that 'authentic, traditional and local culture in many parts of the world is being battered out of existence by the indiscriminate dumping of large quantities of slick commercial and media products, mainly from the United States' (Tunstall, 1977: 57).

Nkrumah on neo-colonialism

> Even the cinema stories of fabulous Hollywood are loaded. One has only to listen to the cheers of an African audience as Hollywood's heroes slaughter red Indians or Asiatics to understand the effectiveness

of this weapon. For, in the developing continents, where the colonialist heritage has left a vast [number] still illiterate, even the smallest child gets the message contained in the blood and thunder stories emanating from California. And along with murder and the Wild West goes an incessant barrage of anti-socialist propaganda, in which the trade union man, the revolutionary, or the man of dark skin is generally cast as the villain, while the policeman, the gum-shoe, the Federal agent – in a word, the CIA-type spy – is ever the hero . . .

Source: from Nkrumah's book **Neo-Colonialism: The Last Stage of Imperialism**, 1965, quoted in Alleyne, 1995: 11

Cultural or media imperialism?

If imperialism is the dominance of one nation of another, media imperialism is the dominance of one nation's media system by another, and cultural imperialism the dominance of one nation's culture by another. The problem is that the media are the main vehicles for the transfer of cultural values from one nation or society to another. The term 'culture' or 'way of life' is also fraught with definitional problems. Some scholars choose to use media imperialism in a narrow way, examining only the transfer of media products and media practices, while others see the term as synonymous with cultural imperialism.

Supporters of the thesis interpret cultural or media imperialism in a variety of different ways. The work of the American scholar Herbert Schiller (1969) is perhaps most influential in shaping the thesis. Schiller (1969: 9) defines cultural imperialism as the

sum of the processes by which a society is brought into the modern world system and how the dominating stratum is attracted, pressured, forced and sometimes bribed into shaping social institutions to correspond to, or even promote, the values and structures of the dominating centre of the system.

Simply put, he argues the media and media technology are part of a conspiracy by the American military-industrial complex to maintain its economic, political and military domination of the post-war world. In his book *Mass Communications and the American Empire* he documents how the 'imperial network of American economics and finance' uses communications for its defence, entrenchment and expansion. He examines the role of the American military and government in shaping and subsidising the development of new media technologies, documenting how national telecommunications policy in the USA has increasingly become the responsibility of the Department of Defense, and the close links between the US military and major media corporations. Schiller believes aggressive selling of American media products around the world is a means of promoting the American way of life and worldview, thereby helping to maintain US power and influence. The 'Americanisation' of the world is the consequence of the way in which seemingly harmless media products such as Hollywood films or children's cartoon characters re-inforce audiences' attachment to consumerism and the 'American way'.

Donald Duck and imperialist ideology

Two Latin American commentators, Ariel Dorfman and Armand Mattelart, in their study **How to Read Donald Duck: Imperialist Ideology in the Disney Comic**, sought to demonstrate how the seemingly wholesome and innocent world of Walt Disney concealed American imperialist values. From analysis of Disney comics they argue that a catalogue of ideological values are apparent: an obsession with money and 'compulsive consumerism'; racial and stereotypical representations of Third World nations, in particular the 'infantilisation' of the peoples of these countries; anti-communist and anti-revolutionary propaganda; presentation of capitalism as natural, unchangeable and morally justified, and constant reference to the Third World as 'exotic' and a source of wealth, 'there for the taking' by adventurous westerners. The importance of Donald Duck to selling the American way of life around the world was commented on by a leading Hollywood producer in 1950 who advocated the meshing of the cartoon character and diplomacy as part of a Marshall Plan for ideas (see Miller **et al.**, 2001).

Source: adapted from Tomlinson, 1991: 41–5

Critics take issue with Schiller's conspiratorial view of the global pre-eminence of US media products (Collins, 1990; Tracey, 1985). They argue US global media dominance is due to natural advantages. This is sometimes presented in aesthetic terms. American tele-vision programmes are watched in greater number because they are better made, their plots and narrative are more engaging, the production values higher and characters more appealing, which is attributable to the natural talent of those working in the US film and television industry. More significant are the economic advantages enjoyed by the US media and cultural industries. American television programmes, for example, are cheaper than programmes made elsewhere. Television channels all over the world know they can purchase American programmes at a fraction of the cost needed to make local programmes. The low cost of American programmes is due to the large size of the US domestic market. Companies can recoup the costs of making programmes at home and thus what they sell abroad is all profit. This economic advantage, rather than any conspiracy, accounts for the dominance of the global media market by US interests.

While the cultural or media imperialism thesis came to exercise a great hold over the policy makers and peoples of the so-called Third World, many scholars reject the thesis for being too pessimistic. Tracey (1985) attacks the failure to provide empirical evidence in support of the thesis. Much of the research describes the flows of western- or American-made mass media material into a country, with an assumption of ideological and cultural effects (Fejes, 1981). Advocates of the thesis 'simply assume that reading American comics, seeing adverts, watching pictures ... has a direct effect' (Tomlinson, 1991: 44). The thesis, by focusing on texts and company reports rather than the 'realities of individual lives', fails to address the cultural meanings of these flows (Tracey, 1985: 45). The thesis lacks an explanation of how particular values and practices associated with particular media products are reproduced in the consciousness of 'dependent people' as well as within the structures of dependent societies (Reeves, 1993: 63). Research that has been done into audience responses to globally popular TV programmes challenges the thesis. Studies of *Dallas*, once described by the French Minister of Culture as a 'symbol of American cultural imperialism', indicate how a simple, direct and uniform ideological effect from exposure to an imperialist media product is improbable (Tomlinson, 1991: 47). The active engagement of audiences around the world in making sense of *Dallas* casts doubt on the thesis (see Chapter 8). Katz and Liebes (1990) conclude that it is almost impossible to understand how American products are perceived around the world. They argue the thesis rests on three dubious assertions: that there is an American message in the content and form of the media, that the message is perceived by viewers and that it is perceived in the same way by viewers in different countries (quoted in Tomlinson, 1991: 47). By neglecting audiences, cultural imperialism underestimates the challenges to Americanisation or westernisation in different parts of the world. There are many vital currents of opposition or resistance from local communities to cultural dominance (Dowmunt, 1993; Thussu, 1998).

Cultural resistance

Cultural resistance can take many forms. On the one hand, there is the exporting of programmes and material from the South to the West. Companies such as Televisa in Mexico and Globo in Brazil are emerging as genuine global media players, exporting their products around the world. On the other hand, audiences in the global South can be seen as taking whatever messages they want and appropriating them to local conditions. Or peoples in the global South make use of western media technologies in ways relevant and acceptable to themselves and their conditions.

There is also a terminological and ideological confusion over who is doing what to whom in the process of cultural imperialism. The key relationship in the thesis is between the West and the rest. For Vidyarthi (1988: 13) 'the West seeks ideological domination of the developing world, presenting its spiritual values and world outlook as the only rational and indisputable one'. But what are these western values and this western outlook? Latouche (1996) examines the concept of 'the West', unpackaging components such as Christianity, the philosophy of the Enlightenment, the racial superiority of whiteness, and capitalism. Each of these is a highly contested area within western culture and history, making the concept of westernisation problematic. Hence the emphasis on the 'Americanisation' of the world, whereby McDonald's, Coca-Cola, Hollywood and CNN can readily be identified as promoting the American way of life. Putting aside the question of what exactly is meant by the 'American way of life', the concept of Americanisation does address the fact that concerns about US cultural influence are equally, if not more, keenly expressed and experienced in Europe. Europeans have been expressing their anxieties about the impact of US media and cultural products since the inflow of Hollywood films and US jazz music in the 1920s and 1930s. The crucial problem is in what ways and to what extent do films, music and programmes such as those from *Star Trek* to *Bonanza* represent American values and the American way of life. How do they convey these values? This has led some to ask whether we should talk about cultural imperialism in terms of national media products. Rather they link media values to the spread of capitalism.

Schiller and his colleagues emphasise the importance of the media in the promotion of consumerism. Mattelart (1979) examines the role of the multi national firms in the control of global culture. The dumping of media and cultural products around the world is part of the process of hooking people into the capitalist system, encouraging them to become consumers, thereby enhancing the conditions to sell more. Consumerism, however, is often conflated with the American way of life: it is 'American-style consumption' imposed by US business in partnership with government. Sklair (1993: 31) argues to identify cultural imperialism with the USA or US capitalism is 'a profound and profoundly mystifying error'. Rather the ideology of consumerism is a worldwide phenomenon. The growth of global media firms promoting the ideology of consumerism, often at odds with the nation-state, including their own government, is highlighted. Theorists stress the power of these firms, describing them as 'the lords of the global village' with 'their own political agenda' and

exerting a homogenising power over ideas, culture and commerce that affects populations larger than any in history. Neither Caesar, nor Hitler,

221

Franklin Roosevelt nor any Pope, has commanded as much power to shape the information on which so many people depend ... to make decisions about everything from whom to vote for to what to eat.

(Bagdikian, quoted in Smith, 1991: 25; see Chapter 3)

These firms, according to Sklair (1993), do not define their interests within the national context. They are committed to a global capitalist project and as such are producing a 'transnational capitalist class' comprising company executives and their local affiliates, state bureaucrats, politicians and professionals, and consumerist elites around the world who increasingly owe less and less allegiance to nations and states (see Sklair, 2001).

The end product of cultural imperialism is supposed to be the domination of one culture by another alien culture. Local, authentic and traditional cultures are being battered out of existence by the overwhelming flow of American, western consumerist media products. This raises the problems of understanding what a 'culture' is (Tomlinson, 1991: Chapter 3). The thesis equates cultural identity with national culture. It is national identity that is threatened. But national culture is not as uniform and distinct as the thesis leads one to believe. Within any nation there are minority groupings and differences of subcultures and local identities. This is especially true in many of the recently de-colonised nations. Their fragile national identity is highlighted by linguistic, ethnic and political distinctions. Nigeria, for example, comprises nearly 200 languages and 150 different ethnic groupings. Even countries such as Britain, which have had several centuries of national existence, contain ethnic and linguistic differences. There is also the question of what is 'authentic' and 'traditional' about cultures. Culture is dynamic not static, always in process of change. Outside influences shape cultures, which develop and change over time. It is often impossible to distinguish culture in the modern world as being purely locally produced, as most local cultural practices have 'traces of previous cultural borrowing or influence' that have become assimilated and naturalised (Tomlinson, 1991: 91). Many cultural 'traditions' have been invented in relatively recent times (Hobsbawm and Ranger, 1983). If there is no continuity or uniformity in national cultures then the impact of global media and culture should be seen as simply another part of the dynamic evolution of national identities.

Definitional problems, terminological vagueness, lack of empirical evidence to support the thesis, as well as the belief that the world is more complex than the picture painted by cultural imperialists led to a rethinking of the thesis. The arguments about cultural imperialism became politically bogged down in the debate about a New World Information and Communication Order (NWICO) in the late 1970s and early 1980s. It was the arrival of the new media technologies such as the Internet and the World Wide Web in the 1990s that resulted in renewed interest in the media and global culture. If the cultural or media imperialism thesis is a product of the era of television, then the notion of globalisation emerges out of the world of the new media technologies.

NWICO

In the early 1970s a number of countries from the global South got together to lobby through the United Nations for changes in the international economic system and international information order. Under the Group of 77 they called for political changes in the different fora of the UN, including in the case of information the United Nations Education, Scientific and Cultural Organisation (UNESCO). In 1980 UNESCO produced the MacBride Report, which documented the state of international news and information, and put forward some tentative suggestions for a new information order. Western governments and much of the western media opposed these proposals, arguing they were an infringement on the free flow of information. On losing the argument the USA followed by the UK, withdrew from UNESCO, effectively preventing that body from enacting any sort of change, and the issue eventually died.

GLOBALISATION

More recent thinking about the emergence of a global consciousness or culture is globalisation, which is seen as 'the concept of the 1990s' (Waters, 1995: 1). While describing the process by which economic activity, political values and culture have ceased to be constrained by geography and territory, globalisation emphasises the role of the media. They are seen as 'the shock troops of global cultural revolution' (Curran and Seaton, 1997: 245). New media technologies such as satellites and the Internet represent a 'quantum leap' forward in the capacity of the media to bring people closer together. As opposed to the 1960s and 1970s, media technologies today are producing qualitative changes in the nature of global communication. Whereas cultural imperialists see the flow of information as one-way, globalisation embraces the capacity of audiences to engage in two-way communication via the interactivity of technologies such as the Internet, e-mail and the World Wide Web as well as the growth of information exchange between peoples across national boundaries outside the control of the nation-state. Globalisation adopts a slightly different emphasis in explaining the emergence of a global culture or consciousness. Whereas 'the idea of cultural imperialism contains the notion of a purposeful project – the intended spread of a social system from one centre of power across the globe' – globalisation suggests the 'interconnection and interdependency of all global areas which happens in a far less purposeful way . . . the result of economic and cultural practices which do not of themselves aim at global integration but which nevertheless produce it' (Tomlinson, 1991: 175).

Globalisation theorists such as Giddens argue top-down power is 'losing its edge' in the more open, decentralised and flexible global communication system that is beginning to emerge (quoted in Held, 2000: 10). Technological developments appear to undermine the established political and economic control by enabling smaller organisations as well as individuals to challenge the power of globally dominant organisations.

This is not to say that there is agreement between theorists about the nature of globalisation. Held (2000) distinguishes between 'positive' and 'pessimistic' globalisers. The latter are cultural imperialists applying their thesis to new circumstances, emphasising how the new technologies increase the gap between the world's rich and poor, corporations' control over global culture and media, and the homogenisation of global society. Positive globalisers, on the other hand, argue globalisation is 'more than the diffusion of western institutions across the world in which other cultures are crushed'; it is the emergence of 'world interdependence and planetary consciousness', which will 'inevitably involve conceptions and strategies from non-western settings' (Giddens, quoted in Thompson, 1997: 145). They draw attention to the ability of the new media to revitalise the global society by enabling people to become more involved in global public affairs (Rheingold, 1994; see Chapter 3). They argue the de-regulation of state constraints on the free market has provided a catalyst for the globalisation of media firms, encouraging them to adapt to local markets. Market forces are seen as forcing global media companies to take account of local people and local tastes in making their products. Rather than being at odds with local cultures and identities, globalisation is seen as corresponding with the development of local identities. Broadly speaking, globalisation in this sense does not conceive of global culture as steeped in western values but recognises and acknowledges cultural niches and local abilities. Hamelink (1993: 384–5) labels this view as *pluralist* globalism as it emphasises the maintenance of cultural diversity, while others prefer the term *glocalisation* to describe how the newly emerging global culture embraces demands for localisation. Global culture borrows from a variety of cultures. Neither western nor American nor local, but a *mélange*, a mixture, of many influences from all over the world. Post-modernists have described this mix of different cultural influences and values as 'hybridity'.

Globalisation as a theory recognises the complexity of the contemporary global media environment, and in particular the part media in the 1990s played in preserving, promoting and defending the local. In the United Kingdom, the Welsh fourth channel, *Sianel Pedwar Cymru*, has the remit to support Welsh language and culture. Similarly throughout Europe the media are playing a role in the maintenance of local cultures and identities (see Moragas Spa *et al.*, 1999). New media have allowed a diversity of 'alternative' and 'radical' voices to be heard (Held, 2000: 56). The Zapatistas movement in Mexico was able to communicate with the world, by-passing established media through the use of the Internet. Global firms are bringing indigenous media products to the notice of a global audience – for example, the recent popularity of Cuban and African music. Robins (1997b) notes how musical cultures and media provide good examples of hybridity with examples such as Rasta-Cymru, a Welsh-speaking reggae band. MTV's global rise has been based on adapting to local cultural and linguistic audiences, particularly in Europe (Roe and De Meyer, 2000). Local cultures have also adapted and used western media technology to develop their own identities and/or defeat western ideas. Abu-Lughod (1989) found the introduction of broadcasting into the Bedouin tribes of the Sahara served to bring them closer together and re-invigorate their sense of Bedouin identity. The use of the audio cassette to spread the teachings of Islam in Iran and the Middle East is an example of how new media are associated with the ability of local cultures to resist western influence. With the massive growth of media across the world, the resulting increase in the space to fill has assisted local production, enabling it to grow to the extent that American products are less important in global media terms (Sreberny-Mohammadi, 1991). The blurring of boundaries between media genres, the adaptation of global media to local conditions, the use of new media to resist western values and re-assert local cultures, as well as the contra-flow of material to the West from non-western parts of the world are put forward to support the notion of globalisation as a positive and inclusive phenomenon.

The recurring theme underlying the notion of hybridisation and the mixing of the global and local is the possibility that new identities are emerging (see Hall, 1992). The 'old certainties and hierarchies of identity are called into question in a world of dissolving boundaries and disrupted continuities' (Robins, 1997a: 38). Globalisation in particular is seen as a threat to the nation-state and national identity. This is implied in different ways by all the perspectives on globalisation. National identities are either being eroded by cultural homogenisation or by the strengthening of local or regional identities in reaction to global change, or new hybrid identities are taking their place (Hall, 1992). At the supra-national, national, subnational, local and ethnic levels there are examples of people exploring the possibilities of re-defining their sense of who they are – whether it is the efforts of the European Commission to develop a pan-European identity or the attempts by previously submerged national identities to re-assert themselves, such as in Scotland, Wales, Flanders or Kashmir, or the search by minorities to re-connect themselves to their wider diaspora. Contemporary media are seen as offering people new identities that cut across national boundaries. For most of the post-war period media have been national in their outlook and organisation. Benedict Anderson (1983) in a widely influential piece of work conceives of the nation as an 'imagined political community'. It is imagined because members of the same national community, even the smallest, will never meet one another. Their communion only exists in the minds of one another. Their capacity to imagine their collective identity is made possible by a number of processes, one of the most important being the media and mass communication. The press and subsequently broadcasting enable people to simultaneously imagine they belong to the same national community. For example, the BBC – that is the *British* Broadcasting Corporation – by bringing a large number of people together for national rituals and events such as the monarch's Christmas message, the state opening of Parliament, ministerial broadcasts and sporting events fulfils the sense of belonging to one nation (see Scannell and Cardiff, 1991).

Globalisation undermines national culture and identity in a variety of ways. People in nearly every nation are open to cultural experiences from all over the world. National borders are no longer a barrier to the influx of alien ideas and values. Satellites above and the Internet below have played a crucial part in making the modern nation porous. National governments cannot prevent, regulate nor censor the traffic the information superhighway brings through their countries. Nations 'cannot protect their subjects from images, ideas, tastes even, of which they disapprove' (Curran and Seaton, 1997: 250). In recent years the vast political changes in many parts of the world have been aided and abetted by the messages beamed in by global media – for example, the overthrow of the former communist regimes of eastern Europe. It is now possible to imagine one's collective identity differently, and the media offer a number of possible alternatives to our sense of belonging. The decline of public service or state broadcasting has further weakened the process of imagining the nation (see below).

Traditionalists are sceptical about the claims that globalisation has undermined the nation-state and national identity (Held, 2000). While not arguing that national cultures remain unchanged, the changes associated with globalisation from this perspective are overstated and national continuities understated. Held (2000: 65–71) identifies several examples of the durability of national culture. While public service broadcasting is declining, in many parts of the world it holds its own against commercial channels. Some media remain resolutely national in their character – the press around the world has made few advances in the direction of globalisation. While news gathering may have become global, news remains primarily consumed by national audiences produced by national news media. National regulation has not always proven toothless in the face of global media technologies. History tends to show 'there is nothing dramatically new about recent communication technologies and global communication', putting claims about the information and communication revolution in some perspective (Held, 2000: 71).

No matter how theorists conceive of the impact of global media and culture, whether as modernisation, imperialism or globalisation, the centrality of technology and information to all perspectives is apparent. This has led some commentators to see 'information' as the defining feature of the modern world (Webster, 1995). There is more information than ever before, and it plays a pivotal role in crucial aspects of modern life, both leisure and work. It is the 'dominant ideology of our time, shaping and justifying the actions of business leaders and politicians, and through the media, increasingly shaping the commonsense understanding of our times' (Garnham, 2000: 19). The notion of the 'information society' suggests we are entering or have already entered a new type of society whose differences from previous social systems are a result of the permeation of information, information technologies and the media in our lives. This is a matter of theoretical dispute.

INFORMATION SOCIETY

The explosion of information and media in social circulation is apparent for all to see. 'Dazzling new technological opportunities' drive the emergence of the 'information society'. Technology has transformed the nature of information and communication. Previously information was 'manipulated in different places for different purposes from broadcasting to telephones' (Curran and Seaton, 1997: 241). Media and communication technologies were distinct, governed by their own set of political and economic arrangements, and storing and processing information in different places and ways. Today we are witnessing the convergence of telecommunications, computing technologies and media. They are being brought together by digital technology, which enables an unlimited amount of information to be stored, transmitted, gathered and utilised in new ways, and makes feasible the linking together of homes, workplaces and businesses in one global information network. One of the advocates of the brave new digital world, Nicholas Negroponte, sums up the potential for change:

> Early in the next millennium your right or left cufflinks or earrings may communicate with each other by low-orbiting satellites and have more computer power than your present PC. Your telephone won't ring indiscriminately; it will receive and perhaps respond to your incoming calls like a well-trained English butler. Mass media will be re-defined by systems for transmitting and receiving personalised information and entertainment.
>
> (Quoted in MacKay, 2001: 7)

New media entrepreneurs, governments, policy makers and many media practitioners play up the miraculous transformations that are occurring. They are optimistic about the development of the information society, seeing it as an inevitable and beneficial outcome of technological change. Labelled as 'neophiliacs' they embrace and celebrate change. One of them, the world's richest man and pioneer of the new media technologies, Microsoft's Bill Gates, believes in the power of information to challenge prejudice and inequality (quoted in Curran and Seaton, 1997: 244). He shares the same technologically deterministic view as McLuhan (See Chapter 3). The innovations mentioned above must bring about a complete re-configuration of the social world, as their impact is so far-reaching. One of the most influential accounts of the information society came from Daniel Bell as early as 1973. His theory traces the transition from a pre-industrial, through an industrial to a post-industrial society (his label for the information society). In the post-industrial society more people are engaged in work relating to the processing, gathering and storing of information. Their involvement in the service sector contrasts with work in industrial society, which was with machinery primarily in the manufacturing sector, and in pre-industrial society where agricultural work predominated. The knowledge industries of post-industrial society are seen as making work safer, cleaner, better rewarded and more rewarding. The media are a crucial part of this society, which Bell acknowledges although he never discusses their significance (MacKay, 2001: 22–8). Although somewhat dated, Bell's theory typifies the neophiliac view of the information society as driven by techno-logical change and facilitating positive and beneficial social change.

Definitions of information society

A number of labels are used besides 'information society' to describe the social impact of the information and communication revolution – for example, 'post-industrial', 'network' or 'knowledge' society. For Webster (1997) this reflects different ways of defining the information society, each of which are analytically separate. He lists five major definitions.

1. Technological: charts the rise of innovation in information and media technology and the rise of the information superhighway.
2. Economic: describes the growth in the economic value of information activities and the development of the information economy or e-economy.
3. Occupational: examines the changing patterns of occupational activity, focusing on the decline of manufacturing and the growth of the service sector.
4. Spatial: emphasises the growth of networks, which revise time and space relations, with the ability to manage affairs on a global scale and relieved of constraints of time.
5. Cultural: outlines extraordinary increase in information in circulation as a result of more media.

Cultural pessimists reject this rosy picture of the information society. They contend, 'increases in information serve specific interests and thereby serve to perpetuate the status quo' (Webster, 1997). Schiller (1996) argues the information explosion serves to sustain corporate capitalism and reinforce existing inequalities in society (see Webster, 1995: Chapter 5). The development of new information and media technologies is 'decisively influenced by the market pressures of buying, selling and trading in order to make profit' (Webster, 1995). The priority is to extract maximum profit from information and cultural products rather than using them for the public good. Access to these technologies is deter-mined by the ability to pay. The rich can buy into a plethora of information and commu-nication services while the poor are left to consume what Schiller calls 'garbage information' such as mass entertainment and junk mail. For Schiller and other cultural pessimists it is capitalism and not technology that is driving the information society: 'the capitalist system's long-established features are the key architectural elements of the so-called "information society"' (Webster, 1997). The emphasis is on continuity rather than transformation in the social impact of the new technologies. This is also apparent in the views of those who argue the information explosion has increased the power and ability of the state and corporations to control the individual. Drawing from Foucault they stress the heightened surveillance capacities of modern information technologies (see Webster, 1995: Chapters 4 and 6). Rather than de-centralising control into the hands of users, the new information technologies, particularly computing, are producing an elite of 'cyber-crats' whose skills and knowledge enable them to control networks and ultimately society (Dutton, 1999: 24). Others argue that the change wrought by the information society is negative. For example, Blumler (1992) argues the profusion of media and communication is eroding the sense of community as a result of the fragmentation of the mass audience. The media are no longer able to bring people together by the supply of common and shared experiences to the mass audience. Baudrillard (1983) sees the information blizzard causing the collapse of meaning. More information means less meaning, the result of which is confusion and uncertainty (see Chapter 3).

Trying to assess the merits of the arguments of neophiliacs and pessimists is made difficult by the problem of measuring the information society (Webster, 1997). Quantitative measures about the increase in the amount of information in society and the number of people working in the information and service sectors is no basis for designating a new type of society as having emerged. The discussion is also confused by the unproblematic approach taken to information and the information process. Dutton (1999) and Webster (1995) note that much of the thinking about the information society is based on the communication model developed by Shannon and Weaver (1949). This presents the information process as a one-way flow of communication from sender to receiver by a physical channel subject to noise and interference. Information is a transmittable entity, like electricity, which is uniquely re-usable. This ignores the highly 'vexatious' nature of information in everyday life. As people attach different meanings to what they see, hear and read, what information entails is not straightforward. The one-way flow also ignores the interactivity that characterises much of the new information technology. For Dutton (1999: Chapter 2) the theoretical basis for addressing the impact of new media and information technologies is old-fashioned. For others it raises questions about the quality of information.

DUMBING DOWN OR REACHING OUT?

The growth of media and cultural industries and the rise of the information society coincides with a 'pervasive sense of declining cultural, educational and political standards' or 'dumbing down' (Barnett, 1998: 75). Contrary to the perception that the information and communications revolution, and especially the Internet, promises to revitalise democracy and re-invigorate the public sphere the new technologies are seen as 'destroying the pillars of the fourth estate' (Sparks, 2000: 4). According to one commentator these technologies have 'debased our standards of journalism and eroded our capacity for civil discourse' (Sparks, 2000: 4). While there may be more information available, the quality of this information as well as public understanding is declining. This poses a threat to democracy. Public ignorance and apathy is growing as the serious, challenging and truthful is being pushed aside by the trivial, sensational, vulgar and manipulated. The individual citizen's capacity and ability to participate in the political process is diminishing and the impoverishment of public life and the public sphere provides the 'dangerous potential for demagogic manipulation' (Sparks, 2000: 5). Furthermore democratic accountability and transparency is being swamped by spin doctors who have greater scope then ever before to manage news and information. Such views are resonant with those of mass society theorists. In media studies this debate revolves around the notion of 'tabloidisation'.

The rise of tabloid values in the mass media is central to the general concerns about declining standards. Barnett (1998) identifies three separate strands to the tabloidisation argument. First, the demise of the amount of serious material in the media. The emphasis today in the press and broadcasting is on entertainment, showbusiness, celebrities, scandal and prurience. Less attention is paid to politics, economics, the arts, policy and social issues. The private and personal lives of celebrities and ordinary people are taking up more column inches and airtime than political processes and economic and social developments. The success of the *Sun* newspaper in Britain, the *Jerry Springer Show* in the USA, the reality TV format epitomised by *Big Brother* developed in The Netherlands and exported to the world and magazines such as *Hello!* can all be used as examples of the 'bad' pushing out the 'good'. Second, the nature of serious and challenging material in the media is being 'debased through various packaging and presentational strategies to make it more populist'. The claim is made that stories are increasingly 'bright, light and trite'. Stories are shorter and pictures more prominent or telegenic while the language used is simpler and less wordy. Soundbite journalism, driven by the need for pictures and entertainment, is increasing its hold over serious newspapers, prestigious news bulletins and current affairs programmes. There is 'a retreat from investigative journalism and the reporting of hard news to the preferred territory of "softer" and "lighter" stories' (Franklin, 1997: 4). Third, serious news, information and programming are less prominent. The shift of ITN news from 10 pm to 11 pm, the graveyard slot of Sunday late evening for BBC's flagship current affairs programme *Panorama*, the virtual disappearance of arts programmes from primetime and the increased prominence of 'human interest' stories on newspaper front pages are some examples. The 'serious, analytical or more difficult stories are still being covered but are being relegated to the margins of the TV and radio schedules or the inside pages of newspapers and magazines' (Barnett, 1998: 7).

The evidence to support such claims is a matter of dispute (see Barnett, 1998; McNair, 1998; Sparks, 2000; Tulloch, 2000, for discussion). Much of the dispute centres on different interpretations of what is meant by 'serious' material and what constitutes quality in media coverage. Critics of tabloidisation are attacked for their elitism. They seek to foist their own elite conceptions of news and programming on to the rest of society. Tabloid news, according to one commentator, 'means news led by the audience's interests – less pompous, less pedagogic, less male; more human, more vivacious, more demotic' (quoted in McNair, 1998: 122). Defenders of tabloidisation seek to 'validate the interests and beliefs of the people who consume' the tabloid media (Sparks, 2000: 25). Rather than interpret tabloidisation as the degradation of the public sphere, it can be seen as simply one consequence of mass democracy, with positive and negative features (McNair, 1998: 122). Some go further, arguing the tabloid media are potentially deeply subversive. Fiske (1992) suggests the content of the tabloid media 'offers an alternative reality to the official one and carries utopianized fantasies of emancipation from the constraints of poverty and perceived social failure'. Langer (1998) sees the irreverence of the tabloid media as having the potential to destabilise the dominant ideological order established by the serious news (both quoted in Sparks, 2000: 25). Norris (2000) argues the rise of tabloid values in the media simply represents the diversification in the channels, levels and formats of political communication. Quality journalism and thoughtful coverage of policy debates 'remain strong and flourishing', only now they exist alongside the 'tabloid trash' that makes up most of the increase in the amount of news. By focusing on the 'excesses in the popular end of the market' critics lose sight of the overall changes in the information environment (Norris, 2000: 14–15). She argues the opportunities to learn about public affairs today are greater than ever before and the tabloid media provide a different way of learning about public affairs. The focus on personalities might open up issues that otherwise are seen as remote, dry and abstract in the hands of the serious media. The 'conversational style and the friendliness and familiarity' of the tabloid media are seen as having a 'democratising' function (Sparks, 2000: 26–7) thereby contributing to the enrichment of the public sphere.

Those arguing for the downward drift of the press and television attribute the development to a number of factors: increased competition, the relaxation of regulation, the increased importance of advertising in editorial decisions and the rise of the PR industry (Barnett, 1998). Perhaps the most significant discussion has been around de-regulation and the decline of public service broadcasting. Public service broadcasting is a distinctive model of broadcasting that emerged in Europe in the 1920s. European nations, at the advent of radio, rejected both the unregulated, free market model developing in the United States as well as the directly regulated, state-controlled system emerging in the Soviet Union. A variety of public service broadcasting systems developed across the continent, some of which placed broadcasting in a closer relationship with the state than others. This model was developed in many other countries around the world, especially in the wake of de-colonisation in the 1950s and 1960s. Throughout its history the model has been interpreted to take account of the particular social, political and economic realities of time and place. However, a range of technological, financial, political and social factors has gradually eroded support for public service broadcasting since 1980. Broadcasting, as a result, has undergone considerable change, with technological developments and new regulatory mechanisms ushering in a world of multi-channel, market-driven television. This has brought about a re-adjustment of broadcasting structures, output and audiences.

Theory of public service

The goals of public service broadcasting vary from country to country and have changed over time. Associated with the first Director General of the BBC, John Reith, public service broadcasting basically regards information as a social good not a commodity. Broadcasting serves the community not the market. Several principles are seen as providing the foundations on which public service broadcasting operates. As a valuable public property the government should regulate – but not directly run – broadcasting to maintain standards and diversity of programming. It should be financed through public funds such as the licence fee to guarantee its independence of the market and the pressure of making a profit. It should serve the interests of the nation, and not any particular social group or vested interest. Broadcasters should be politically and publicly accountable. The broadcasting service should be universal and everyone should be able to have access to it.

The relaxation of regulation, and not just in public service systems, has led to the loosening or removal of the obligations on broadcasters to produce particular kinds of programming. For example, no longer is ITV obliged to broadcast current affairs in primetime. The decline of high-quality current affairs on British television is attributable to the changes in regulation, as in the new de-regulated world high audience ratings are more important that uncovering miscarriages of justice, exposing political wrong-doing or explaining the dangers of the new world order. Increased competition is the main feature of the new broadcasting order, forcing broadcasters into a new and more consumerist relationship with their viewers (Barnett, 1998: 83–4). This means giving the audience more and more of what they want, preventing the making of those programmes that challenge conventional wisdoms and educate people about the world around them. Proponents of de-regulation stress the greater choice that increased competition brings. No longer do ordinary viewers have to watch what others think they should. De-regulation ensures their tastes are catered for and if they want to watch more trash than serious television then that is what democracy is all about. Opponents respond that choice is limited. There may be more channels but what they broadcast is increasingly similar. They point to how the new cable and satellite channels simply re-package and re-sell existing products.

The debate about public service broadcasting is seen as crucial in the midst of the information and communication revolution. Garnham (1990) mounts a strong defence of the model on the grounds that information benefits society and the public at large rather than the private individual. The media can only be socially responsible, politically independent and publicly accountable through public service. Garnham (1990: 131) accepts that in practice public service broadcasters such as the BBC have not always discharged their responsibilities effectively or to their full potential, preferring to serve the interests of the rich and powerful than represent a diversity of voices in society. In other words public service broadcasting has not always contributed to the expansion of the public sphere. But public service does allow broadcasters to address viewers as citizens, imparting a sense of the social value of information and communication, whether as a platform for political debate or a means of ensuring democratic accountability. Its continuation is essential if the information and communications revolution is to benefit society as a whole. Critics, however, argue the death of public service television is imminent. For some it is already dead: in Tracey's words public service broadcasting is a 'corpse on leave' and any attempt to save it is more akin to 'the preservation of primeval bugs in amber than the continuation of any vibrant cultural species' (1995: 33).

The argument over the demise of public service and serious news pre-supposes there is a process of change occurring. Some scholars draw attention to the continuities in the 'dumbing down' debate (see Tulloch, 2000). Concerns over declining standards in the media have been prevalent since the middle of the nineteenth century (see Chapter 1). Matthew Arnold's denunciation of the 'New Journalism' of the 1880s centred on less attention being paid to parliament and politics and more to sport, gossip, crime and sex (Sparks, 2000: 18). Similarly the arrivals of the *Daily Mail* in 1896 and commercial television, ITV, in Britain in 1955 were lambasted for their debasement of British culture or devaluation of public life (see Williams, 1998). While the actual nature and content of the press and media may be different today, the debate about the impact of new forms of journalism and media content on culture, society and the democratic process has a long lineage. There is a lesson for media theory here. Those wrestling with the impact of new media technology and new media forms and content in the era of modernity have much in common with contemporary theorists trying to make sense of globalisation and the rise of the information society.

BIBLIOGRAPHY

Abercrombie, N. (1996) *Television and Society*. London: Polity Press.

Abercrombie, N. and Longhurst, B. (1998) *Audiences*. London: Sage.

Abercrombie, N., Hill, S. and Turner, B. (1980) *The Dominant Ideology Thesis*. London: George Allen & Unwin.

Abu-Lughod, L. (1989) Bedouins, cassettes and technologies of public culture, *Middle East Report* **159**, 7–11.

Adler, R. (1975) Understanding television: an overview of the literature of the medium as a social and cultural force, in Adler, R. and Cater, D. (eds) *Television as a Social Force*. New York: Praeger.

Adorno, T. (1957) Television and the pattern of mass culture, in Rosen, B. and White, D. (eds) *Mass Culture: The Popular Arts in America*. Glencoe, IL: Free Press.

Adorno, T. and Horkheimer, M. (1973) *Dialectics of Enlightenment*. London: Allen Lane.

Aggarwala, N. (1990) A third world perspective on news, in Martin, L. and Hiebert, R. (eds) *Current Issues in International Communication*. New York: Longman.

Alasuutari, P. (1999) *Rethinking the Media Audience*. London: Sage.

Allan, S. (1999) *News Culture*. Buckingham: Open University Press.

Alleyne, M. (1995) *International Power and International Communication*. London: Macmillan.

Althusser. L. (1971) *Lenin and Philosophy and Other Essays*. London: Verso.

Alvarado, M., Gutch, R. and Wollen, T. (1987) *Learning the Media*. London: Macmillan.

Anderson, A. (1993) Source–media relations: the production of the environmental agenda, in Hansen, A. (ed.) *The Mass Media and Environmental Issues*. Leicester: Leicester University Press.

Anderson, B. (1983) *Imagined Communities*. London: Verso.

Anderson, D. and Sharrock, W. (1979) Biasing the news: technical issues in 'Media Studies', *British Journal of Sociology* **13**(3), 367–85.

Ang, I. (1985) *Watching 'Dallas': Soap Opera and the Meolodramatic Imagination*. London: Methuen.

Ang, I. (1991) *Desperately Seeking the Audience*. London: Routledge.

Ang, I. (1995) The nature of the audience, in Downing, J., Mohammadi, A. and Sreberny-Mohammadi, A. (eds) *Questioning the Media*. London: Sage (2nd edn).

Ang, I. (ed.) (1996) *Living Room Wars*. London: Routledge.

Ang, I. (1998) The performance of the sponge: mass communication theory enters the postmodern world, in Brants, K., Hermes, J. and Van Zoonen, L. (eds), *The Media in Question*. London: Sage.

Ang, I. and Hermes, J. (1991) Gender and/in media consumption, in Curran, J. and Gurevitch, M. (eds) *Mass Media and Society*. London: Arnold.

Angell (1922) *The Press and the Organisation of Society*. London: Labour Publishing Society.

Aronson, J. (1970) *The Press and the Cold War*. Indianapolis: Bobbs-Merrill.

Bagdikian, B. (1992) *The Media Monopoly*. Boston: Beacon Press (4th edn).

Baistow, T. (1985) *Fourth Rate Estate*. London: Pluto.

Bandura, A. (1965) Influence of models' reinforcement contingencies on the acquisition of imitative responses, *Journal of Personality and Social Psychology* **1**, 589–95.

Baran, S. and Davies, D. (1995) *Mass Communications Theory*. Belmont, California: Wadsworth.

Barker, M. (1989) The lost world of stereotypes, in O'Sullivan, T. and Jewkes, Y. (eds) *The Media Studies Reader*. London: Arnold. (Reprint from *Comics: Ideology, Power and the Critics*. Manchester: Manchester University Press, 1989.)

Barker, M. (1998) Critique: audiences 'r' us, in Dickinson, R., Harindranath, R. and Linne, O. (eds) *Approaches to Audiences*. London: Arnold.

Barker, M. (2001) The Newson Report: a case study in 'common sense', in Barker, M. and Petley, J. (eds) *Ill Effects: The Media/Violence Debate*. London: Routledge.

Barker, M. and Brooks, K. (1998) *Knowing Audiences: 'Judge Dredd', its Fans, Friends and Foes*. Luton: University of Luton Press.

Barker, M. and Petley, J. (2001) *Ill Effects: The Media/Violence Debate*. London: Routledge.

Barnett, S. (1998) Dumbing down or reaching out, in Seaton, J. (ed.) *Politics and the Media*. Oxford: Blackwell.

Barrat, D. (1986) *Media Sociology*. London: Tavistock.

Barthes, R. (2000) [1957] *Mythologies*. London: Vintage Classics.

Bass, A. (1969) Redefining the gatekeeper concept, *Journalism Quarterly* **46**, 69–72.

Baudrillard, J. (1983) *Simulations*. New York: Semiotext(e).

Bayley, E. (1981) *Joe McCarthy and the Press*. Wisconsin: University of Wisconsin Press.

Beharrel, P. and Philo, G. (eds) (1977) *Trade Unions and the Media.* London: Macmillan.

Bell, A. (1991) *The Language of the News Media.* Oxford: Blackwell.

Benjamin, W. (1970) *Illuminations.* London: Jonathan Cape.

Bennett, T. (1982) Theories of the media, theories of society, in Gurevitch, M., Bennett, T., Curran, J. and Woollacott, J. (eds) *Culture, Society and the Media.* London: Methuen.

Berelson, B. (1952) *Content Analysis in Communication Research.* Glencoe, IL: Free Press.

Berelson, B. (1959) The state of communications research, *Public Opinion Quarterly* **23**, 1–6.

Berger, S. and Luckmann, T. (1967) *The Social Construction of Reality.* Harmondsworth: Penguin.

Berkowitz, L. and Rawlings, E. (1963) Effects of film violence on inhibitions against subsequent aggression, *Journal of Abnormal Psychology* **66**.

Bernays, E. (1923) *Crystallising Public Opinion.* New York: Boni and Liveright.

Bignell, J. (1997) *Media Semiotics: An Introduction.* Manchester: Manchester University Press.

Birt, J. and Jay, P. (1975) A bias against understanding, *Times*, 28 February/3 September/ 1 October.

Bleske, G. (1991) Ms Gates takes over, *Newspaper Research Journal* **12**, 88–97.

Blumler, J. (1992) *Television and the Public Interest.* London: Sage.

Blumler, J. and Gurevitch, M. (1986) Journalists' orientations of political institutions: the case of parliamentary broadcasting, in Golding, P., Murdock, G. and Schlesinger, P. (eds) *Communicating Politics: Mass Communications and the Political Process.* Leicester: Leicester University Press.

Blumler, J. and Katz, E. (eds) (1974) *The Uses of Mass Communications.* California: Sage.

Booker, W. (1998) *Teach Yourself Cultural Studies.* London: Hodder & Stoughton.

Bourdieu, P. (1984) *Distinction: A Social Critique of the Judgement of Taste.* London: Routledge.

Boyce, D.G. (1978) The fourth estate: a reappraisal, in Boyce, D.G., Curran, J. and Wingate, P. (eds) *Newspaper History: From the 17th Century to the Present Day.* London: Constable.

Boyd Barrett, O. (1995) Early theories in media research, in Boyd Barrett, O. and Newbold, C. (eds) *Approaches to Media: A Reader.* London: Arnold.

Boyd Barrett, O. and Newbold, C. (1995) *Approaches to Media: A Reader.* London: Arnold.

Branston, G. and Strafford, R. (1996) *The Media Student's Book.* London: Routledge.

Breed, W. (1955) Social control in the newsroom: a functional analysis, *Social Forces* **33**, 326–35.

Bromley, M. (1997) The end of journalism? Changes in workplace practices in the press and broadcasting in the 1990s, in Bromley, M. and O'Malley, T. (eds) *A Journalism Reader.* London: Routledge.

Bromley, M. (1998) The 'tabloiding' of Britain: 'quality' newspapers in the 1990s, in Stevenson, H. and Bromley, M. (eds) *Sex, Lies and Democracy: the Press and the Public.* London: Longman.

Bromley, M. and O'Malley, T. (1997) *A Journalism Reader.* London: Routledge.

Brown, R. (1970) Approaches to the historical development of mass media studies, in Tunstall, J. (ed.) *Media Sociology.* London: Constable.

Brunt, R. and Jordin, M. (1982) The politics of 'bias': how television audiences view current affairs, in Hawthorn, J. *Propaganda, Persuasion and Polemic.* London: Arnold.

Burgelin, O. (1972) Structural analysis and mass communication, in McQuail, D. (ed.) *The Sociology of Mass Communication.* London: Penguin.

Burke, P. (2000) *A Social History of Knowledge.* London: Polity Press.

Burnett, D. (1996) *The Global Jukebox.* London: Routledge.

Burns, T. (1977) *The BBC: Public Institution and Private World.* London: Macmillan.

Busby, L. (1975) Sex-role research on the mass media, *Journal of Communication* (Autumn), 107–31.

Buss, A. (1961) *The Psychology of Aggression.* New York: John Wiley.

Cantril, H., Gaudet, H. and Herzog, H. (1940) *The Invasion from Mars.* Princeton, NJ: Princeton University Press.

Carey, James (1989) *Communication as Culture.* London: Routledge.

Carey, John (1992) *Intellectuals and the Masses.* London: Penguin.

Chalaby, J. (1996) Journalism as an Anglo-American invention, *European Journal of Communication* **11**(3), 320–6.

Chibnall, S. (1977) *Law and Order News.* London: Tavistock Press.

Cohen, B. (1963) *The Press and Foreign Policy.* Princeton, NJ: Princeton University Press.

Cohen, S. (1987) [1973] *Folk Devils and Moral Panics.* Oxford: Blackwell.

Collett, P. and Lamb, R. (1986) *Watching People Watching Television.* London: Independent Broadcasting Authority (IBA).

Collins, R. (1990) *Television: Policy and Culture.* London: Unwin Hyman.

Collins, R. and Murroni, C. (1996) *New Media, New Policies.* London: Polity Press.

Connell, I. (1984) Fabulous powers: blaming the media, in Masterman, L. (ed.) *Television Mythologies: Stars, Shows and Signs.* London: Comedia.

Connell, I. (1978) Monopoly capitalism and the media, in Hibbin, S. (ed.) *Politics, Ideology and the State.* London: Lawrence and Wishart.

Cook, P. (ed.) (1987) *The Cinema Book.* London: British Film Institute (BFI).

Cooper, L. (1932) *The Rhetoric of Aristotle.* New York: Appleton-Century Company.

Corner, J. (1991) Meaning, genre and context: the problematics of "public knowledge" in new audience studies, in Curran, J. and Gurevitch, M. (eds) *Mass Media and Society.* London: Edward Arnold.

Corner, J. (1997) Media Studies and the 'knowledge problem', *Screen* **36.2** (Summer), 147–55.

Corner, J. (1998) *Studying the Media: Problems of Theory and Method.* Edinburgh: Edinburgh University Press.

Corner, J., Schlesinger, P. and Silverstone, R. (1998) *International Media Research.* London: Routledge.

Craig, R. (1994) Why are there so many communication theories?, in Levy, M. and Gurevitch, M. (eds) *Defining Media Studies.* Oxford: Oxford University Press.

Craig, T. and Petley, J. (2001) Invasion of the Internet abusers: marketing fears about the information superhighway, in Barker, M. and Petley, J. (eds) *Ill Effects: the Media/Violence Debate.* London: Routledge.

Croteau, D. and Hoynes, W. (1997) *Media/Society: Industries, Images and Audiences.* London: Pine Forge Press.

Cruz, J. and Lewis, J. (eds) (1994) *Viewers, Listeners, Readers: Audiences and Cultural Reception.* Boulder: Westview.

Cubitt, S. (1985) 'Top of the Pops': the politics of the living room, in Masterman, L. (ed.) *TV Mythologies.* London: Comedia.

Curran, C. (1979) *A Seamless Robe.* London: Collins.

Curran, J. (1977) Capitalism and control of the press 1800–1975, in Curran, J., Gurevitch, M. and Woollacott, J. (eds) *Mass Communication and Society.* London: Arnold.

Curran, J. (1978) Advertising and the press, in Curran, J. (ed.) *The British Press: A Manifesto.* London: Macmillan.

Curran, J. (1980) Advertising as a patronage system, in Christian, H. (ed.) *The Sociology of Journalism and the Press.* Keele: University of Keele.

Curran, J. (1990) The new revisionism in mass communication research: a reappraisal, *European Journal of Communication* **5**, 135–64.

Curran, J. (1991) Mass media and democracy: a reappraisal, in Curran, J. and Gurevitch, M. (eds) *Mass Media and Society*. London: Edward Arnold.

Curran, J. (1992) Culturalist perspectives of news organisations: a reappraisal and a case study, in Ferguson, M. (ed.) *Public Communication: The New Imperatives*. London: Sage.

Curran, J. (1996) Rethinking mass communication, in Curran, J., Morley, D. and Walkerdine, V. (eds) *Cultural Studies and Communications*. London: Arnold.

Curran, J. (2000) *Media Organisations in Society*. London: Arnold.

Curran, J., Gurevitch, M. and Woollacott, J. (1977) *Mass Communication and Society*. London: Edward Arnold.

Curran, J., Douglas, A. and Whannell, G. (1981) The political economy of the human interest story, in Smith, A. (ed.) *Newspapers and Democracy*. Cambridge, MA: MIT Press.

Curran, J., Gurevitch, M. and Woollacott, J. (1982) The study of the media: theoretical approaches, in Gurevitch, M., Bennett, T., Curran, J. and Woollacott, J. (eds) *Culture, Society and the Media*. London: Methuen.

Curran, J. and Seaton, J. (1991) *Power without Responsibility*. London: Routledge (4th edn).

Curran, J. and Seaton, J. (1997) *Power without Responsibility*. London: Routledge (5th edn).

Dahlgren, P. and Sparks, C. (1992) *Journalism and Popular Culture*. London: Sage.

Deacon, D. and Golding, P. (1994) *Taxation and Representation: The Media, Political Communication and the Poll Tax*. London: John Libbey.

De Fleur, M. and Ball-Rokeach, S. (1989) *Theories of Mass Communication*. London: Longman.

Dewe-Mathews, T. (1994) *Censored – What They Didn't Allow You to See and Why: The Story of Film Censorship in Britain*. London: Chatto and Windus.

Dewey, J. (1927) *The Public and its Problems*. Chicago: Swallow Press.

Docherty, D., Morrison, D. and Tracey, M. (1993) Scholarship as silence, in Levy, M. and Gurevitch, M. (eds) *Defining Media Studies*. Oxford: Oxford University Press.

Dorfman, A. and Mattelart, A. (1975) *How to Read Donald Duck: Imperialist Ideology in the Disney Comic*. New York: International General.

Dowmunt, T. (1993) *Channels of Resistance: Global Television and Local Empowerment*. London: British Film Institute (BFI).

Durant, A. (1991) Noises off screen: could a crisis of confidence be good for Media Studies?, *Screen* **32.4** (Winter), 407–28.

Dutton, W. (ed.) (1999) *Society on the Line: Information Politics in the Digital Age*. Oxford: Oxford University Press.

Dworkin, A. (1981) *Pornography: Men Possessing Women*. London: the Women's Press.

Dyer, R. (1977) *Gays and Film*. London: British Film Institute (BFI).

Dyson, K. and Homolka, W. (1995) *Culture First!* London: Cassell.

Eagleton, T. (1991) *Ideology: An Introduction*. London: Verso.

Eco, U. (1966) Narrative structure in Fleming, in Buono, E. and Eco, U. (eds) *The Bond Affair*. London: MacDonald.

Eldridge, J., Kitzinger, J. and Williams, K. (1997) *The Mass Media and Power in Modern Britain*. Oxford: Oxford University Press.

Elliott, P. (1972) *The Making of a Television Series*. London: Constable.

Elliott, P. (1974) Uses and gratifications research: a critique and sociological alternative, in Blumler, J. and Katz, E. (eds) *The Uses of Mass Communication*. London: Sage.

Elliott, P. (1978) Professional ideology and organisational change: the journalist since 1800, in Boyce, D.G., Curran, J. and Wingate, P. (eds) *Newspaper History: From the 17th Century to the Present Day*. London: Constable.

Entman, R. (1989) *Democracy without Citizens: Media and the Decay of American Politics*. New York: Oxford University Press.

Epstein, E. (1974) *News from Nowhere*. New York: Vintage Books.

Ettema, J. and Whitney, J. (eds) (1982) *Individuals in Mass Media Organisations*. California: Sage.

European Commission (1999) *Images of Women in the Media*. Luxembourg: EC.

Fejes, F. (1981) Media imperialism: an assessment, *Media, Culture and Society* **3**(3), 281–9.

Ferguson, M. (1990) *Public Communication: the New Imperatives*. London: Sage.

Ferguson, M. and Golding, P. (eds) (1997) *Cultural Studies in Question*. London: Sage.

Ferguson, R. (1998) *Representing 'Race'*. London: Arnold.

Ferrante, J. (1992) *Global Sociology*. Belmont, CA: Wadsworth.

Feshbach, S. and Singer, J. (1971) *Television and Aggression*. San Fransisco: Jossey-Bass.

Feuer, J. (1987) Genre study and television, in Allen, R. (ed.) *Channels of Discourse*. London: Methuen.

Fishman, M. (1981) *Manufacturing the News*. Austin, TX: University of Texas Press.

Fiske, J. (1982) *Introduction to Communication Studies*. London: Routledge.

Fiske, J. (1986) Television: polysemy and popularity, *Critical Studies in Mass Communication* **34**, 391–408.

Fiske, J. (1987a) *Television Culture*. London: Methuen.

Fiske, J. (1987b) British Cultural Studies and television, in Allen, R. (ed.) *Channels of*

Discourse. London: Methuen.

Fiske, J. (1989a) *Reading the Popular*. London: Unwin Hyman.

Fiske, J. (1989b) *Understanding the Popular*. London: Unwin Hyman.

Fiske, J. (1992) Popularity and the politics of information, in Dahlgren, P. and Sparks, C. (eds) *Journalism and Popular Culture*. London: Sage.

Foucault, M. (1977) *Discipline and Punishment*. London: Allen Lane.

Fowler, R. (1991) *Language in the News*. London: Routledge.

Franklin, B. (1997) *Newszak & News Media*. London: Arnold.

Fraser, N. (1992) Rethinking the public sphere, in Calhoun, C. (ed.) *Habermas and the Public Sphere*. Cambridge, MA.: MIT Press.

Fulcher, J. and Scott, J. (1999) *Sociology*. Oxford: Oxord University Press.

Gallagher, M. (1982) Negotiation of control in media organizations and occupations, in Gurevitch, M., Bennett, T., Curran, J. and Woollacott, J. (eds) *Culture, Society and the Media*. London: Methuen.

Gallagher, M. (1992) Women and men in the media, *Communications Research Trends* **12**(1).

Gamman, L. and Marshment, M. (eds) (1988) *The Female Gaze*. London: The Women's Press.

Gandy, O. (1982) *Beyond Agenda Setting*. Norwood, NJ: Ablex.

Gans, H. (1979) *Deciding What's News*. New York: Pantheon Books.

Garnham, N. (1983) Media Studies in Britain remain marginal, *Journalism Studies Review* July, 33–5.

Garnham, N. (1990) *Capitalism and Communication*. London: Sage.

Garnham, N. (1995) Political economy and cultural studies: reconciliation or divorce, *Critical Studies in Mass Communication* **12**, 62–71.

Garnham, N. (2000) *Emancipation, the Media and Modernity*. Oxford: Oxford University Press.

Gauntlett, D. (1998) Ten things wrong with the 'effects model', in Dickinson, R., Harindranath, R. and Linne, O. (eds) *Approaches to Audiences*. London: Arnold.

Gauntlett, D. (2001) The worrying influence of 'Media Effects' Studies, in Barker, M. and Petley, J. (eds) *Ill Effects: The Media/Violence Debate*. London: Routledge.

Gerbner, G. (1992) Violence and terror in and by the media, in Raboy, M. and Dagenais, B. (eds) *Media, Crisis and Democracy*. London: Sage.

Gerbner, G., Gross, L., Morgan, M. and Signorielli, N. (1982) The 'mainstreaming' of America: violence profile No 11, *Journal of Communication* **30**, 10–29.

Gerbner, G., Gross, L., Morgan, M. and Signorielli, N. (1984) Charting the mainstream:

television's contributions to political orientations, *Journal of Communication* **32**, 100–27.

Gieber (1956) Across the desk: a study of 16 telegraph editors, *Journalism Quarterly* **33**, 423–32.

Gillespie, M. (1995) *Television, Ethnicity and Cultural Change*. London: Routledge.

Gitlin, T. (1978) Media sociology: the dominant paradigm, *Theory and Society* **6**, 205–53. (Reprinted in *Mass Communication Review Yearbook*, Vol. 2, 1978.)

Gitlin, T. (1980) *The Whole World is Watching: Mass Media in the Making and Unmaking of the New Left*. Berkeley: University of California Press.

Gitlin, T. (1991) The politics of communication and the communication of politics, in Curran, J. and Gurevitch, M. (eds) *Mass Media and Society*. London: Arnold.

Glasgow Media Group (1976) *Bad News*. London: Routledge.

Glasgow Media Group (1980) *More Bad News*. London: Routledge.

Glasser, T. (1985) Objectivity precludes responsibility, in Hiebert, R. and Reuss, C. (eds) *Impact of Mass Media: Current Issues*. London: Longman.

Glover, D. (1984) *The Sociology of the Mass Media*. Ormskirk: Causeway.

Goldenberg, E. (1975) *Making the Papers*. Lexington: D.C. Heath.

Golding, P. (1977) Media professionalism in the Third World: a transfer of ideology, in Curran, J., Gurevitch, M. and Woollacott, J. (eds) *Mass Communication and Society*. London: Edward Arnold.

Golding, P. (1994) The communication paradox: inequality at the national and international levels, *Media Development* **4**, 7–11.

Golding, P. and Elliott, P. (1979) *Making the News*. London: Longman.

Golding, P. and Murdock, G. (1978) Theories of communication and theories of society, *Communication Research* **5**(3), 339–56.

Golding, P. and Murdock, G. (1990) Screening out the poor, in Willis, J. and Wollen, T. (eds) *The Neglected Audience*. London: British Film Institute (BFI).

Golding, P. and Murdock, G. (2000) [1991] Culture, communication and political economy, in Curran, J. and Gurevitch, M. (eds) *Mass Media and Society*. London: Edward Arnold.

Goode, E. and Ben-Yehuda, N. (1994) *Moral Panics: The Social Construction of Deviance*. Oxford: Blackwell.

Goodwin, A. (1988) *Media Studies for Adults*. London: British Film Institute (BFI).

Gray, A. (1992) *Video Playtime: The Gendering of a Leisure Technology*. London: Routledge.

Gray, A. (1999) Audience and reception research in retrospect: the trouble with audiences, in Alasuutari, P. (1999) *Rethinking the Media Audience*. London: Sage.

Grossberg, L. (1995) Cultural Studies vs political economy: is anybody else bored with this debate?, *Critical Studies in Mass Communication* (March), 72–81.

Grossberg, L., Wartella, E. and Whitney, D.C. (1998) *Media Making: Mass Media in a Popular Culture*. London: Sage.

Gunter, B. (1997) *Measuring Bias on Television*. Luton: John Libbey.

Gurevitch, M., Bennett, T., Curran, J. and Woollacott, J. (1982) *Culture, Society and the Media*. London: Methuen.

Gurevitch, M. and Blumler, J. (1977) Linkages between mass media and politics, in Curran, J., Gurevitch, M. and Woollacott, J. (eds) *Mass Communication and Society*. London: Arnold.

Hall, S. (1973) Encoding and decoding in the television discourse, BCCCS Occasional Papers.

Hall, S. (1074) Media power: the double bind, *Journal of Communication* (Autumn), 19–27.

Hall, S. (1975) Encoding and decoding in the television discourse, *Education and Culture* **6**, Strasbourg: Council of Europe.

Hall, S. (1977) Culture, the media and the ideological effect, in Curran, J., Gurevitch, M. and Woollacott, J. (eds) *Mass Communication and Society*. London: Edward Arnold.

Hall, S. (1978) Newspapers, parties and classes, in Curran, J. (ed.) *The British Press: A Manifesto*. London: Macmillan Press.

Hall, S. (1980) Encoding/decoding, in Hall, S., Hobson, D., Lowe, A. and Willis, P. (eds) *Culture, Media, Language* London: Hutchinson.

Hall, S. (1982) The rediscovery of 'ideology': return of the repressed in Media Studies, in Gurevitch, M., Bennett, T., Curran, J. and Woollacott, J (eds) *Culture, Society and the Media*. London: Methuen.

Hall, S. (1992) The question of cultural identity, in Hall, S., Held, D. and McGrew, T. (eds) *Modernity and its Futures*. London: Polity.

Hall, S. and Jefferson, T. (eds) (1976) *Resistance through Rituals: Youth subcultures in Post War Britain*. London: Heinemann.

Hall, S., Connell, I. and Curti, L. (1976) The 'unity' of current affairs television, *Cultural Studies* **9**, 51–93.

Hall, S., Critcher, C., Jefferson, T., Clarke, J. and Roberts, B. (1978) *Policing the Crisis*. London: Macmillan.

Halloran, J. (1969) *The Effects of Television*. London: Panther.

Halloran, J., Brown, R. and Chaney, D. (1970) *Television and Delinquency*. Leicester:

University of Leicester Press.

Hamelink, C. (1983) *Cultural Autonomy in Global Communication*. New York: Longman.

Hamelink, C. (1995a) Globalism and national sovereignty, in Nordenstreng, K. and Schiller, H. (eds) *Beyond National Sovereignty: International Communication in the 1990s*. Norwood, NJ: Ablex.

Hamelink, C. (1995b) Information imbalance across the globe, in Downing, J., Mohammadi, A., and Sreberny-Mohammadi, A. (eds) *Questioning the Media*. London: Sage (2nd edn).

Hansen, A., Cottle, S., Negrine, R. and Newbold, C. (1998) *Mass Communication Research Methods*. London: Macmillan.

Hardt, H. (1992) *Critical Communications Studies: Communication History and Theory in America*. London: Routledge.

Harms, J. and Dickens, D. (1996) Postmodern Media Studies: analysis or symptom, *Critical Studies in Mass Communication* **13**, 210–27.

Hartley, J., Goulden, H. and O'Sullivan, T. (1985) *Making Sense of the Media*. London: Comedia.

Hartley, J. (1992) *The Politics of Pictures*. London: Routledge.

Hartmann, P. and Husbands, C. (1974) *Racism and the Mass Media*. London: Davis Poynter.

Heath, S. (1981) *Questions of Cinema*. London: Macmillan.

Hebdige, D. (1979) *Subculture: The Meaning of Style*. London: Methuen.

Held, D. (2000) *A Globalizing World? Culture, Economics, Politics*. London: Routledge.

Herman, E. and Chomsky, N. (1988) *The Political Economy of the Mass Media*. New York: Pantheon Books.

Herman, E. and McChesney, R. (1997) *The Global Media*. London: Cassell.

Herman, E. (1998) The propaganda model revisited, in McChesney, R.W., Wood, E.M. and Foster, J.B. (eds) *Capitalism in the Information Age*. New York: Monthly Review Press.

Herzog, H. (1944) What do we really know about day-time serial listeners?, in Lazarsfeld, P. (ed.) *Radio Research*. New York: Duell, Sloan and Pearce.

Hetherington, A. (1985) *News, Newspapers and Television*. London: Macmillan.

Hirsch, P. (1972) Occupational, organisational and institutional models in mass media research: toward an intergrated framework, in Kline, G. and Tichenor, P. (eds) *Current Perspectives in Mass Communication Research*. London: Sage.

Hobsbawm, E. and Ranger, T. (1983) *The Invention of Tradition*. Cambridge: Cambridge

University Press.

Hobson, D. (1980) Housewives and the mass media, in Hall, S., Hobson, D., Lowe, A. and Willis, P. (eds) *Culture, Media, Language.* London: Hutchinson.

Hobson, D. (1982) '*Crossroads': The Drama of a Soap Opera.* London: Methuen.

Hoge, J. (1985) Business and the media: stereotyping each other, in Hiebert, R. and Reuss, C. (eds) *Impact of Mass Media: Current Issues.* London: Longman.

Hoggart, R. (1958) *The Uses of Literacy.* London: Pelican.

Hood, S. (1972) The politics of television, in McQuail, D. (ed.) *Sociology of Mass Communications.* Harmondsworth: Penguin.

Hood, S. (1980) *On Television.* London: Pluto Press (1st edn).

Hood, S. and Tabary-Peterssen, T. (1997) *On Television.* London: Pluto (4th edn).

Hoogvelt, A. (1997) *Globalisation and the Postcolonial World: The New Political Economy of Development.* London: Macmillan.

Hovland, C., Janis, I. and Kelley, H. (1953) *Communication and Persuasion.* New Haven, Conn.: Yale University Press.

Howitt, D. (1982) *Mass Media and Social Problems.* Oxford: Pergamon Press.

Inglis, F. (1990) *Media Theory: An Introduction.* Oxford: Blackwell.

Innis, H. (1950) *Empire and Communication.* Toronto: Toronto University Press.

Innis, H. (1951) *The Bias of Communication.* Toronto: Toronto University Press.

Iyengar, S. and Kinder, D. (1987) *News That Matters.* Chicago: University of Chicago Press.

Iyengar, S. and Reeves, R. (1997) *Do the Media Govern? Politicians, Voters and Reporters in America.* London: Sage.

Iyengar, S., Peters, M.D. and Kinder, D. (1982) Experimental demonstrations of the 'not-so-minimal' consequences of television news programs, *American Political Science Review* **76**, 848–58.

Jankowski, N. and Wester, F. (1991) The qualitative tradition in social science inquiry: contributions to mass communications research, in Jensen, K.B. and Jankowski, N. (eds) *A Handbook of Qualitative Methods for Mass Communication Research.* London: Routledge.

Janus, N. (1977) Research on sex-roles in the mass media: toward a critical approach, *Insurgent Sociologist* **7**(3), 19–32.

Jensen, K.B. and Jankowski, N. (eds). (1991) *A Handbook of Qualitative Methods for Mass Communications Research.* London: Routledge.

Johnstone, J., Slawski, E. and Bowman, W. (1976) *The News People.* Urbana: University of Illinois Press.

Jones, M. (1997) Media violence and children revisited, *Sociology Review* (September), 20–1.

Journal of Communication (1983) Special Edition: Ferment in the Field, *Journal of Communication* **33**(3).

Journal of Communication (1993a) The future of the field I, *Journal of Communication* **43**(3).

Journal of Communication (1993b) The future of the field II, *Journal of Communication* **43**(4).

Jowett, G. and O'Donnell, J. (1998) *Propaganda and Persuasion*. London: Sage Third Edition.

Katz, E. (1959) Mass communication research and the study of culture, *Studies in Public Communication* **2**, 1–6.

Katz, E. and Lazarsfeld, P. (1955) *Personal Influence: The Part Played by People in the Flow of Information*. New York: Free Press.

Katz, E. and Liebes, T. (1990) *The Export of Meaning*. New York: Oxford University Press.

Keane, J. (1991) *The Media and Democracy*. London: Polity Press.

King, J. and Stott, M. (1977) *Is This Your Life? Images of Women in the Media*. London: Virago.

Kitzinger, J. (1993) Understanding AIDS: media messages and what people know about AIDS, in Eldridge, J. (ed.) *Getting the Message*. London: Routledge.

Kitzinger, J. (1997) Media influence, *Sociology Review* (April), 6–10.

Kitzinger, J. (1999) A sociology of media power: key issues in audience reception research, in Philo, G. (ed.) *Message Received*. London: Longman.

Kitzinger, J. and Skidmore, P. (1995) Playing safe: media coverage of child sex abuse prevention strategies, *Child Abuse Review* **4**, 47–56.

Klapper, J. (1960) *The Effects of Mass Communication*. New York: Free Press.

Kocher, R. (1986) Bloodhounds or missionaries: role definitions of German and British journalists, *European Journal of Communication* **1**, 43–64.

Koss, S. (1984) *The Rise and Fall of the Political Press*, Vols I and II. London: Macmillan.

Kress, G. (1985) *Linguistic Processes in Socialcultural Practice*. Sydney: Deakin University Press.

Kuhn, T. (1970) *The Structure of Scientific Revolutions*. Chicago: Chicago University Press.

Kumar, K. (1977) Holding the middle ground, in Curran, J., Gurevitch, M. and Woollacott, J. (eds) *Mass Communications and Society*. London: Edward Arnold.

Lang, G. and Lang, K. (1981) Watergate: an exploration of the agenda building process, *Mass Communications Review Yearbook*. London: Sage.

Lang, G. and Lang, K. (1983) *The Battle for Public Opinion: the President, the Press and the Polls during Watergate*. New York: Columbia University Press.

Langer, J. (1998) *Tabloid Television*. London: Routledge.

Lapsey, R. and Westlake, M. (1988) *Film Theory: An Introduction*. Manchester: Manchester University Press.

Larrain, J. (1979) *The Concept of Ideology*. London: Hutchinson.

Lasswell, H. (1927) *Propaganda Technique in the World War*. New York: Peter Smith.

Lasswell, H. (1948) The structure and function of communication in society, in Schramm, W. and Roberts, D. (eds) *The Process and Effects of Mass Communication*. Urbana: University of Illinois Press.

Latouche, S. (1996) *The Westernisation of the World*. London: Polity Press.

Lazarsfeld, P. and Merton, R. (1948) Mass communication, popular taste and organised social action, in Bryson, L. (ed.) *The Communication of Ideas*. New York: Harper.

Lazarsfeld, P., Berelson, B. and Gaudet, H. (1948) *The People's Choice*. New York: Columbia Press.

Leavis, F. (1930) *Mass Civilisation and Minority Culture*. London: Chatto and Windus.

Lerner, D. (1958) *The Passing of Traditional Society*. New York: Free Press.

Lewis, J. (1991) *The Ideological Octopus: An Exploration of Television and Its Audience*. London: Routledge.

Lewis, J. (1997) What counts in Cultural Studies, *Media, Culture and Society* **19**, 83–97.

Levy, M. and Gurevitch, M. (1994) *Defining Media Studies*. Oxford: Oxford University Press.

Lichtenberg, J. (2000) 'In Defence of Objectivity' revisited, in Curran, J. and Gurevitch, M. (eds) *Mass Media and Society*. London: Arnold.

Lichter, S., Rothman, S. and Lichter, L. (1986) *The Media Elite: America's New Powerbrokers*. Bethesda, MD: Adler and Adler.

Lippmann, W. (1922) *Public Opinion*. New York: Harcourt Brace.

Lippmann, W. (1925) *The Phantom Public*. New York: Harcourt Brace.

Lippmann, W. (1965) *Public Opinion*. New York: Free Press.

Lippman, W. and Merz, C. (1920) A test of the news *The New Republic* (4 August).

Livingstone, S. (1998) Audience research at the crossroads, *European Journal of Cultural Studies* **1**(2), 193–217.

Lorimer, R. (1994) *Mass Communications: A Comparative Introduction*. Manchester: Manchester University Press.

Lull, J. (1990) *Inside Family Viewing*. London: Routledge.

Lull, J. (2000) *Media, Communication, Culture: a Global Approach*. London: Polity Press.

Lyotard, J. (1984) *The Postmodern Condition*. Manchester: Manchester University Press.

McChesney, R. (1994) Critical communications research at the crossroads, in Levy, M. and Gurevitch, M. (eds) *Defining Media Studies*. Oxford: Oxford University Press.

McCombs, M. (1981) The agenda setting approach, in Nimmo, D. and Sanders, K. (eds) *Handbook of Political Communication*. California: Sage.

McCombs, M. and Shaw, D. (1972) The agenda setting function of the mass media, *Public Opinion Quarterly* **36**, 176–87.

Machin, D. (2002) *Ethnographic Research Methods for the Media*. London: Arnold.

MacKay, H. (2001) *Investigating the Information Society*. Milton Keynes: Open University Press.

McLuhan, M. (1994) *Understanding Media*. London: Ark.

McLuhan, M. and Fiore, Q. (1968) *War and Peace in the Global Village*. San Francisco: Hardwire.

McLennan, G. (1991a) *Marxism and the Methodologies of History*. London: New Left Books.

McLennan, G. (1991b) Politics and power, in McLennan, G. (ed.) *The Power of Ideology*. Buckingham: Open University Press.

McLeod, J., Kosicki, G. and Pan, Z. (1991) On understanding and misunderstanding media effects, in Curran, J. and Gurevitch, M. (eds) *Mass Media and Society*. London: Edward Arnold (2nd edn).

McDonnell, K. and Robins, K. (1980) Marxist cultural theory: the Althusserian smokescreen, in Clarke, S. *One Dimensional Marxism: Althusser and the Politics of Culture*. London: New Left Books.

McGregor, B. (1997) *Live, Direct and Biased? Making TV News in the Satellite Age*. London: Edward Arnold.

McLellan, D. (1971) *The Thoughts of Karl Marx*. London: Macmillan.

McNair, B. (1998) *The Sociology of Journalism*. London: Arnold.

McQuail, D. (1984) With the benefit of hindsight: reflections on uses and gratifications research, *Critical Studies in Mass Communication* **1**(2), 177–93.

McQuail, D. (1986) Is media theory adequate to the challenge of new communications technologies, in Ferguson, M. (ed.) *New Communication Technologies and the Public Interest*. London: Sage.

McQuail, D. (1987) *Mass Communication Theory*. London: Sage (2nd edn).

McQuail, D. (1992) *Media Performance: Mass Communications and the Public Interest*. London: Sage.

McQuail, D. (1994) *Mass Communication Theory*. London: Sage (3rd edn).

McQuail, D (2000) *Mass Communication Theory*. London: Sage (4th edn).

McQuail, D., Blumler, J. and Brown, R. (1972) The television audience: a revised perspective, in McQuail, D (ed.) *Sociology of Mass Communication*. Harmondsworth: Penguin.

McRobbie, A. (2000) The return to cultural production: case study – fashion journalism, in Curran, J. and Gurevitch, M. (eds) *Mass Media and Society*. London: Arnold.

Maddox, B. (1996) Beware the rise in hands-off lessons, *The Times*, 3 April.

Maltby, R. (1995) *Hollywood Cinema*. Oxford: Blackwell.

Manning, P. (2001) *News and News Sources*. London: Sage.

Marx, K. and Engels, F. (1974) *Selected Works*. London: Lawrence and Wishart.

Mattelart, A. (1979) *Multinational Corporations and the Control of Culture*. Falmer: Harvester Press.

Mattelart, A. (1989) *Advertising International*. London: Routledge.

Mattelart, A. and Mattelart, M. (1998) *Theories of Communication*. London: Sage.

Merton, R. (1949) *Social Theory and Social Structure*. Glencoe, IL: Free Press.

Meyrowitz, J. (1994) Images of media: hidden ferment – and harmony – in the field, in Levy, M. and Gurevitch, M. (eds) *Defining Media Studies* Oxford: Oxford University Press. (1994).

Miliband, R. (1973) *The State in Capitalist Society*. London: Quartet Books.

Miller, T., Govil, N., McMurria, J. and Maxwell, R. (2001) *Global Hollywood*. London: British Film Institute (BFI).

Mills, C. Wright (1957) *The Power Elite*. Oxford: Oxford University Press.

Mitchell, J. (1975) *Psychoanalysis and Feminism*. Harmondsworth: London.

Modleski, T. (1982) *Loving with a Vengeance: Mass-produced Fantasies for Women*. London: Methuen.

Moores, S. (1988) The box on the dresser: memories of early radio and everyday life, *Media, Culture and Society* **10**, 23–40.

Moores, S. (1996) *Satellite Television and Everyday Life*. Luton: John Libbey.

Moragas Spa, M., Garitaonandia, C. and Lopez, B. (eds) (1999) *Television on your Doorstep*. Luton: University of Luton Press.

Morgan, G. (1992) The sociology of organisations, *Sociology Review* (February), 17–20.

Morgan, M. (1989) Television and democracy, in Angus, I. and Jhally, S. (eds) *Cultural Politics in Contemporary America*. London: Routledge.

Morley, D. (1980) *The 'Nationwide' Audience*. London: British Film Institute (BFI).

Morley, D. (1986) *Family Television: Cultural Power and Domestic Leisure*. London: Comedia.

Morley, D. (1992) *Television, Audience and Cultural Studies*. London: Routledge.

Morley, D. (1995) Theories of consumption in Media Studies, in Miller, D. (ed.) *Acknowledging Consumption*. London: Routledge.

Morley, D. (1996) Populism, revisionism and the new audience research, in Curran, J., Morley, D. and Walkerdine, V. (eds) *Cultural Studies and Communication*. London: Arnold.

Morley, D. (1999) To boldly go . . . the 'third generation of reception studies' in Alasuutari, P. (ed.) *Rethinking the Media Audience*. London: Sage.

Morley, D. and Brunsdon, C. (1978) *Everyday Television: the 'Nationwide' Study*. London: British Film Institute (BFI).

Morley, D. and Silverstone, R. (1990) Domestic communication, *Media, Culture and Society* **12**, 31–55.

Mosco, V. (1996) *The Political Economy of Communication*. London: Sage.

Mowlana, H. (1996) *Global Communication in Transition: The End of Diversity?* London: Sage.

Mulvey, L. (1975) Visual pleasure and narrative cinema, *Screen* **16**(3), 16–18.

Mungham, G. and Williams, K. (1987) BBC: A question of balance, *Mediaworld* (December/January), 18–20.

Murdock, G. (1980) Class, power and the press: problems of conceptualisation and evidence, in Christian, H. (ed.) *The Sociology of Journalism and the Press*. Keele: Keele University.

Murdock, G. (1982a) Large corporations and the control of the communications industries, in Gurevitch, M., Bennett, T., Curran, J. and Woollacott, J. (eds) *Culture, Society and the Media*. London: Methuen, 118–150.

Murdock, G. (1982b) Mass communication and social violence: a critical review of recent research trends, in Marsh, P. and Campbell, A. (eds) *Aggression and Violence*. Oxford: Blackwell.

Murdock, G. (1990) Redrawing the map of the communications industries: concentration and ownership in the era of privatisation, in Ferguson, M (ed.) *Public*

Communication: The New Imperatives. London: Sage.

Murdock, G. (1992) Citizens, consumers and the public culture, in Skovmand, M. and Schroeder, K. (eds) *Media Cultures.* London: Routledge.

Murdock, G. (1994) The new mogul empires: media concentration and control in the age of convergence, *Media Development* **4**, 3–6.

Murdock, G. (2000a) Reconstructing the ruined tower: contemporary communications and questions of class, in Curran, J. and Gurevitch, M. (eds) *Mass Media and Society.* London: Edward Arnold.

Murdock, G. (2000b) Digital futures: European television in the age of convergence, in Witen, J., Murdock, G and Dahlgren, P. (eds) *Television Across Europe: A Comparative Introduction.* London: Sage.

Murdock, G. (2001) Reservoirs of dogma: an archaeology of popular anxieties, in Barker, M. and Petley, J. (eds) *Ill Effects: The Media/Violence Debate.* London: Routledge.

Murdock, G. and Golding, P. (1973) For a political economy of mass communications, in Miliband, R. and Saville, J. (eds) *Socialist Register.* London: Merlin.

Murdock, G. and Golding, P. (1977) Capitalism, communications and class relations, in Curran, J., Gurevitch, M. and Woollacott, J. (eds) *Mass Communications and Society.* London: Edward Arnold.

Murdock, G. and McCron, R. (1978) Television and teenage violence, *New Society* **14** (December), 632–3.

Neale, S. (1980) *Genre.* London: British Film Institute (BFI).

Neale, S. (2000) *Genre and Hollywood.* London: Routledge.

Negrine, R. (1989) *Politics and the Mass Media in Britain.* London: Sage.

Negroponte, N. (1996) *Being Digital.* London: Hodder & Stoughton.

Negus, K. (1999) *Music Genres and Corporate Cultures.* London: Routledge.

Newburn, T. and Hagell, A. (1995) Violence on screen, *Sociology Review* (February) 7–10.

Noble, G. (1975) *Children in Front of the Small Screen.* London: Constable.

Norris, P. (2000) *A Virtuous Circle: Political Communication in Post Industrial Societies.* Cambridge: Cambridge University Press.

O'Connor, A. and Downing, J. (1995) Culture and communication, in Downing, J., Mohammadi, A. and Sreberny-Mohammadi, A. (eds) *Questioning the Media.* London: Sage (2nd edn).

Open University (1977a) *Mass Communication and Society* (course reading, Block Four Unit 10, Patterns of Ownership: Questions of Control), Milton Keynes: Open University Press.

Open University (1977b) *Mass Communication and Society* (course reading, Block Four Unit 11, Organisations and Occupations), Milton Keynes: Open University Press.

O'Sullivan, T., Dutton, B. and Rayner, P. (1998) *Studying the Media*. London: Arnold (2nd edn).

O'Sullivan, T., Hartley, J., Saunders, D., Montgomery, M. and Fiske, J. (1994) *Key Concepts in Communications and Cultural Studies*. London: Routledge.

O'Sullivan, T. and Jewkes, Y. (eds) (1997) *The Media Studies Reader*. London: Arnold.

Packard, V. (1957) *The Hidden Persuaders*. London: Longman.

Paletz, D. and Entman, R. (1981) *Media, Politics, Power*. New York: Free Press.

Parenti, M. (1986) *Inventing Reality: The Politics of the Mass Media*. New York: St Martin's Press.

Park, R. (1922) *The Immigrant Press and Its Control*. New York: Harper.

Park, R. (1923) The natural history of the newspaper, *The American Journal of Sociology* **XXIX**(3), 273–89.

Pearson, G. (1983) *Hooligan: A History of Respectable Fears*. London: Macmillan.

Pearson, G. (1984) Falling standards: a short, sharp history of moral decline, in Barker, M. (ed.) *The Video Nasties: Freedom and Censorship in the Media*. London: Pluto Press.

Perkins, T. (1979) Rethinking stereotypes, in Barrett, M., Corrigan, P., Kuhn, A. and Wolff, J. (eds) *Ideology and Cultural Production*. London: Croom Helm.

Perry, D. (1996) *Theory and Research in Mass Communication: Contexts and Consequences*. New York: Lawrence Erlbaum.

Pettman, R. (1996) *Understanding International Political Economy*. London: Lynne Reinner.

Philo, G. and Miller, D. (2001) *Market Killing*. London: Longman.

Philo, G., Beharrel, P., Davis, H. and Hewitt, J. (1982) *Really Bad News*. London: Writers and Readers.

Pickering, M. (2001) *Stereotyping*. London: Palgrave.

Pilger, J. (1992) *Distant Voices*. London: Verso.

Pilger, J. (1995) All right on the night, *Guardian*, 31 March.

Pilger, J. (1998) *Distant Voices*. London: Vintage.

Postman, N. (1985) *Amusing Ourselves to Death*. London: Methuen.

Price, S. (1993) *Media Studies*. London: Pitman Publishing.

Radway, J. (1984) *Reading the Romance: Women, Patriarchy and Popular Literature*. Chapel Hill: University of North Carolina Press.

Redhead, S. (1993) *Rave Off: Police and Deviance in Contemporary Youth Culture.* London: Avebury.

Reeves, G. (1993) *Communications and the 'Third World'.* London: Routledge.

Rheingold, H. (1994) *The Virtual Community.* London: Secker and Warburg.

Robins, K. (1996) *Into the Image.* London: Routledge.

Robins, K. (1997a) What in the world is going on?, in DeGuy, P. (ed.) *Production of Culture, Cultures of Production.* London: Sage.

Robins, K. (1997b) What is globalisation?, *Sociology Review* (February), 2–6.

Roe, K. and De Meyer, G. (2000) Music television: MTV Europe, in Wieten, J., Murdock, G. and Dahlgren, P. (eds) *Television Across Europe: A Comparative Introduction.* London: Sage.

Rogers, E. (1962) *The Diffusion of Innovations.* Glencoe, IL: Free Press.

Rogers, E. (1969) *Modernisation Among Peasants: The Impact of Communications.* New York: Holt, Reinhart and Winston.

Rogers, E. and Dearing, J. (1988) Agenda-setting research: where has it been, where is it going, *Mass Communication Review Yearbook.* London: Sage, 555–94.

Romano, C. (1986) WHAT? The grisly truth about bare facts, in Manoff, R.K. and Schudson, M. (eds) *Reading the News.* New York: Pantheon Books.

Root, J. (1986) *Open the Box.* London: Comedia.

Rosten, L. (1937) *The Washington Correspondents.* New York: Harcourt Brace.

Rosten, L. (1941) *Hollywood: The Movie Colony, the Movie Makers.* New York: Harcourt Brace.

Rothenbuhler, E. (1994) Argument for a Durkheimian theory of the communicative, in Levy, M. and Gurevitch, M. (eds) *Defining Media Studies.* Oxford: Oxford University Press.

Rowland, W. (1983) *The Politics of TV Violence: Policy Uses of Communication Research.* London: Sage.

Ruddock, A. (2001) *Understanding Audience: Theory and Method.* London: Sage.

Ryall, T. (1975) Teaching through genre, *Screen Education* **17**, 27–33.

Seaton, J. and Pimlott, B. (eds) (1987) *The Media in British Politics.* London: Avebury.

Scammell, M. (1993) *Designer Politics.* London: Macmillan.

Scannell, P. and Cardiff, D. (1991) *A Social History of Broadcasting.* Oxford: Blackwell.

Schiller, H. (1969) *Mass Communication and the American Empire.* Boston: Beacon Press.

Schiller, H. (1989) *Culture Inc. The Corporate Takeover of Public Expression.* Oxford: Oxford University Press.

Schiller, H. (1996) *Information Inequality*. London: Routledge.

Schlesinger, P. (1980) Between sociology and journalism, in Christian, H. (ed.) *The Sociology of Journalism and the Press*. Keele: University of Keele, 341–70.

Schlesinger, P. (1987) *Putting 'Reality' Together* London: Methuen (2nd edn).

Schlesinger, P. (1990) Rethinking the sociology of journalism: source strategies and the limits of media centrism, in Ferguson, M. (ed.) *Public Communications: The New Imperatives*. London: Sage.

Schlesinger, P. and Tumber, H. (1994) *Reporting Crime: The Media Politics of Criminal Justice*. Oxford: Clarendon.

Scholte, J. (2000) *Globalization: A Critical Introduction*. London: Blackwell.

Schorr, D. (1985) Go get some milk and cookies and watch the murders on television, in Hiebert, R.E. and Reuss, C. (eds) *Impact of Mass Media*. New York: Longman.

Schramm, W. (1964) *Mass Media and National Development*. California: Stanford University Press.

Schudson, M. (1978) *Discovering the News: A Social History of American Newspapers*. New York: Basic Books.

Schudson, M. (1989) The sociology of news production, *Media, Culture and Society* **11**, 263–82.

Schudson, M. (1995) *The Power of News*. Cambridge, MA; Harvard University Press.

Schudson, M. (2000) 'The Sociology of News Production' revisited – again, in Curran, J. and Gurevitch, M. (eds) *Mass Media and Society*. London: Arnold.

Seaman, W. (1992) Active audience theory: pointless populism, *Media, Culture and Society* **14**, 301–11.

Seaton, J. and Pimlott, B. (1987) *The Media in British Politics*. Aldershot: Avebury.

Severin, W. with Tankard, J. (1988) *Communication Theories: Origins, Methods and Uses*. London: Longman (2nd edn).

Shannon, C. and Weaver, W. (1949) *The Mathematical Theory of Communication*. Urbana, IL: University of Illinois Press.

Shively, J. (1992) Cowboys and Indians: perceptions of western films among American Indians and Anglos, *American Sociological Review* **57**, 725–34.

Shoemaker, P. (1991) *Gatekeeping*. London: Sage.

Shoemaker, P. and Reese, S. (1991) *Mediating the Message: Theories of Influences on Media Content*. London: Longman.

Sigal, L. (1973) *Reporters and Officials*. Lexington: D.C. Heath.

Sigelman, L. (1973) Reporting the news: an organisational analysis, *American Journal of Sociology* **79**, 132–51.

Sinclair, J. (1990) From 'modernisation' to cultural dependence: mass communication and the Third World, in Martin, L.J. and Hiebert, R. (eds) *Current Issues in International Communication*. New York: Longman.

Sinclair, U. (1919) *The Brass Check: A Study in American Journalism*, published by author.

Sklair, L. (1993) Consumerism drives the global mass media system, *Media Development* **2**, 30–4.

Sklair, L. (2001) *The Transnational Capitalist Class*. Oxford: Blackwell.

Smith, A. (1978) The long road to objectivity and back again: the kinds of truth we get in journalism, in Boyce, D.G., Curran, J. and Wingate, P. (eds) *Newspaper History: From the 17th Century to the Present Day*. London: Constable.

Smith, A. (1980) *The Geopolitics of Information*. Oxford: Oxford University Press.

Smith, A. (1991) *The Age of Behemoths: The Globalization of Mass Media Firms*. New York: Twentieth Century Fund.

Smythe, D. (1977) Communications: blind spot of western Marxism, *Canadian Journal of Political and Social Theory* **1**, 120–7.

Snider, P. (1967) 'Mr Gates' revisited: A 1966 version of the 1949 case study, *Journalism Quarterly* **44**, 419–27.

Sorlin, P. (1994) *The Mass Media*. London: Routledge.

Sparks, C. (2000) Introduction, in Sparks, C. and Tulloch, J. (eds) *Tabloid Tales: Global Debates over Media Standards*. Lanham, MD: Rowman and Littlefield.

Spichal, S. and Sparks, C. (1994) *Journalists for the 21st Century*. Norwood, NJ: Ablex.

Sreberny-Mohammadi, A. (1991) The global and local in international communications, in Curran, J. and Gurevitch, M. (eds) *Mass Media and Society*. London: Arnold.

Steeves, H. (1987) Feminist theories and Media Studies, *Critical Studies in Mass Communication* **4**, 95–135.

Stevenson, N. (1995) *Understanding Media Cultures*. London: Sage.

Storey, J. (2001) *Cultural Theory and Popular Culture: An Introduction*. London: Prentice Hall (3rd edn).

Street, J. (2001) *Mass Media, Politics and Democracy*. London: Palgrave.

Strinati, D. (1995) *An Introduction to Theories of Popular Culture*. London: Routledge.

Strinati, D. (2000) *An Introduction to Studying Popular Culture*. London: Routledge.

Sturmer, C. (1993) MTV's Europe: an imaginary continent, in Dowmunt, T. (ed.)

Channels of Resistance: Global Television and Local Empowerment London: British Film Institute (BFI).

Sutcliffe, T. (1997) This is essentially the latest flowering of a long British intellectual tradition – non-conformist self-flagellation, *Independent*, 17 July.

Swingewood, A. (1977) *The Myth of Mass Culture*. London: Macmillan.

Swingewood, A. (1998) *Cultural Theory and the Problem of Modernity*. London: Macmillan.

Taylor, L. and Willis, A. (1999) *Media Studies: Texts, Institutions and Audiences*. London: Blackwell.

Taylor, P. (1997) *Investigating Culture and Identity*. London: HarperCollins.

Thompson, J. (1990) *Ideology and Modern Culture*. London: Polity Press.

Thompson, J. (1995) *The Media and Modernity*. London: Polity Press.

Thompson, K. (ed.) (1997) *Media and Cultural Regulation*. London: Sage.

Thompson, K. (1998) *Moral Panics*. London: Routledge.

Thussu, D. (ed.) (1998) *Electronic Empires: Global Media and Local Resistance*. London: Arnold.

Thussu, D. (2000) *International Communication*. London: Edward Arnold.

Tiffen, R. (1989) *News and Power*. Sydney: Allen and Unwin.

Todorov, T. (1977) *The Poetics of Prose*. Oxford: Blackwell.

Toffler, A. (1980) *The Third Wave*. London: Pan Books.

Tolson, A. (1996) *Mediations: Text and Discourse in Media Studies*. London: Arnold.

Tomlinson, J. (1991) *Cultural Imperialism*. London: Pinter Press.

Tomlinson, J. (1997) Internationalism, globalization and cultural imperialism, in Thompson, K. (ed.) *Media and Cultural Regulation*. London: Sage.

Traccy, M. (1985) The poisoned chalice? International television and the idea of dominance, *Daedalus* **114**(4), 17–56. (Reprinted in O'Sullivan and Jewkes, Y. (eds) (1997) *The Media Studies Reader*. London: Arnold.)

Tracey, M. (1995) *The Decline and Fall of Public Service Broadcasting*. Oxford: Oxford University Press.

Tuchman, G. (1972) Objectivity as strategic ritual, *American Journal of Sociology* **77**, 660–70.

Tuchman, G. (1978a) *Making News*. New York: Free Press.

Tuchman, G. (1978b) Introduction: the symbolic annihilation of women, in Tuchman, G., Daniels, A. and Benet, J. (eds) (1978) *Hearth and Home: Images of Women in the Mass*

Media. New York: Oxford University Press.

Tuchman, G. (1991) Qualitative methods in the study of news, in Jensen, K.B and Jankowski, N. (eds) *A Handbook of Qualitative Methods for Mass Communications Research*. London: Routledge.

Tuchman, G., Daniels, A. and Benet, J. (eds) (1978) *Hearth and Home: Images of Women in the Mass Media*. New York: Oxford University Press.

Tudor, A. (1974) *Theories of Film*. London: Secker and Warburg.

Tudor, A. (1979) On alchohol and the mystique of media effects, in Cook, J. and Lewington, M. (eds) *Images of Alcoholism*. London: British Film Institute (BFI). (Reprinted in O'Sullivan, T. and Jewkes, Y. (eds) (1997) *The Media Studies Reader*. London: Arnold, 174–81.)

Tulloch, J. (2000) The eternal recurrence of new journalism, in Sparks, C. and Tulloch, J. (eds) *Tabloid Tales: Global Debates over Media Standards*. Lanham, MD: Rowman and Littlefield.

Tunstall, J. (1970) Introduction, in Tunstall, J. (ed.) *Media Sociology*. London: Constable.

Tunstall, J. (1971) *Journalists at Work. Specialist Correspondents: Their News Organisations, News Sources and Competitor-Colleagues*. London: Constable.

Tunstall, J. (1977) *The Media are American: Anglo-American Media in the World*. London: Constable.

Tunstall, J. (1983) *The Media in Britain*. London: Constable.

Tunstall, J. (ed.) (2001) *Media Occupations and Professions: A Reader*. Oxford: Oxford University Press.

Tunstall, J. and Palmer, M. (1991) *Media Moguls*. London: Routledge.

Tunstall, J. and Machin, D. (2000) *The Anglo-American Media Connection*. Oxford: Oxford University Press.

Turow, J. (1997) *Media Systems in Society: Understanding Industries, Strategies and Power*. London: Longman.

Van Dijk, T. (1998) *Ideology*. London: Sage.

Van Zoonen, L. (1988) Rethinking women and the news, *European Journal of Communication* **3**, 35–53.

Van Zoonen, L. (1994) *Feminist Media Studies*. London: Sage.

Vidyarthi, G. (1988) *Cultural Neocolonialism*. New Delhi: Allied Publishing.

Wagg, S. (1987) Mass communications: the debate about ownership and control, *Social Studies Review* (March), 15–20.

Ward, I. (1995) *Politics of the Media.* Sydney: Macmillan.

Wasko, J. (1994) *Hollywood in the Information Age.* London: Polity Press.

Waters, D. (1995) *Globalisation.* London: Routledge.

Watson, J. (1998) *Media Communication: An Introduction to Theory and Process.* London: Macmillan.

Watson, J. and Hill, A. (1993) *A Dictionary of Communication and Media Studies.* London: Edward Arnold.

Watts, D. (1997) *Political Communication Today.* Manchester: Manchester University Press.

Weaver, D. (1998) *The Global Journalist.* New Jersey: Hampton Press.

Weaver, D. and Wilhoit, G. (1991) *The American Journalist: A Portrait of US News People and Their Work,* Bloomington: Indiana University Press (2nd edn).

Weaver, D. and Wilhoit, G. (1996) *The American Journalist in the 1990s: US News People and the End of an Era.* Mahwah, NJ: Erlbaum.

Weber, M. (1976) *The Protestant Ethic and the Rise of Capitalism.* London: Allen and Unwin.

Weber, M. (2001) [1918] Political journalists, in Tunstall, J. (ed.) *Media Occupations and Professions.* Oxford: Oxford University Press.

Webster, F. (1995) *Theories of the Information Society.* London: Routledge.

Webster, F. (1997) The information society?, *Sociology Review* (November), 21–4.

Westergaard, J. (1977) Power, class and the media, in Curran, J., Gurevitch, M. and Woollacott, J. (eds) *Mass Communications and Society.* London: Edward Arnold.

Whale, J. (1980) *Politics and the Mass Media.* London: Fontana.

Wheen, F. (1999) *Karl Marx.* London: Fourth Estate.

Whitaker, B. (1981) *News Ltd: Why You Can't Read All About it.* London: Minority Press Group.

White, D. (1950) The 'gatekeeper': a case study in the selection of news, *Journalism Quarterly* **27**, 383–90.

Williams, G. (1994) *Britain's Media: How They are Related.* London: Campaign for Press and Broadcasting Freedom.

Williams, K. (1998) *Get Me A Murder a Day: A History of Mass Communication in Britain.* London: Arnold.

Williams, K. (1992) Something more important than truth: the ethics of war reporting in Belsey, A. and Chadwick, R. (eds) *The Ethics of Journalism and the Media.* London: Routledge.

Williams, R. (1961) *The Long Revolution*. London: Penguin.

Willis, P. (1977) *Learning to Labour*. Farnborough, Hants: Saxon House.

Wirth, L. (1948) Consensus and mass communication, *American Sociological Review* **13**(1), 1–15.

Wise, R. (2000) *Multimedia: A Critical Introduction*. London: Routledge.

Wober, M. (1998) Cultural indicators: European reflections on a research paradigm, in Dickinson, R., Harindranath, R. and Linne, O. (eds) *Approaches to Audiences*. London: Arnold.

Woollacott, J. (1982) Meanings and messages, in Gurevitch, M., Bennett, T., Curran, J. and Woollacott, J. (eds) *Culture, Society and the Media*. London: Methuen.

Wright, C. (1960) *Mass Communication: A Sociological Perspective*. New York: Random House.

Zynda, H. (1981) A form of low life – how films portray press, *Journalism Studies Review* (July), 6–12.

INDEX

Note: page numbers in bold refer to diagrams